THE CLAY SANSKRIT LIBRARY

FOUNDED BY JOHN & JENNIFER CLAY

GENERAL EDITOR

SHELDON POLLOCK

EDITED BY

ISABELLE ONIANS

WWW.CLAYSANSKRITLIBRARY.ORG
WWW.NYUPRESS.ORG

Artwork by Robert Beer.
Typeset in Adobe Garamond Pro at 10.25 : 12.3+pt.
Editorial input from Dániel Balogh, Ridi Faruque,
Chris Gibbons, Tomoyuki Kono & Eszter Somogyi.
Printed and Bound in Great Britain by
TJ Books Ltd, Cornwall on acid free paper

LIFE OF THE BUDDHA

by AŚVAGHOṢA

TRANSLATED BY

Patrick Olivelle

NEW YORK UNIVERSITY PRESS

JJC FOUNDATION

2009

First Edition 2008

The Clay Sanskrit Library is co-published by
New York University Press
and the JJC Foundation.

Further information about this volume
and the rest of the Clay Sanskrit Library
is available at the end of this book and
on the following Websites:
www.claysanskritlibrary.org
www.nyupress.org

ISBN 978-0-8147-6216-5

Library of Congress Cataloging-in-Publication Data
Aśvaghoṣa
[Buddhacarita.English & Sanskrit]
Life of the Buddha / by Aśvaghoṣa;
translated by Patrick Olivelle. – 1st ed.
p. cm. – (The Clay Sanskrit Library)
Poem.

In English and Sanskrit (romanized) on facing pages.
Includes bibliographical references and index.
ISBN 978-0-8147-6216-5
1. Gautama Buddha–Poetry.
I. Olivelle, Patrick.
II. Title.
BQ1606.B8322E54 2007
294.3'823–dc22
2007025032

CONTENTS

CSL CONVENTIONS

Sanskrit Alphabetical Order

Vowels:	*a ā i ī u ū ṛ ṝ ḷ ḹ e ai o au ṃ ḥ*
Gutturals:	*k kh g gh ṅ*
Palatals:	*c ch j jh ñ*
Retroflex:	*ṭ ṭh ḍ ḍh ṇ*
Dentals:	*t th d dh n*
Labials:	*p ph b bh m*
Semivowels:	*y r l v*
Spirants:	*ś ṣ s h*

Guide to Sanskrit Pronunciation

a	b*u*t
ā, â	f*a*ther
i	s*i*t
ī, î	f*ee*
u	p*u*t
ū, û	b*oo*
ṛ	vocalic *r*, American p*ur*dy or English p*re*tty
ṝ	lengthened *ṛ*
ḷ	vocalic *l*, ab*le*
e, ê, ē	m*a*de, esp. in Welsh pronunciation
ai	b*i*te
o, ô, ō	r*o*pe, esp. Welsh pronunciation; Italian s*o*lo
au	s*ou*nd
ṃ	*anusvāra* nasalizes the preceding vowel
ḥ	*visarga*, a voiceless aspiration (resembling the English *h*), or like Scottish lo*ch*, or an aspiration with a faint echoing of the last element of the preceding vowel so that *taiḥ* is pronounced *taih*^{i}
k	lu*ck*
kh	blo*ckh*ead
g	*g*o
gh	bi*gh*ead
ṅ	a*n*ger
c	*ch*ill
ch	mat*chh*ead
j	*j*og
jh	aspirated *j*, he*dgeh*og
ñ	ca*ny*on
ṭ	retroflex *t*, *t*ry (with the tip of tongue turned up to touch the hard palate)
ṭh	same as the preceding but aspirated
ḍ	retroflex *d* (with the tip

	of tongue turned up to touch the hard palate)
ḍh	same as the preceding but aspirated
ṇ	retroflex *n* (with the tip of tongue turned up to touch the hard palate)
t	French *t*out
th	ten*t h*ook
d	*d*inner
dh	guil*dh*all
n	*n*ow
p	*p*ill
ph	u*ph*eaval
b	*b*efore
bh	a*bh*orrent
m	*m*ind
y	*y*es
r	trilled, resembling the Italian pronunciation of *r*
l	*l*inger
v	*w*ord
ś	*sh*ore
ṣ	retroflex *sh* (with the tip of the tongue turned up to touch the hard palate)
s	hi*ss*
h	*h*ood

CSL Punctuation of English

The acute accent on Sanskrit words when they occur outside of the Sanskrit text itself, marks stress, e.g., Ramáyana. It is not part of traditional Sanskrit orthography, transliteration, or transcription, but we supply it here to guide readers in the pronunciation of these unfamiliar words. Since no Sanskrit word is accented on the last syllable it is not necessary to accent disyllables, e.g., Rama.

The second CSL innovation designed to assist the reader in the pronunciation of lengthy unfamiliar words is to insert an unobtrusive middle dot between semantic word breaks in compound names (provided the word break does not fall on a vowel resulting from the fusion of two vowels), e.g., Maha·bhárata, but Ramáyana (not Rama·áyana). Our dot echoes the punctuating middle dot (·) found in the oldest surviving samples of written Indic, the Ashokan inscriptions of the third century BCE.

The deep layering of Sanskrit narrative has also dictated that we use quotation marks only to announce the beginning and end of every direct speech, and not at the beginning of every paragraph.

CSL Punctuation of Sanskrit

The Sanskrit text is also punctuated, in accordance with the punctuation of the English translation. In mid-verse, the punctuation will not alter the sandhi or the scansion. Proper names are capitalized. Most Sanskrit meters have four "feet" (*pāda*); where possible we print the common *śloka* meter on two lines. In the Sanskrit text, we use French *Guillemets* (e.g., *«kva saṃcicīrṣuḥ?»*) instead of English quotation marks (e.g., "Where are you off to?") to avoid confusion with the apostrophes used for vowel elision in sandhi.

SANDHI

Sanskrit presents the learner with a challenge: *sandhi* (euphonic combination). Sandhi means that when two words are joined in connected speech or writing (which in Sanskrit reflects speech), the last letter (or even letters) of the first word often changes; compare the way we pronounce "the" in "the beginning" and "the end."

In Sanskrit the first letter of the second word may also change; and if both the last letter of the first word and the first letter of the second are vowels, they may fuse. This has a parallel in English: a nasal consonant is inserted between two vowels that would otherwise coalesce: "a pear" and "an apple." Sanskrit vowel fusion may produce ambiguity.

The charts on the following pages give the full sandhi system.

Fortunately it is not necessary to know these changes in order to start reading Sanskrit. All that is important to know is the form of the second word without sandhi (pre-sandhi), so that it can be recognized or looked up in a dictionary. Therefore we are printing Sanskrit with a system of punctuation that will indicate, unambiguously, the original form of the second word, i.e., the form without sandhi. Such sandhi mostly concerns the fusion of two vowels.

In Sanskrit, vowels may be short or long and are written differently accordingly. We follow the general convention that a vowel with no mark above it is short. Other books mark a long vowel either with a bar called a macron (*ā*) or with a circumflex (*â*). Our system uses the

VOWEL SANDHI

Final vowels: a	ā	i	ī	u	ū	ṛ	e	ai	o	au	*Initial vowels:*
' â	" â	y a	y a	v a	v a	r a	e '	ā a	o '	āv a	a
' ā	" ā	y ā	y ā	v ā	v ā	r ā	a ā	ā ā	a ā	āv ā	ā
' ê	" ê	' î	" î	v i	v i	r i	a i	ā i	a i	āv i	i
' ē	" ē	' ī	" ī	v ī	v ī	r ī	a ī	ā ī	a ī	āv ī	ī
' ô	" ô	y u	y u	' û	" û	r u	a u	ā u	a u	āv u	u
' ō	" ō	y ū	y ū	' ū	" ū	r ū	a ū	ā ū	a ū	āv ū	ū
a' r	a" r	y ṛ	y ṛ	v ṛ	v ṛ	' ṝ	a ṛ	ā ṛ	a ṛ	āv ṛ	ṛ
' âi	" âi	y e	y e	v e	v e	r e	a e	ā e	a e	āv e	e
' āi	" āi	y ai	y ai	v ai	v ai	r ai	a ai	ā ai	a ai	āv ai	ai
' âu	" âu	y o	y o	v o	v o	r o	a o	ā o	a o	āv o	o
' āu	" āu	y au	y au	v au	v au	r au	a au	ā au	a au	āv au	au

CONSONANT SANDHI

Permitted finals: k	ṭ	t	p	ṅ	n	m	*(Except āḥ/aḥ)* ḥ/r	āḥ	aḥ	*Initial letters:*
k	ṭ	t	p	ṅ	n	ṃ	ḥ	āḥ	aḥ	k/kh
g	ḍ	d	b	ṅ	n	ṃ	r	ā	o	g/gh
k	ṭ	c	p	ṅ	ṃś	ṃ	ś	āś	aś	c/ch
g	ḍ	j	b	ṅ	ñ	ṃ	r	ā	o	j/jh
k	ṭ	ṭ	p	ṅ	ṃṣ	ṃ	ṣ	āṣ	aṣ	ṭ/ṭh
g	ḍ	ḍ	b	ṅ	ṇ	ṃ	r	ā	o	ḍ/ḍh
k	ṭ	t	p	ṅ	ṃs	ṃ	s	ās	as	t/th
g	ḍ	d	b	ṅ	n	ṃ	r	ā	o	d/dh
k	ṭ	t	p	ṅ	n	ṃ	ḥ	āḥ	aḥ	p/ph
g	ḍ	d	b	ṅ	n	ṃ	r	ā	o	b/bh
ṅ	ṇ	n	m	ṅ	n	ṃ	r	ā	o	*nasals* (n/m)
g	ḍ	d	b	ṅ	n	ṃ	r	ā	o	y/v
g	ḍ	d	b	ṅ	n	ṃ	*zero*[1]	ā	o	r
g	ḍ	l	b	ṅ	l̃[2]	ṃ	r	ā	o	l
k	ṭ	c ch	p	ṅ	ñ ś/ch	ṃ	ḥ	āḥ	aḥ	ś
k	ṭ	t	p	ṅ	n	ṃ	ḥ	āḥ	aḥ	ṣ/s
gg h	ḍḍ h	dd h	bb h	ṅ	n	ṃ	r	ā	o	h
g	ḍ	d	b	ṅ/ṅṅ[3]	n/nn[3]	m	r	ā	a[4]	*vowels*
k	ṭ	t	p	ṅ	n	m	ḥ	āḥ	aḥ	*zero*

[1]ḥ or r disappears, and if a/i/u precedes, this lengthens to ā/ī/ū. [2]e.g. tān+lokān=tāl̃ lokān.
[3]The doubling occurs if the preceding vowel is short. [4]Except: aḥ+a=o '.

macron, except that for initial vowels in sandhi we use a circumflex to indicate that originally the vowel was short, or the shorter of two possibilities (*e* rather than *ai*, *o* rather than *au*).

When we print initial *â*,	before sandhi that vowel was *a*
î or *ê*,	*i*
û or *ô*,	*u*
âi,	*e*
âu,	*o*
ā,	*ā*
ī,	*ī*
ū,	*ū*
ē,	*ī*
ō,	*ū*
ai,	*ai*
āu,	*au*
', before sandhi there was a vowel *a*	

When a final short vowel (*a*, *i*, or *u*) has merged into a following vowel, we print ' at the end of the word, and when a final long vowel (*ā*, *ī*, or *ū*) has merged into a following vowel we print " at the end of the word. The vast majority of these cases will concern a final *a* or *ā*. See, for instance, the following examples:

What before sandhi was *atra asti*	is represented as *atr' âsti*
atra āste	*atr' āste*
kanyā asti	*kany" âsti*
kanyā āste	*kany" āste*
atra iti	*atr' êti*
kanyā iti	*kany" êti*
kanyā īpsitā	*kany" ēpsitā*

Finally, three other points concerning the initial letter of the second word:

(1) A word that before sandhi begins with *ṛ* (vowel), after sandhi begins with *r* followed by a consonant: *yatha" rtu* represents pre-sandhi *yathā ṛtu*.

(2) When before sandhi the previous word ends in *t* and the following word begins with *ś*, after sandhi the last letter of the previous word is *c*

and the following word begins with *ch*: *syāc chāstravit* represents pre-sandhi *syāt śāstravit*.

(3) Where a word begins with *h* and the previous word ends with a double consonant, this is our simplified spelling to show the pre-sandhi form: *tad hasati* is commonly written as *tad dhasati*, but we write *tadd hasati* so that the original initial letter is obvious.

COMPOUNDS

We also punctuate the division of compounds (*samāsa*), simply by inserting a thin vertical line between words. There are words where the decision whether to regard them as compounds is arbitrary. Our principle has been to try to guide readers to the correct dictionary entries.

Exemplar of CSL Style

Where the Devanagari script reads:

कुम्भस्थली रक्षतु वो विकीर्णसिन्धूररेणुर्द्विरदाननस्य ।
प्रशान्तये विघ्नतमश्छटानां निष्ठ्यूतबालातपपल्लवेव ॥

Others would print:

kumbhasthalī rakṣatu vo vikīrṇasindūrareṇur dviradānanasya /
praśāntaye vighnatamaśchaṭānāṃ niṣṭhyūtabālātapapallaveva //

We print:

kumbha|sthalī rakṣatu vo vikīrṇa|sindūra|reṇur dvirad'|ānanasya
praśāntaye vighna|tamaś|chaṭānāṃ niṣṭhyūta|bāl'|ātapa|pallav" êva.

And in English:

May Ganésha's domed forehead protect you! Streaked with vermilion dust, it seems to be emitting the spreading rays of the rising sun to pacify the teeming darkness of obstructions.

("Nava·sáhasanka and the Serpent Princess" 1.3)

PREFACE

THIS PROJECT started with a casual conversation with Richard Gombrich several years ago in which I expressed an interest in translating the *Buddhacarita* for the Clay Sanskrit Library series. Richard probably took my comments more seriously than I did at the time, and several months later asked me whether I was still interested in this translation. I am grateful to Richard for giving this project to me; it has been such a fun assignment and a great learning experience.

Many individuals helped me with this translation, sharing their knowledge and expertise. I am grateful to the students in my advanced Sanskrit seminar in the Fall of 2006 with whom I read the first four chapters of the *Buddhacarita*: Ishan Chakrabarti, Matthew Dasti, Justin Fifield, Christopher Handy, Peter Knapczyk, Elliott McCarter, Urmila Patil, and Vijay Pattisapu. They provided me with valuable insights and helped me fine-tune the translation. Alf Hiltebeitel was already working on the concept of dharma in the *Buddhacarita* and Ashva·ghosha's knowledge of the epics, and he shared his knowledge and writing with me. Other friends who assisted me in various ways include Joel Brereton, Oliver Freiberger, and Gregory Schopen.

My wife, Suman, as usual provided a close reading of the entire manuscript and caught numerous mistakes and typos.

To all a heartfelt thanks.

PATRICK OLIVELLE
Austin, February 2007

INTRODUCTION

Ashva·ghosha, according to tradition, was a brahmin who converted to Buddhism and became a Buddhist monk. Internal evidence of his extant works shows that he was a learned man well versed both in the Brahmanical texts, mythology, ritual, and philosophy, and in Buddhist theology and history. In addition to being an erudite theologian, Ashva·ghosha was a gifted poet. In "Life of the Buddha" (*Buddhacarita*), he melds the theological and the poetic into an epic poem that presents Buddhism as the crowning and consummation of the Brahmanical religion, as the means of releasing human beings from the agony of their imprisonment in life, and as the fulfillment of all human aspirations. The poem is an "apologia" for Buddhism against Brahmanical attacks and arguments, an apologia in the form of a finely crafted "Life of the Buddha" from his conception to his Awakening, preaching, and death.

Date and Place of Ashva·ghosha

There is a scholarly consensus that Ashva·ghosha lived in the first century CE. All the evidence for such dating comes from Ashva·ghosha's works themselves and their relationship to other texts of the period. Many of the arguments, therefore, contain a good dose of subjectivity. The only firm date we have is derived from the Chinese translation of "Life of the Buddha" carried out around 420 CE. It is also most likely that Ashva·ghosha is considerably earlier than the most famous of the Sanskrit poets, Kali·dasa, who is dated somewhat tentatively to the fourth century CE.

A case, however, can be made that Ashva·ghosha knew Manu's work on dharma ("Manu's Code of Law," *Mānavadharmaśāstra*), which I have dated to around the second century CE (OLIVELLE 2005: 25). Twice in "Life of the Buddha" (2.16; 8.78) and once in "Handsome Nanda" (*Saundarananda*, 3.41) he compares the age of the Buddha to the golden age of Manu. Ashva·ghosha repeatedly identifies the Buddha with the sun; and he calls Manu the son of the sun. I think this juxtaposition is intentional. Ashva·ghosha compares the Buddha to Svayam·bhu, the Self-existent One (10.2, 10.19), while Manu, the author of "Manu's Code of Law," is identified as the son of Svayam·bhu. Indeed, the treatise on dharma that Manu imparted is said to have been actually composed by his father Svayam·bhu (Manu 1.3, 58). In this context, it is significant that Ashva·ghosha puts these words in the mouth of the Buddha: "I have no teacher. I have obtained Nirvana; I am not the same as others. Know that I am the Self-existent (*svayaṃ/bhū*) with respect to dharma (15.4)." The Buddha is higher than Manu with respect to dharma; the Buddha is Svayam·bhu himself, the very author of the original treatise on dharma. The Buddha's dharma is thus the original and eternal dharma, surpassing that of Manu, which is implicitly an inferior and degenerate dharma.

A further clue comes from Ashva·ghosha's use of the theology of debt (OLIVELLE 1993: 46–53) to defend the position that a man should take to asceticism only in old age. These words are put in the mouth of the counselor of Buddha's father (9.65–66):

A man is released from his debts
to his ancestors through offspring,
to seers through studying the Vedas,
and to the gods through sacrifice;
A man is born with these three debts,
whoever has become released from these,
for him alone, they say, there is release.
Release is open to one, experts say,
who strives following this sequence of rules;
Those who desire release violating that sequence,
only get fatigued though they expend much effort.

Although the theology of debt is alluded to in the "Maha·bhárata," it is Manu who for the first time uses this theology to defend his position that the orders of life (*āśrama*s) are to be followed sequentially as an individual grows old and that renunciation is limited to old age.[1] That freedom from debt is a precondition for undertaking the life of freedom (mendicancy) echoes Manu. Indeed, one can see that these two verses of Ashva·ghosha parallel the two verses of Manu (6.35–36):

Only after he has paid his three debts,
should a man set his mind on release;
if he devotes himself to release without paying them,
he will proceed downward.
Only after he has studied the Vedas according to rule,
fathered sons in keeping with the Law,
and offered sacrifices according to his ability,
should a man set his mind on release.

Note also Ashva·ghosha's use of the term *mokṣa* (release, liberation) in the technical meaning given to it by Manu, namely, renunciatory asceticism of a wandering mendicant (see OLIVELLE 2005: 243), rather than simply liberation from the cycle of rebirth. It appears likely that both in the theology and in the vocabulary Ashva·ghosha is here following Manu's text.

If this connection between Ashva·ghosha and Manu is accepted, then he should be assigned to the second rather than to the first century CE. Such a connection also throws light on the theological and apologetic background of Ashva·ghosha's work.

The colophons of both the poems give Sakéta, also known as Ayódhya in what is today eastern Uttar Pradesh, as the birth-place of Ashva·ghosha. The internal evidence of "Life of the Buddha" appears to support this. As JOHNSTON (1984: xvii, xlvii–l) has shown, Ashva·ghosha knew the "Ramáyana" and presents the Buddha as the new Rama. He acknowledges Valmíki as the "first poet" (1.43) and models the departure of the Buddha from his city to the forest after that of Rama. Here the Buddha is explicitly compared to Rama (8.8; 9.9):

When the townsfolk saw the two return
without that bull of the Shakya race
and walking with their bodies drooping,
they shed tears along the path, as when
long ago the chariot of Dásharatha returned.
Then, the chaplain together with the counselor,
left the carriage and came up to him, as the sage
Aurvashéya along with Vama·deva did,
wishing to see Rama living in the forest.

Shuddhódana's lament is compared to that of Dasha·ratha when Rama went into exile (8.81):

Thus did the king,
grieving at being separated from his son,
give up his innate steadfastness comparable to the earth's,
and utter countless lamentations as if he were deranged,
like Dasha·ratha over Rama, as he succumbed to grief.

Irrespective of whether he is assigned to the first or the second century CE, Ashva·ghosha lived during a period when much of north-western and north-central India was under the rule of the Kushánas. They were a group that invaded north-western India from central Asia and established a strong empire during the second half of the first century CE. The significant aspect of this empire is that the Kushána rulers became Buddhists and strong patrons of Buddhist institutions. We find this especially in the public visual presence of Buddhism in the architecture of the Kushána period, a time when few Hindu/Brahmanical structures were present. Foreign rule and Buddhist rule represented by the Kushánas, including the in-your-face challenge of Buddhist public monuments, were a double challenge to the Brahmanical conception of society, kingship, and the place of the brahmin community within society.

Many rulers in the preceding four or five centuries had been partial to non-Brahmanical religious movements, especially the Buddhist. Beginning with the Maurya empire and Ashóka, the Brahmanical self-definition was increasingly challenged and their position within the socio-political structures weakened. Recent scholarship, represented by MADELEINE BIARDEAU, ALF HILTEBEITEL, and

James Fitzgerald, has seen the Brahmanical epics as implicit answers to the Buddhist challenge. I have argued that the legal text of Manu should also be seen as a Brahmanical response to this challenge (Olivelle 2005: 37–41). This Brahmanical "counter-reformation" was bound to attract Buddhist responses, and "Life of the Buddha" can be seen as one such response. It is interesting to note that, perhaps taking a page from the early Buddhist works on the life and activities of the Buddha, the two famous Indian epics are essentially the life and deeds of Rama and Yudhi·shthira, the former, significantly, the *dhārmika* (dharmic king) and the latter the son and incarnation of Dharma. We can detect a response when Ashva·ghosha calls the Buddha the image of dharma or dharma in visible form (10.6, 10.19) and explicitly identifies him with dharma (7.35).

The backdrop to Ashva·ghosha's work, I believe, is also the contemporary socio-political reality and the Brahmanical responses, both theological and literary, to that reality. His "Life of the Buddha" can be best interpreted as an apologetic work presenting the Buddhist response to Brahmanical attacks. Ashva·ghosha was well-positioned to undertake this task, for he was clearly well-versed in Brahmanical texts, mythologies, and theologies. His audience, therefore, was not simply his fellow Buddhists but also the broader educated public of his day, especially the Brahmanical intelligentsia. The form of his response, a finely crafted epic poem, was also probably intended to reach a broad, diverse, and educated audience. Citations of his work by later writers on aesthetics and the imitation of his poems by major Brahmanical poets, including Kali·dasa,[2] show that Ashva·ghosha largely achieved his aim.

Works of Ashva·ghosha

There are two extant works of Ashva·ghosha, "Life of the Buddha" and "Handsome Nanda." Both are written in verse and intended to be poetic works (*kāvya*) of distinction. Indeed, these are the two earliest extant *kāvya*s in Sanskrit. "Handsome Nanda" is a *kāvya* in eighteen cantos narrating the story of the long and complicated path to conversion of Buddha's half-brother Nanda and his wife Súndari. The only other work that can be confidently ascribed to Ashva·ghosha is the *kāvya Śāriputraprakaraṇa*, a play in nine acts about the conversion of the Buddha's two chief disciples, Shari·putra and Maudgalyáyana. Only a few passages of this work are extant.

Numerous other works are attributed to Ashva·ghosha in Tibetan and Chinese traditions. The probability that any of these, which deal principally with topics of Maha·yana theology, are authentic works of our poet is extremely slim.

Considering the poetic merits of the two extant *kāvya*s, JOHNSTON (1984: xix) is of the opinion that "Handome Nanda" is the later and more developed work of Ashva·ghosha: "the handling of the *Saundarananda* is altogether more mature and assured than that of the *Buddhacarita*, whose effect is often marred by repetitions of the same words or phrases, or even of a whole *pāda*, in a way that the *kavi*s of the classical age sedulously avoided."

Theology and Apologetics of "Life of the Buddha"

Reading "Life of the Buddha" as a Buddhist response to Brahmanical challenges,[3] we can detect two major thrusts in Ashva·ghosha's argument.

First, he presents the Buddha's doctrine, the dharma discovered through his Awakening, as the consummation of the Brahmanical religion. He reads the history of the Brahmanical tradition as a preparation for the arrival of the Buddha; Brahmanism anticipates the Buddha, and Buddhism is the fulfillment of Brahmanism. It is wrong, therefore, to place them in opposition to each other, to see them as adversaries. This is not a new argument of Ashva·ghosha; the canonical literature already presents the Buddha as the crowning of the Brahmanical tradition. Nor is this unusual in the history of religions, especially when a new religious movement seeks to define itself against an older inherited tradition. Thus, the "new testament" of the Jesus movement presented itself as the fulfillment of the prophesies embedded in the older Jewish tradition, branding its texts as the "old testament." Coming as he does from within the Brahmanical tradition, Ashva·ghosha's stance is quite understandable; he wants to remain both a brahmin and a Buddhist, just as the early Christians wanted to be both Jews and Christians. That Ashva·ghosha was imbued with the Brahmanical scholastic mentality and tradition is evident in his use of the expression *iti smṛtaḥ* ("such is the authoritative tradition," or "so states an authoritative text of tradition")[4] so common in Brahmanical texts.

Second, Ashva·ghosha engages in a polemic against the inherited tradition, demonstrating how doctrines, divinities, and holy men of Brahmanism are defective and untrustworthy as spiritual guides. The dharma of the Buddha has not only fulfilled but also superseded the Brahmanical dharma. Ashva·ghosha has to walk a fine line in this dual argument, because the one can often undercut the other. On the one hand, Brahmanism is viewed positively as preparatory to the Buddhist message, and, on the other, it is presented as depraved, immoral, and superseded.

Ashva·ghosha, however, is careful to observe that the Buddha's dharma, although opposed to the current practices of Brahmanism, is not something entirely new and novel. It is a dharma that was discovered by past Buddhas; Siddhártha's discovery is only the most recent in a long line. His dharma, therefore, is both new and ancient. As he tells his groom Chanda (6.19):

This was the firm resolution,
as you know, of our ancestors;
do not grieve for me as I walk
on this path, that is my patrimony.

Buddha's Dharma as Consummation of Brahmanism

Ashva·ghosha's presentation of the Buddha's dharma as the consummation and fulfillment of the Brahmanical tradition is made implicitly and indirectly rather than openly. He does not come out directly and tell his audience that the Buddha's dharma is what brahmins have been waiting for all these centuries. Indeed, his is the manner in which most Indian authors, especially the Brahmanical ones, deal with their opponents. Buddhism, for example, is never mentioned explicitly either in the epics or in the work of Manu; it is always in the background, and without taking into account that backdrop the full significance of the text cannot be understood.

The most explicit statements come in the narration of Siddhártha's birth. The focus is on the extraordinary marks on the baby's body, marks that Buddhist theology interpreted as the signs of a Great Man (*mahā/puruṣa*), and on the miraculous events that accompanied his birth. The first to reflect on these are learned brahmins probably attached to the royal household, and they announce (1.34–36):

The signs on the body of this illustrious one,
with the brilliance of gold, the radiance of a lamp,
foretell that he'll be either an Awakened Seer,
or a World Conqueror on the earth among men.
Should he desire world sovereignty through
might and right,
he will stand on earth at the head of all kings,
like the light of the sun,
at the head of all heavenly lights.
Going to the forest, should he seek release,
by his knowledge and truth he will vanquish
all doctrines and stand on earth, like Meru,
the king of mountains, among all the hills.

The seer Ásita is the second to interpret these signs. Seeing Ásita with tears in his eyes, Shuddhódana is alarmed, fearing a danger to his infant son. But Ásita is crying for himself, because he knows that he will die before he can hear the Buddha's dharma. Ásita predicts that the infant will become a Buddha, a Fully Awakened One (1.69–75):

For quitting his realm, detached from pleasures,
realizing the truth through arduous efforts,
This sun of knowledge will blaze forth,
in this world to dispel
the darkness of delusion.
From this sea of grief,
strewn with the foam of sickness,
with waves of old age
and fearsome tides of death,
He will rescue with the mighty boat of knowledge
this stricken world carried away by the current.
The living world that's tormented by thirst will drink
from the lofty stream of dharma flowing from him;
A stream that is made cool by mental trance,
a stream whose current is wisdom,
whose banks are steadfast discipline,
whose chakra·vaka *ducks are vows.*
To those who are tormented by suffering,
ensnared by the objects of sense,
roaming through samsara's wild tracks,
This one will proclaim the way to release,
as to travelers who've lost their way.
Upon men in this world who are being scorched
by the fire of passion, whose fuel
is the objects of the senses,
He'll pour relief with the rain of dharma,

like a rain cloud pouring down rain,
at the end of the summer heat.
With the irresistible supreme blow
of the true dharma, he will burst open
The door whose bolt is thirst and whose panels
are delusion and torpor,
so that creatures may escape.
Gaining full Awakening, this king of dharma
will release the world from bondage,
A world bound up with the snares of its own delusion,
a world overcome by grief,
a world that has no refuge.

These are two major representatives of the Brahmanical tradition. The first are wise and learned brahmins, the keepers of the tradition.[5] The second is Ásita, identified as a "great seer" (*maha"/ṛṣi*: 1.49) and described as a "*brahman*-knower blazing with the splendor of *brahman* and the splendor of his ascetic toil" (1.50). Being a seer, he is identified with the very founders of the Vedic tradition. The term *brahman* here probably refers to the Veda; thus an expert in the Vedas authenticates the dharma the Buddha will discover. From the very heart, therefore, of the Brahmanical tradition the future Buddha receives affirmation and authentication. Significantly, the wise brahmins declare that Siddhártha will become an "Awakened Seer," placing him squarely within the tradition of Brahmanical holy men. Ásita is said to be "yearning for dharma" (1.49), implicitly stating that he, and therefore the Vedic tradition, did not have the fullness of dharma. That fullness can come only from the Awakened One.

Gods are a third level of authority within the Brahmanical tradition, and at every step of Siddhártha's life gods affirm his uniqueness and facilitate his path toward Awakening. Miracles abound at his birth, and gods bow their heads and hold up a white parasol over him (1.17). Gods and divine serpents are said to be thirsty for his dharma (1.18, 1.24). As Siddhártha leaves home for the wilderness, gods facilitate his departure (5.47, 5.81, 5.86). And just before his Awakening they scold Mara and affirm that Siddhártha has vanquished him and his cohorts (13.56). Brahmanical gods give legitimacy to the Buddha's claim to omniscience and authority to his dharma. We see this also in the visual remains from the Kushána period where the Buddha is often flanked by Brahma and Indra, the creator and the king among the gods. In "Life of the Buddha" itself Siddhártha is equated with Indra and identified with *svayaṃ/bhū*, the Self-existent One, which is a reference to the creator god Brahma.[6]

Even more significant, however, is the implicit undercurrent of the entire text that compares the Buddha to significant Brahmanical figures of the past. Thus, his extraordinary birth is compared to that of other famous kings of the past who had unusual births (1.10). Siddhártha's departure to the forest parallels that of Rama: Shuddhódana's grief is similar to that of Dasha·ratha; the mission of the minister and chaplain to bring Siddhártha back is compared to that of Aurvashéya and Vama·deva, who were commissioned to bring back Rama.[7] Shuddhódana himself compares his grief to that of Rama's father (8.79, see also 8.81 cited above):

I envy the king who was Indra's friend,
the wise son of King Aja;
When his son went to the forest, he went to heaven,
without living a miserable life
and shedding futile tears.

A theme that runs through the text is that the young and the recent can surpass the old and the ancient. In the very first Canto, the brahmin prognosticators tell Shuddhódana that the young can surpass the old, sons can outdo their fathers, and give many examples from the Brahmanical past to illustrate this truth (1.46). They conclude:

So, age and lineage are not a yardstick;
anyone anywhere may attain
pre-eminence in the world;
Among kings and seers there are many deeds
not performed by the elders
but accomplished by their sons.

This is clearly a defensive posture in Ashva·ghosha's "apologia," showing that it is quite legitimate for the "recent" Buddha to challenge and surpass the ancient Brahmanical wisdom.

The Buddha's dharma, then, is not in opposition to the Brahmanical tradition; it is not a "heterodox" religion. Ashva·ghosha presents it as representing the highest aspirations of that tradition, as the fulfillment of its deepest yearnings, as its crowning achievement.

Refutation of Brahmanical Arguments

Even though Ashva·ghosha sought to present Buddhism as an integral part of Brahmanism, the reality was that there was an ongoing debate between the two traditions. This is evident in the literary traditions,[8] but the opposition probably was manifested also within the political, social, and economic reality as well. But "Life of the Buddha" is concerned principally with the intellectual challenges to the Buddhist dharma, especially to the Buddhist view of the ascetic life as the highest religious aspiration and the only mode of life that can lead a person to final liberation from the phenomenal life of suffering.

On the one hand, Ashva·ghosha presents Brahmanical objections to the Buddhist dharma and the Buddhist responses to them in several speeches and dialogues by various interlocutors. On the other hand, Ashva·ghosha addresses issues of religious modes of life and philosophies and technologies of liberation within Brahmanism to demonstrate their inadequacy with regard to final liberation. I will deal with these two aspects of his argument separately.

The first of these interlocutors is a young man named Udáyin, the son of the king's chaplain, who will also present Brahmanical arguments against the Buddha's decision to renounce. Udáyin is a young urbane gentleman, an educated brahmin and friend of Prince Siddhártha. His focus is on *kāma*, the sensual pleasures that a young person of wealth and power should indulge in. This accords with the efforts of Shuddhódana to surround his son with pleasure and comforts so that Ásita's prediction that he will repair to the forest would not come true. In Canto 4 we see Prince

Siddhártha, who had already seen the signs that pointed to the suffering and impermanent nature of life, surrounded by royal courtesans in a lovely royal park. Their job was to entertain the prince and draw him into a life of sensual indulgence. What is significant in Udáyin's comments for the Brahmanical argument, however, is that engaging in pleasures during youth is presented as a duty within the "triple set" (*tri/varga*), the three goals that a human being should pursue; *kāma* is the first of these to be followed in one's youth. Udáyin presents examples of ancient sages and seers who engaged in sex; there really is nothing wrong with it! Shuddhódana himself takes up this theme in his objection to a young man taking to the ascetic life; it can be dangerous, because a young man is unable to control his senses (5.30–31):

Turn back, my son, from this resolution,
for it's not the time for you
to give yourself to dharma;
For, when you're young and your mind is fickle,
there're many dangers, they say,
in the practice of dharma.
As objects of sense tend to excite his senses,
as he can't be firm facing the hardships of vows,
A young man's mind turns away from the wilderness,
above all as he is not used to solitude.

This is a fine segue to the next argument: the ascetic life is best undertaken when someone is old. This is in keeping with the classical formulation of the *āśrama* system which sees the four as stages of life through which a man passes as he grows old (Olivelle 1993). Renunciation of the world and the pursuit of liberation are reserved for old age. Once again Shuddhódana articulates this position well (5.32–33):

But for me it is the time for dharma,
after conferring on you sovereignty,
you who possess the marks of sovereignty
O lover of dharma;
But if you leave your father by violating
the right order, you whose courage is firm,
your dharma will turn into adharma.
So, give up this resolution of yours,
give yourself for now to household dharma;
For, when one goes to the ascetic grove
after he has enjoyed the joys of youth,
it's truly a wonderful sight!

The Chaplain too, as he conveys to the prince his father's arguments, articulates the Brahmanical position that the *āśramas* should be undertaken in the proper order; violating that order, as Siddhártha has done, is against dharma. So, the Buddha's wish to follow the dharma is itself an *a/dharma*—a refrain that we hear frequently in the Brahmanical objections (9.14):

I know that you have resolved to follow dharma,
and, I realize, this will be your future goal;
but I am burnt up by this fire, the fire of grief,
for you have gone to the forest at the wrong time.

The king's counselor also reiterates this point. Their objection is not to Siddhártha taking to renunciation but to the untimely nature of his decision. Indeed, the counselor is patronizing when he says that Siddhártha may have made this foolish decision because he was unfamiliar with the duties inherent in the "triple set" (9.53–54):

It is not that this decision of yours
to practice dharma is not right,
just that this is not the right time;
For, to condemn your old father to grief
is surely not your dharma,
you who delight in dharma.
Perhaps your mind is not too sharp,
or not conversant with
dharma, wealth, and pleasure;
That you leave to win an unseen result,
disdaining the object before your eyes.

The importance of following the "triple set" is also the focus of King Shrenya's argument that Siddhártha should return home and become king. The three goals should be followed sequentially and in the proper order; violation of that order invites ruin (10.28–30):

Choose, therefore, any one of these options,
devote yourself as prescribed
to dharma, wealth, and pleasure;
For by inverting here the triple set
through passion one goes to ruin
here and in the hereafter.
For when pleasure impairs wealth and dharma,
when wealth suppresses dharma and pleasure,
Or when dharma wipes out pleasure and wealth,

one should abandon it, if one wishes
to attain the goal in its entirety.
By pursuing, therefore, the triple set,
make this lovely body of yours bear fruit;
For when a man gains in their entirety
dharma, wealth, and pleasure, they say
he has achieved the purpose of
human life in its entirety.

The triple set is also connected explicitly with the pursuit of asceticism in old age (10.34):

Surely, when you are old you can practice dharma,
old age lacks capacity to enjoy pleasures;
And, therefore, they assign pleasure for youth,
wealth for the middle-aged,
and dharma for the old.

Yasho·dhara's lament (8.32, 8.61) at her husband abandoning her with an infant child is heart-rending; and that is its intent. But there are elements of her forceful tirade that represent a Brahmanical argument. Siddhártha's wife is his partner in dharma (*saha/dharma/cāriṇī*); and this makes perfect sense if we see the sacrificial and ritual regimen of Brahmanism as the central focus of dharma. Only a married man accompanied by his wife can perform the major ritual acts of the Brahmanical religion. Yasho·dhara presents her case forcefully. Siddhártha's practice of dharma, that is, his ascetic practices, will not provide him with dharma, that is, spiritual merit (8.61):

If it is his wish to practice dharma,
abandoning me without protector,
forsaking me, his partner in dharma;
From where can he obtain dharma
when he desires ascetic toil
without his partner in dharma?

She accuses him of being selfish in not permitting her to share in his dharma, and she presents the examples of former kings who entered the forest accompanied by their wives[9] (8.62–63):

Perhaps he has not heard of former kings,
his forefathers such as Maha·sudársha,
who repaired to the forest with their wives;
For that's the reason why he wants
to practice dharma without me.
Perhaps he does not see that in sacrifices
both husband and wife are consecrated
and are sanctified by the Vedic rites,
that the two enjoy the fruits of these rites,
equally even in the afterlife;
That's the reason why he acts selfishly
with respect to dharma concerning me.

Finally, there is the argument that the pursuit of liberation is not confined to world-renouncing ascetics; history tells us that even householders have attained liberation. The argument here is one we hear frequently in the epics: if knowledge is the cause of liberation, then the emblems of the ascetic life are useless. One can obtain that knowledge in any station of life. Thus the "Bhagavad Gita" (5.3) calls a householder who engages in ritual activities with inner detachment a *nitya/saṃnyāsī*, someone who is a continuous renouncer. The chaplain reports this argument of Shuddhódana (9.18–21):

And this dharma is achieved not just in forests;
ascetics do achieve it even in cities;
in this regard the means are effort and intent;
forest and emblems are the marks of a coward.
Kings, even while remaining householders
cradled in the lap of royal fortune
crowns upon their heads
pearl strings on shoulders
arms bound with bracelets
have won the dharma of release—
Bali and Vajra·bahu,
the younger brothers of Dhruva,
Vaibhrája, Ashádha, and Anti·deva,
Jánaka, likewise, the king of Vidéha,
Druma of Shalva and the Sénajit kings—
Know that these householder kings were well trained
in dharma rules leading to highest bliss;
therefore, you should enjoy both together,
lordship over mind and royal fortune.

In refuting one by one these arguments, viewed by Siddhártha as specious, he sets out the central thesis of the Buddhist dharma: life is suffering, life is impermanent, death looms large, one cannot wait until old age to achieve release. The message is one of anguish, anxiety, and urgency. This again is not something completely new; a very similar message is presented by a son arguing on the same topic with his father in a fine "Maha·bhárata" passage (12.169). Siddhártha articulates this position to Udáyin (4.97–8):

O how steady and strong your mind must be
that you see substance in fleeting pleasures,
That, seeing these creatures on the path of death,
you are attached to sensual pleasures
in the midst of the most frightful dangers.
I, however, am timid, much perturbed,
as I think of the dangers
of old age, sickness, and death;
I find no peace or content, much less joy,
seeing the world with fire as if ablaze.

He tells his father that he will remain at home if Shuddhódana can be a surety with regard to four things, if he can guarantee these four outcomes (5.34–35):

If you will become a surety for me
in four things, O King,
I will not go to the ascetic grove.
My life shall never be subject to death,
disease shall not steal this good health of mine,
Old age shall never overtake my youth,
no mishap shall rob this fortune of mine.

He rejects the examples from history that Udáyin cites. They have no authority with regard to dharma. These men cannot be eminent or exemplary when their behavior is so reprehensible (4.90–91):

What you say about those eminent men,
that they were also given to pleasures;
It should indeed cause us all anxiety,
that these men also have succumbed to death!
No true eminence exists in my view,
where death exists as a general trait,
Where attachment to sense objects persists,
or where self-possession is not attained.

Clearly, waiting for old age to pursue liberation is not an option. The *āśrama* system may be fine social organization, but it fails to answer the anxieties buried in the hearts of those seeking to break out of the bondage of old age, sickness, and death. There is no wrong time to pursue bliss (9.37–38):

From the time a man comes out of the womb
death is set to slay him at every stage;
So how could His Lordship, in his love for his son,
say that I went to the forest at the wrong time?
There is a wrong time to enjoy pleasures,
a time is ordained also for obtaining wealth;
Time tears up this world all the time;
but there is no appointed time
for what produces final bliss.

He explicitly rejects the dharma based on following the "triple set," calling it an evil and unable to satisfy the ultimate yearning of the human heart (11.58):

As to what you said to me that the triple set
when followed in its entirety
is for humans the highest good;

My view on this is that it's truly an evil,
for the triple set is fleeting
and fails to satisfy.

Finally, Siddhártha rejects out of hand the very possibility of attaining liberation while remaining a king and a householder. The office of the king is filled with dangers to the spiritual life (9.40–41):

How can it be right for a wise man to accept
kingship that is delusion's dwelling place,
Where anxiety, pride, and fatigue lurk, and damage
to dharma by mistreating other men?
For a kingdom is charming yet full of dangers,
like a golden castle that is on fire,
like exquisite food that's mixed with poison,
like a lotus pond filled with crocodiles.

And he dismisses the scriptures and traditions that record household kings who attained liberation (9.48–50):

As for the scripture that householder kings
have attained release,
that cannot be!
The dharma of release, where calm prevails,
And the dharma of kings, where force prevails—
how far apart are they!
If a king delights in calm, his realm falls apart,
if his mind is on his realm, his calm is destroyed;
For calmness and fierceness are incompatible,
like the union of fire and water, heat and cold.
So, certainly, either those kings
gave up their realms and obtained calm,

Or remaining within the realm, they projected
release to a non-final state,
because their senses were controlled.

Besides rejecting the Brahmanical arguments against renunciation and the Buddhist dharma, Ashva·ghosha takes up the issue of Brahmanical techniques and philosophies pertaining to liberation. Siddhártha as a brand new ascetic visits (Canto 6) a Brahmanical hermitage with ascetics engaged in a variety of austere practices (*tapas*). The ascetics explain the kinds of vows they undertake, the pain they endure. But Siddhártha observes that all their pain and suffering only lead to temporary states of happiness; they work so much for so little (7.20–21):

Pain is basic to the many types of ascetic toil,
while heaven is the highest reward of ascetic toil;
And yet, all the worlds are subject to change;
such toil in hermitages
only to gain so little!
They forsake their dear kin and objects of sense
and for the sake of heaven practice restraint;
Yet parted from that, they are destined to go
only to states of bondage even more dire.

He points out the contradiction in what they are doing, for if bodily pain is dharma, then bodily bliss should be *a/dharma*; yet they seek bliss by means of pain (7.26):

But, if dharma here consists of bodily pain,
then bodily bliss should be adharma*;*

So when by dharma one attains bliss hereafter,
dharma here bears the fruit of adharma*!*

When the ascetics implore him to remain with them, Siddhártha states forthrightly that his goal is very different from the lower ones they have set for themselves (7.48):

But your dharma aims at attaining heaven;
and my desire is to be free from rebirth.
So I have no wish to live in this forest,
for the dharma of cessation is opposed
to the dharma of continued existence.

Once again Ashva·ghosha produces an authoritative Brahmanical voice to put the stamp of Brahmanical approval on the path Siddhártha has taken. This brahmin is made authoritative by his bodily appearance, just like the infant Siddhártha (7.51–52):

But a certain tall brahmin among them,
used to lying on ash, wearing a topknot,
with reddish eyes, wearing a bark garment,
with a thin long nose and a water pot,
made this oration:
Wise one, your resolve is truly magnificent,
in that, still young, you have seen the peril of birth;
For, having examined well heaven and release,
one who sets his mind on release,
he alone does truly exist!

The philosophical side of Brahmanism is represented by Aráda, who teaches a form of Sankhya doctrine. Clearly at this time it was the major philosophy within the broad

Brahmanical tradition represented by the "Maha·bhárata" and especially the "Bhagavad Gita." Siddhártha is again dismissive of this knowledge that, according to him, leads only half way; it does not produce final bliss and liberation. The main problem for him is the presence of a permanent soul within the Sankhya philosophy (12.69–71):

I have listened to this subtle knowledge
that grows progressively more and more pure;
But since the field-knower is not forsaken,
I think it is short of the absolute.
For, although the knower of the field is freed
from Primal nature and Transformations,
Yet I think it still has the quality
of giving birth and serving as a seed.
For, though the soul, being wholly pure,
you consider to be released;
Yet, because the causal roots are present,
it will once again become unreleased.

Dharma as Site of Contention

HILTEBEITEL (2006: 235) remarks that "It is a surprising point to have to make that Ashva·ghosha would be centrally concerned with dharma, but others seem to have missed it." By "others" he means modern scholars of Ashva·ghosha. It is, indeed, surprising that even JOHNSTON, whose edition and translation of "Life of the Buddha" and his long and detailed introduction to it remain the single most important contribution to Ashva·ghosha studies up to this day, does not deal with this topic at all. Reading "Life of the

Buddha" closely, one cannot fail to notice not only the frequency with which he used the term dharma (130 times in the first thirteen Cantos) but also how he plays with the diverse meanings the term had within the religious discourses of his day. From the recent studies of dharma in the epics and the legal tradition (Olivelle 2004), it is very clear that this term had become the central site of contention among the various religious movements. The question was: Whose dharma is the best, the fullest, and the most authentic?

The period "Between the Empires," the Maurya and the Gupta, roughly the last four centuries BCE and the first four CE, was a time of great intellectual ferment (Olivelle 2006). The picture painted in general introductions to Indian religions of an unchanging India, of an immutable perennial philosophy, is simply an illusion. What Bimal Matilal has said of the Indian intellectual tradition in general applies in spades to this period: "The tradition was self-conscious. It has been interpreting and re-interpreting itself over the ages. It is hardly a new phenomenon. The myth is tied up with the Indologist's romantic search for a classical, pure form of Hinduism (or Buddhism as the case may be), and is little better than a dream" (Ganeri 2002: 40). It was not sufficient for the inquiring minds of the period that something should be considered authoritative simply because it is found in the scriptures of one or another tradition, or even in the Vedas. Ashva·ghosha compares the back-and-forth movement of a demonic woman to the mind of a fickle man moving from one scripture to another (13.49). There were various scriptures competing for attention. Siddhártha rejects out of hand the scriptures, here probably the Vedas, on which the Brahmanical arguments against renunciation are based (4.83), calling them "unfounded" (9.76). Shuddhódana's advisors are aware that there is a deep controversy between the various rules of the Vedic scriptures and the views of Siddhártha; they present their mission to bring him back as a battle between these two sides (8.85):

Let a battle then be waged here on many fronts
between your son and the diverse rules of scripture.

It is within this context of inquiry and debate that we must see the controversies surrounding dharma. Ashva·ghosha presents the arguments from the Buddhist and the Brahmanical sides as a controversy centered on the correct definition of dharma. It is not so much that some definitions of dharma are considered false. Ashva·ghosha presents the array of meanings in which his interlocutors used the term, all of them legitimate at some level. What he wants to emphasize, however, is that no dharma can prevent the pursuit of the highest dharma, the dharma that Siddhártha pursues, the dharma that he preaches once he has become the Buddha. Lower level conceptions of dharma cannot be obstacles on the path to the highest dharma, the "true dharma" of Buddhism called *sad/dharma*.[10]

At the highest level, then, dharma (Dh1)[11] is the truth and the way that was the content of the Buddha's Awakening. Thus, the insight into the law of dependent origination he obtained at his Awakening is described as "the excellent dharma he had seen," which is his best companion (14.99).[12] The reference is to Dh1 when divine serpents are said to be "thirsty for dharma" (1.19), divine beings are said to be "eager for dharma" (1.24), and Ásita is said to be "yearning for dharma" (1.49). Ásita also refers to Dh1 when he calls the Buddha "this king of dharma" (1.75) and laments that he will not live to hear this "absolute dharma" (1.76). This is the "lofty stream of dharma" (1.71) that the world longs to drink from, the "rain of dharma" (1.73) that will relieve the world burning with the fire of passion.

Closely linked to Dh1 is the use of dharma (Dh2) with reference to leaving home and family and devoting oneself completely to the pursuit of liberation within an ascetic mode of life. Thus at 3.24 when it is said that Siddhártha "will give up kingship and follow the dharma," or when at 10.33 he is asked to wait until he is old to "practice dharma," or when at 5.30 he is told that it is not the right time to "follow dharma," it is clear that the reference is to the ascetic way of life, even though what exact form it would take is left unclear. It appears that for Ashva·ghosha dharma as such, that is, when the term is used without additional qualifications, has the meaning of Dh2. Thus at least one meaning of dharma used in the "triple set" appears to be identical with Dh2. I think this meaning is broad enough to cover the hermits living in forest hermitages, as also wandering mendicants. Thus Siddhártha tells the hermits that he does not know "this method of dharma" (7.12), and that he is "still a novice in dharma" (7.46).

A different meaning is evident in the use of dharma (Dh3) to indicate the proper behavior pattern and the proper sequence in which various duties should be undertaken. This is the more traditional meaning of dharma found in the Brahmanical *dharma/śāstras*. The opposite of Dh3 dharma is *a/dharma*, both the violation of that dharma and the sin and demerit one acquires as a result. Thus, Shuddhódana admonishes his son that if he pursues dharma in violation of the proper order, he will be committing an *a/dharma*: "if you leave your father violating the proper order ... your dharma will turn into *a/dharma*" (5.32). At 9.14 the Chaplain tells the prince to give up Dh2 dharma "for the sake of dharma itself." Clearly, there is a battle being waged within the very bosom of dharma. Ashva·ghosha presents the conflicts between the various forms of dharma, as when following Dh2 dharma is a violation of Dh3 dharma. He rejects, however, the Brahmanical resolution proposed: follow the various dharmas during different periods of life, which is the solution offered also by the *āśrama* system in the classical formulation of Manu. The power of the call of Dh1 and Dh2 dharma eliminates the claims of any other form of dharma. This is a point made also in the ascetical texts of the Brahmanical tradition itself, as when the *Jābālopaniṣad* (IV) says that a person may renounce "on the very day that he becomes detached" regardless of whether he has fulfilled any other obligation or not. Siddhártha himself gives a similar response to his groom Chanda (6.21): "no time is improper for pursuing dharma (Dh2), when life is so insecure."

Often dharma is qualified as belonging to or within the domain of a particular category of people or a particular goal toward which it is directed. Although the kinds of dharma comprehended within this usage are many, I will call this usage Dh4, because here dharma is explicitly confined to a specific sphere.[13] Thus, Ashva·ghosha speaks of *mokṣa/dharma* (dharma of liberation; 9.19, 9.48), *nivṛtti/dharma* (dharma of cessation; 7.48), *rāja/dharma* (dharma of kings; 9.48), and *gṛhastha/dharma* (householder's dharma: 5.33).

Within Dh4 dharma, however, the householder's dharma (which I will call Dh5 and which includes a substantial segment of the royal dharma) is often singled out in opposition to the Dh2 dharma. The opposition between Dh2 and Dh5 is at the heart of the debates within "Life of the Buddha." In an interesting sleight of hand, Shrenya tells Siddhártha that if he wants to practice dharma then he should go ahead and perform sacrifices (10.39), which will take him to the zenith of heaven. Thus, dharma is sacrifice, as also the other attendant duties of a Brahmanical householder. It is in this sense that Yasho·dhara calls herself Siddhártha's *saha/dharma/cāriṇī*, "companion in the performance of dharma" (8.61). She then challenges his desire to practice dharma (Dh2) without his partner in dharma (Dh5), concluding that in this way he will not acquire dharma, for he is acting selfishly in his quest (8.63). The clearest oppositon of these two kinds of dharma is given at 7.48 where Siddhártha opposes the dharma of cessation (*nivṛtti/dharma*) to the dharma of continued worldly existence (*pravṛtti/dharma*).

While defining dharma per se as Dh5, the Brahmanical interlocutors can divide Dh2 into two separate aspects: the ascetic lifestyle and the goal of liberation. These two aspects are intermingled within the compound *mokṣa/dharma*. Thus Siddhártha is told that "this dharma (Dh2 as liberation) is achieved not only in the forest" (9.18); examples of householder kings who became liberated are given as proof (9.19).

It is also in this context of redefining what dharma may mean that we come across another universal and ethical meaning of dharma (Dh6) as "compassion for all creatures" (9.17). It appears that it is this superior dharma (Dh6) that Shuddhódana invokes in asking his son to abandon his resolve to follow dharma (Dh2) "for the sake of dharma (Dh6) itself" (9.15) asking him to "show kindness to this unlucky father of yours, for dharma is compassion for all creatures" (9.17).

"Life of the Buddha," then, presents what Shuddhódana's wise counselor calls a "battle waged on many fronts" between Siddhártha, the Buddha-to-be, and the diverse rules of Vedic scriptures. The most prominent front of this battle centers on the interpretation of dharma. The triumph of the Buddha's dharma, called appropriately *sad/dharma* (the true dharma or the real dharma, 1.74), over the other interpretations is the ultimate "apologia" for Buddhism presented by Ashva·ghosha. It is significant that Ashva·ghosha's narrative of the life of the Buddha ends not with his death but with the erection of eighty thousand *stūpa*s enshrining the Buddha's relics by the Emperor Ashóka. The conversion and religious activities of Ashóka signal the final triumph of the Buddha's doctrine in that "battle waged on many fronts." The inclusion of Ashóka in Ashva·ghosha's narrative also indicates the importance of the Emperor in the historical imagination of early Buddhism.

Note on the Text and Translation

No student or translator of the *Buddhacarita* can ignore the monumental work of E.H. JOHNSTON; his work stands as the solid foundation on which contemporary scholars build. One may then question the need for a new translation of this text. The reason is given by JOHNSTON himself, when he confesses: "My translation is a pedestrian affair, designed to be read with the text and to explain its meaning, not to transmute [transmit?] its spirit and literary quality into an alien tongue" (JOHNSTON 1984: iii). I have attempted to convey the literary spirit of the text in this new translation within the limits of my ability, while maintaining accuracy.

One departure from my other translations of Sanskrit texts concerns the pivotal concept of dharma. In my other translations I have regularly translated all Sanskrit terms, including dharma. In Ashva·ghosha's vocabulary and argument, however, dharma is used deliberately with so many meanings and nuances that it would have been futile to capture these varying significations in the translation; English does not have a sufficiently rich vocabulary for this purpose. Therefore, I have kept the words dharma and its opposite *a/dharma* in the translation, inviting thereby the reader to see the different contexts and meanings of this central term.

The Sanskrit text of the *Buddhacarita* has been preserved, unfortunately, in only a single incomplete manuscript. It contains the first thirteen cantos and part of the fourteenth canto of the text. This manuscript was the basis for all the editions of the *Buddhacarita*, including the one JOHNSTON used for his translation. The entire text of the *Buddhacarita* exists in both Chinese and Tibetan translations. JOHNSTON has made use of these to critically edit the Sanskrit text. In the first canto also, the first seven verses, as well as verses 25–40, are missing in the Sanskrit manuscript. A few of these verses have been reconstructed into Sanskrit by JOHNSTON on the basis of the Chinese and Tibetan translation; these I have given within square brackets. My rendering of these verses missing in the Sanskrit manuscript, as well as the summaries of the last cantos, are based on JOHNSTON's translations from the Chinese and Tibetan.

In his argument for the superiority of the Buddhist dharma, Ashva·ghosha alludes to numerous Brahmanical myths, legends, and stories. Without at least a basic familiarity with this mythological background, it is difficult to follow his argument. I have tried to give as much of this background as possible in the notes to the translation, within the confines imposed by the format of this series. Ashva·ghosha also mentions numerous names of seers, holy persons, gods, and the fauna and flora of India. These are listed in the Glossary of Names.

Notes

1 The connection between old age and asceticism is found in a variety of literature (see OLIVELLE 1993: 112–22). Space does not permit me to provide detailed evidence; however, it is Manu who first uses the theology of debts *(ṛṇa)* to provide theological grounding to this view. This theology was already used by Baudháyana as an argument against the *āśrama* system as a whole and against celibate asceticism (OLIVELLE 1993: 86–91).

2 For a detailed discussion of this, see JOHNSTON (1984: lxxix–xcviii).

3 When I refer to "Brahmanical challenges" or "Brahmanical arguments" I do not mean that they are actually articulated by brahmins within the *Buddhacarita*. Many of these arguments are made by individuals who are not brahmins—Kings Shuddhódana and Shrénya, Yasho·dhara, and Chanda—but the arguments present the Brahmanical party line.

4 See 12.21, 12.29, 12.35, 12.63. At 12.82 we have simply *smṛtaḥ*.

5 Note also that his first converts too are brahmins (Canto 16). Especially noteworthy is the Buddha's victory over Áuruvila Káshyapa and his disciples, and the conversion of Sankhya ascetics (Canto 17), including Maudgalyáyana and his other chief disciples, as well as the major Sankhya teachers Pañcha·shikha and Ásuri (Canto 21) and Subhádra, the last of his converts (Canto 26).

6 See also Canto 17 where gods headed by Brahma are said to have lived in Venu·vana in the company of the Buddha and his disciples.

7 As Hiltebeitel (2006: 249) notes, in four of the thirteen conversations of the Buddha relating to dharma Ashva·ghosha relates the prince's departure directly to the *Rāmāyaṇa*.

8 See my earlier comments on the Sanskrit epics and Manu, which are seen increasingly as apologetical works directed primarily at Buddhism.

9 This argument parallels the one made by Madri and Kunti in the *Mahābhārata* (MBh, Critical Edition (CE) 1.110.26) in their effort to accompany their common husband, Pandu, into the forest: "Surely there are other *āśramas*, O bull of the Bháratas, that you can pursue together with us, your wives according to dharma." This *āśrama* is, of course, the third one of the forest hermit.

10 The term *sad/dharma* occurs five times in the *Buddhacarita*: 1.49, 1.74, 6.31, 13.1, 13.31.

11 I will use Dh1, Dh2 etc. to indicate the different meanings of dharma within the *Buddhacarita* for heuristic purposes, even

though I do not intend within the compass of this introduction to deal exhaustively with these meanings.

12 This section is found only in the Chinese and Tiberan translations.

13 The is the usage we find in the Brahmanical *dharma/śāstras* whey they speak of *jāti/dharma* (dharma of castes), *deśa/dharma* (dharma of regions), *rāja/dharma* (dharma of kings), and the like.

Abbreviations

MBh CE = *Mahābhārata* Pune critical edition
MBh CSL = *Mahābhārata* Clay Sanskrit Library edition

Bibliography

BRONKHORST, J. 2005. "Aśvaghoṣa and Vaiśeṣika." In *Buddhism and Jainism: Essays in Honour of Dr. Hojun Nagasaki on His Seventieth Birthday*. Kyoto: Heirakuji Shoten, pp. 235–41.

CHARPENTIER, J. 1914. "Sagengeschichtliches aus dem Arthaśāstra des Kauṭilya." *Wiener Zeitschrift fur die Kunde Morgenländes* 28: 211–34.

COVILL, L. 2007. *Handsome Nanda (Saundarananda)*. New York: New York University Press & JJC Foundation.

COWELL, E.B. 1894. *The Buddha-Karita or Life of Buddha by Asvaghosha*. Reprint. New Delhi: Cosmo, 1977.

DAVE, K.N. 2005 (1985). *Birds in Sanskrit Literature*. Second Edition. Delhi: Motilal Banarsidass.

DE JONG, J.W. 1954. "L'Épisode d'Asita dans le Lalitavistara." *Asiatica, Festschrift F. Weller*. Leipzig, pp. 312–25.

EDGERTON, F. 1953. *Buddhist Hybrid Grammar and Dictionary*. New Haven: Yale University Press.

GANERI, J. (ed.) 2002. *The Collected Essays of Bimal Krishna Matilal: Ethics and Epics*. Delhi: Oxford University Press.

HILTEBEITEL, A. 2006. "Aśvaghoṣa's Buddhacarita: The First Known Close and Critical Reading of the Brahmanical Sanskrit Epics." *Journal of Indian Philosophy* 34: 229–86.

JOHNSTON, E.H. 1930. "Some Sāṃkhya and Yoga Conceptions of the Śvetāśvatara Upaniṣad." *Journal of the Royal Asiatic Society*, pp. 855–78.

———. 1975. *The Saundarananda of Aśvaghoṣa*. Combined reprint of 1928 and 1932 editions. Delhi: Motilal Banarsidass.

———. 1984. *Aśvaghoṣa's Buddhacarita, or Acts of the Buddha*. Combined reprint of 1936. Delhi: Motilal Banarsidass.

KHOSLA, S. 1986. *Aśvaghoṣa and His Times*. New Delhi: Intellectual Publishing House.

KRAMRISCH, S. 1981. *The Presence of Śiva*. Princeton: Princeton University Press.

MALALASEKERA, G.P. 1937–38. *Dictionary of Pāli Proper Names*. 2 vols. London: John Murray.

MANI, V. 1975. *Purāṇic Encyclopaedia*. Delhi: Motilal Banarsidass.

MITRA, R. 1877. *The Lalita Vistara or Memoirs of the Early Life of Śākya Siṃha*. Bibliotheca Indica. Calcutta: Baptist Mission Press.

O'FLAHERTY, W.D. 1981. *Śiva the Erotic Ascetic*. Paperback reprint of 1973. Oxford: Oxford University Press.

OLIVELLE, P. 1993. *The Āśrama System: History and Hermeneutics of a Religious Institution*. New York: Oxford University Press.

———. 1998. *The Early Upaniṣads: Annotated Text and Translation*. South Asia Research Series. New York: Oxford University Press.

———. 2004. *Dharma: Studies in Its Semantic, Cultural, and Religious History*. Published as a special volume in *Journal of Indian Philosophy* vol. 32, nos. 5–6. Forthcoming: Delhi: Motilal Banarsidass.

———. 2005. *The Law Code of Manu*. Oxford World's Classics. Oxford: Oxford University Press.

———. 2006. *Between the Empires: Society in India 300 BCE to 400 CE*. South Asia Research. New York: Oxford University Press.

———. 2007. "The Term vikrama in the Vocabulary of Aśvaghoṣa." In *Pramāṇakīrtiḥ. Papers Dedicated to Ernst Steinkellner on the Occasion of his 70th Birthday*. Wiener Studien zur Tibetologie und Buddhismuskunde, no. 70. Vienna: Arbeitskreis für tibetische und buddhistische Studien, Universität Wien, pp. 587–96.

SCHOTSMAN, I. 1995. *Aśvaghoṣa's Buddhacarita: The Life of the Buddha*. Sarnath, Varanasi: Central Institute of Higher Tibetan Studies.

SHULMAN, D. 1986. 'Terror of Symbols and Symbols of Terror: Notes on the Myth of Śiva as Sthāṇu.' *History of Religions* 26: 101–24.

THOMAS, E.J. 1949. *The Life of the Buddha as Legend and History*. 3rd edition. London: Routledge & Kegan Paul.

LIFE OF THE BUDDHA

CANTO 1

THE BIRTH OF THE LORD

1.1 [Aikṣvāka Ikṣvāku|sama|prabhāvaḥ
Śākyeṣv a|śakyeṣu viśuddha|vṛttaḥ
priyaḥ śarac|candra iva prajābhyaḥ
Śuddhodano nāma babhūva rājā.]

[tasy' Êndra|kalpasya babhūva patnī
- - - - - - - - - - -
Padm" êva lakṣmīḥ pṛthiv" îva dhīrā
Māy" êti nāmn" ân|upam" êva Māyā.]

[- - - - - - - - - - -
- - - - - - - - - - -
tataś ca vidy" êva samādhi|yuktā
garbaṃ dadhe pāpa|vivarjitā sā.]

[- - - - - - - - - - -
- - - - - - - - - - -
- - - - - - - - - - -
na tan|nimittaṃ samavāpa tāpam.]

1.5 [sā tasya deva|pratimasya devī
garbheṇa vaṃśa|śriyam udvahantī
- - - - - - - - - - -
- - - - - - - - - - -.]

[sā Lumbinīṃ nāma van'|ânta|bhūmiṃ
citra|drumāṃ Caitrarath'|âbhirāmām
- - - - - - - - - - -
- - - - - - - - - - -.]

In Ikshváku's line, equal to Ikshváku in might, 1.1
among the invincible Shakyas, was born a king,
loved by his people like the autumn moon,
pure in conduct, Shuddhódana by name.

That equal of Indra had a wife like Shachi herself;
her splendor paralleled his might;
she was as pretty as Padmá, as steadfast as the Earth,
Maya by name, like the peerless Maya herself.

That ruler of men, sporting with his queen,
enjoyed, as it were, Váishravana's sovereign might;
free from sin, then, she produced the fruit
of her womb,
as knowledge does, when united with trance.

Before she conceived she saw in a dream
a white elephant king
entering her body, yet she did not
thereby feel any pain.

Maya, then, the queen of that god-like king, 1.5
her womb bearing the glory of his line,
by her purity freed from delusion,
sorrow and fatigue, set her mind
on visiting that faultless grove.

Seeking a lonely grove suited for trance,
she asked the king to go to Lúmbini,
and to stay in that grove
with trees of every kind,
as lovely as the Cháitraratha grove.

[āry'|āśayāṃ tāṃ - - - - - -
vijñāya kautūhala|harṣa|pūrṇaḥ
śivāt purād bhūmi|patir jagāma
tat|prītaye n' âpi vihāra|hetoḥ.]

tasmin vane śrīmati rāja|patnī
prasūti|kālaṃ samavekṣamāṇā
śayyāṃ vitān'|ôpahitāṃ prapede
nārī|sahasrair abhinandyamānā.

tataḥ prasannaś ca babhūva Puṣyas
tasyāś ca devyā vrata|saṃskṛtāyāḥ
pārśvāt suto loka|hitāya jajñe
nir|vedanaṃ c' âiva nir|āmayaṃ ca.

1.10 ūror yath" Āurvasya Pṛthoś ca hastān
Māndhātur Indra|pratimasya mūrdhnaḥ
Kakṣīvataś c' âiva bhuj'|âṃsa|deśāt
tathā|vidhaṃ tasya babhūva janma.

krameṇa garbhād abhiniḥsṛtaḥ san
babhau cyutaḥ khād iva yony|a|jātaḥ
kalpeṣv an|ekeṣu ca bhāvit'|ātmā
yaḥ saṃprajānan suṣuve na mūḍhaḥ.

dīptyā ca dhairyeṇa ca yo rarāja
bālo ravir bhūmim iv' âvatīrṇaḥ
tath" âtidīpto 'pi nirīkṣyamāṇo
jahāra cakṣūṃṣi yathā śaś'|âṅkaḥ.

Noting that her intention was noble,
because she was endowed with piety,
the king, filled with both wonder and delight,
departed from that auspicious city
to please her and not as a pleasure trip.

In that lovely grove, knowing that the time
for delivery was at hand, the queen went
to a bed covered with a canopy,
to the welcome words of thousands of maids.

Then, as Pushya turned propitious, a son was born
from the side of the queen consecrated by rites,
without pain and without ill,
for the welfare of the world.

As Aurva from the thigh, 1.10
as Prithu from the hand,
as Mandhátri from the head,
  he who was Indra's peer,
as Kakshívat from the armpit,
  so was this birth.*

When in due course he emerged from the womb,
but did not emerge through the birth canal,
he gleamed as if he'd fallen from the sky;
through untold eons he had nurtured his self,
so he was born aware, not oblivious.

With luster and fortitude he did gleam,
as if the young sun had come down to earth;
though dazzlingly bright, he captured the eyes
of those who gazed on him, just like the moon.*

sa hi sva|gātra|prabhay" ôjjvalantyā
dīpa|prabhāṃ bhāskaravan mumoṣa
mah"|ârha|jāmbūnada|cāru|varṇo
vidyotayām āsa diśaś ca sarvāḥ.

an|ākulāny ubja|samudgatāni
niṣpeṣavad vyāyata|vikramāṇi
tath" âiva dhīrāṇi padāni sapta
sapta'|rṣi|tārā|sa|dṛśo jagāma.

1.15 «bodhāya jāto 'smi, jagadd|hit'|ârtham
antyā bhav'|ôtpattir iyaṃ mam' êti»
catur|diśaṃ siṃha|gatir vilokya
vāṇīṃ ca bhavy'|ârtha|karīm uvāca.

khāt prasrute candra|marīci|śubhre
dve vāri|dhāre śiśir'|ôṣṇa|vīrye
śarīra|saṃsparśa|sukh'|ântarāya
nipetatur mūrdhani tasya saumye.

śrīmad|vitāne kanak'|ôjjval'|âṅge
vaiḍūrya|pāde śayane śayānam
yad|gauravāt kāñcana|padma|hastā
yakṣ'|âdhipāḥ saṃparivārya tasthuḥ.

[adṛśya|bhāvā]ś ca div'|âukasaḥ khe
yasya prabhāvāt praṇataiḥ śirobhiḥ
ādhārayan pāṇḍaram ātapa|traṃ
bodhāya jepuḥ param'|āśiṣaś ca.

With the dazzling splendor of his body,
he robbed the light of lamps, just like the sun;
with the charming color of costliest gold,
he lit up all the quarters of the sky.

He looked like the stars of the seven seers,*
as he took seven steps that were steady,
lifted up evenly and straight,
stretched out wide and firmly set down.

"For Awakening I am born, 1.15
for the welfare of the world;
This indeed is the last coming
into existence for me!"

Looking at the four quarters with a lion's mien,
he uttered these words, foretelling what was to come.

From the sky two streams of water came down,
limpid like the rays of the sun and moon,*
they fell, one warm and one cold, on his lovely head,
to give refreshment to his body by their touch.

He slept in a bed with a splendid canopy,
with feet of beryl, with its sides glistening with gold;
yaksha chiefs stood there surrounding him reverently,
golden lotuses in their hands.

Heavenly beings, remaining invisible,
their heads bowed because of his majesty,
held a white parasol in the sky over him,
and gave their best blessings for his Awakening.

mah'|ôragā dharma|viśeṣa|tarṣād
buddheṣv atīteṣu kṛt'|âdhikārāḥ
yam avyajan bhakti|viśiṣṭa|netrā
mandāra|puṣpaiḥ samavākiraṃś ca.

1.20 Tathāgat'|ôtpāda|guṇena tuṣṭāḥ
śuddh'|âdhivāsāś ca viśuddha|sattvāḥ
devā nanandur vigate 'pi rāge
magnasya duḥkhe jagato hitāya.

yasya prasūtau giri|rāja|kīlā
vāt'|āhatā naur iva bhūś cacāla
sa|candanā c' ôtpala|padma|garbhā
papāta vṛṣṭir gaganād an|abhrāt.

vātā vavuḥ sparśa|sukhā mano|jñā
divyāni vāsāṃsy avapātayantaḥ
sūryaḥ sa ev' âbhyadhikaṃ cakāśe
jajvāla saumy'|ârcir an|īrito 'gniḥ.

prāg|uttare c' āvasatha|pradeśe
kūpaḥ svayaṃ prādur|abhūt sit'|âmbuḥ
antaḥ|purāṇy āgata|vismayāni
yasmin kriyās tīrtha iva pracakruḥ.

dharm'|ârthibhir bhūta|gaṇaiś ca divyais
tad|darśan'|ârthaṃ vanam āpupūre
kautūhalen' âiva ca pāda|pebhyaḥ
puṣpāṇy a|kāle 'pi [nipātitāni.]

Thirsty for the excellent dharma, mighty serpents,
who for Buddhas past
    had performed this same function,
fanned him, their eyes exuding devotion,
and sprinkled him with *mandára* blossoms.

Gladdened by the eminence of Tathágata's birth,* 1.20
the gods of the pure realm, their spirits purified,*
rejoiced, even though in them the passions were stilled,
for the welfare of the world plunged in suffering.

At his birth the earth,
pegged down by the mountain king,*
shook like a ship tossed around by the wind;
and from a cloudless sky fell a shower
filled with lotuses blue and red,
and with the scent of sandalwood.

Charming breezes blew, pleasing to the touch,
bringing down showers of garments divine;
the very same sun gleamed ever more bright,
fire blazed without flicker with graceful flames.

In the north-east corner of the dwelling
a well with cool water sprang on its own;
ladies of the seraglio, utterly amazed,
performed the rituals there, as at a sacred ford.

Eager for dharma, throngs of divine beings
filled that grove to obtain his sight;
though out of season, in their zeal,
they threw down flowers from the trees.

1.25 [- - - - - - - - - - -
- - - - - - - - - - -
- - - - - - - - - - -
- - - - - - - - - - -]

[- - - - - - - - - - -
- - - - - - - - - - -
- - - - - - - - - - -
- - - - - - - - - - -]

[- - - - - - - - - - -
- - - - - - - - - - -
- - - - - - - - - - -
- - - - - - - - - - -]

[- - - - - - - - - - -
- - - - - - - - - - -
- - - - - - - - - - -
- - - - - - - - - - -]

[- - - - - - - - - - -
- - - - - - - - - - -
- - - - - - - - - - -
- - - - - - - - - - -]

1.30 [- - - - - - - - - - -
- - - - - - - - - - -
- - - - - - - - - - -
- - - - - - - - - - -]

At that time vicious animals lived together 1.25
without injuring each other;
and those diseases common among men,
they too were cured without any effort.

The birds and deer muffled their cries,
with calm waters the rivers flowed,
the quarters became clear, cloudless sparkled the sky,
and the drums of the gods resounded in the air.*

When the Teacher was born for the release of all,
total peace enveloped the entire world,
as if a lord had come in a time of turmoil;
only Kama, the god of love, did not rejoice.

When he saw the wondrous birth of his son,
the king, although steadfast, was much perturbed;
and from his love two streams of tears surged forth,
rising from apprehension and delight.

The queen was overcome with fear and joy,
like a mixed stream of water, hot and cold;
both because her son's power was other than human,
and because of a mother's natural weakness.

The pious old women failed to comprehend, 1.30
seeing only reasons for alarm;
cleansing themselves and doing rites for good luck,
they petitioned the gods for good fortune.

[- - - - - - - - - - -
- - - - - - - - - - -
- - - - - - - - - - -
- - - - - - - - - - -]

[- - - - - - - - - - -
- - - - - - - - - - -
- - - - - - - - - - -
- - - - - - - - - - -]

[- - - - - - - - - - -
- - - - - - - - - - -
- - - - - - - - - - -
- - - - - - - - - - -]

[- - - - - - - - - - -
- - - - - - - - - - -
- - - - - - - - - - -
- - - - - - - - - - -]

1.35 [- - - - - - - - - - -
- - - - - - - - - - -
- - - - - - - - - - -
- - - - - - - - - - -]

[- - - - - - - - - - -
- - - - - - - - - - -
- - - - - - - - - - -
- - - - - - - - - - -]

Brahmins famed for learning, eloquence, and conduct,
heard about these omens and they examined them;
their faces beaming with wonder and elation,
they said this to the king gripped by both fear and joy:

"On earth for their peace men desire
no distinction beyond a son;
this lamp of yours is the lamp of your clan,
so rejoice and prepare today a feast.

So, be firm and joyful, don't be anxious,
for your clan will flourish without a doubt;
the one born here, your son, is the leader
of those beset by suffering in the world.

The signs on the body of this illustrious one,
with the brilliance of gold, the radiance of a lamp,
foretell that he'll be either an Awakened Seer,
or a World Conqueror on the earth among men.

Should he desire world sovereignty through 1.35
might and right,
he will stand on the earth at the head of all kings,
like the light of the sun,
at the head of all heavenly lights.

Going to the forest, should he seek release,
by his knowledge and truth he will vanquish
all doctrines and stand on earth, like Meru,
the king of mountains, among all the hills.

[- - - - - - - - - - -
- - - - - - - - - - - -
- - - - - - - - - - -
- - - - - - - - - - - -]

[- - - - - - - - - - -
- - - - - - - - - - - -
- - - - - - - - - - -
- - - - - - - - - - - -]

[- - - - - - - - - - -
- - - - - - - - - - - -
- - - - - - - - - - -
- - - - - - - - - - - -]

1.40 [- - - - - - - - - - -
- - - - - - - - - - - -
- - - - - - - - - - -
nidarśanāny] atra ca no nibodha.

yad rāja|śāstraṃ Bhṛgur Aṅgirā vā
na cakratur vaṃśa|karāv ṛṣī tau
tayoḥ sutau saumya sasarjatus tat
kālena Śukraś ca Bṛhas|patiś ca.

As pure gold is the best of all metals,
Meru of mountains, ocean of waters,
moon of planets, sun of fires,
so your son is the best of men.

His eyes gaze steadily without blinking,*
they are limpid and wide, blazing yet mild,
They are steady and with long black lashes;
how can these eyes of his not see all things?"

The king then told those twice-born men:

"Why do we see these wondrous signs in him,
and not in previous noble kings?"

The brahmins then said this to him:

"Wisdom, deeds of wide acclaim, 1.40
and the fame of kings:
there's no earlier or later with respect to these.
For every effect there's a cause;
that's the way nature operates;
learn from us parallels to this.

The treatise on kings that Bhrigu
and Ángiras failed to compose,
two seers who established dynastic lines,
Was authored in due course, my lord,
by their sons, Shukra and Brihas·pati.*

Sārasvataś c' âpi jagāda naṣṭaṃ
vedaṃ punar yaṃ dadṛśur na pūrve;
Vyāsas tath" âinaṃ bahudhā cakāra
na yaṃ Vasiṣṭhaḥ kṛtavān a|śaktiḥ.

Vālmīkir ādau ca sasarja padyaṃ
jagrantha yan na Cyavano maha"|rṣiḥ
cikitsitaṃ yac ca cakāra n' Âtriḥ
paścāt tad Ātreyo ṛṣir jagāda.

yac ca dvijatvaṃ Kuśiko na lebhe
tad Gādhinaḥ sūnur avāpa, rājan;
velāṃ samudre Sagaraś ca dadhre
n' Êkṣvākavo yāṃ prathamaṃ babandhuḥ.

1.45 ācāryakaṃ yoga|vidhau dvi|jānām
a|prāptam anyair Janako jagāma
khyātāni karmāṇi ca yāni Śaureḥ
Śūr'|ādayas teṣv a|balā babhūvuḥ.

tasmāt pramāṇaṃ na vayo na vaṃśaḥ
kaś cit kva cic chraiṣṭhyam upaiti loke;
rājñām ṛṣīṇāṃ ca hi tāni tāni
kṛtāni putrair a|kṛtāni pūrvaiḥ.»

evaṃ nṛpaḥ pratyayitair dvi|jais tair
āśvāsitaś c' âpy abhinanditaś ca
śaṅkām an|iṣṭāṃ vijahau manastaḥ
praharṣam ev' âdhikam āruroha.

Sarásvata proclaimed again the lost Veda,
which men of earlier times had failed to see;
Vyasa, likewise, split it into many sections,
something Vasíshtha could not accomplish.*

Valmíki was the first to create a verse text,
something Chyávana, the great sage,
failed to produce;*
The medical text that Atri failed to produce,
after him the seer Atréya composed.*

The twice-born status that Kúshika could not win
was secured, O king, by the offspring of Gadhin;*
Ságara set the boundaries of the ocean,
which earlier the Ikshvákus could not establish.*

Jánaka taught the Yogic path to twice-born men, 1.45
a position not attained by anyone else;*
And Shura and his kin lacked the strength
to perform
the famous deeds that Shauri accomplished.

So, age and lineage are not a yardstick;
anyone anywhere may attain
pre-eminence in the world;
Among kings and seers there are many deeds
not performed by the elders
but accomplished by their sons."

Thus did those trusted twice-born men
console the king and cheer him up;
he removed unwholesome doubts from his mind
and rose to a still higher level of joy.

prītaś ca tebhyo dvi|ja|sattamebhyaḥ
sat|kāra|pūrvaṃ pradadau dhanāni
«bhūyād ayaṃ bhūmi|patir yath"|ôkto
yāyāj jarām etya vanāni c' êti.»

ath' ô nimittaiś ca tapo|balāc ca
taj janma janm'|ânta|karasya buddhvā
Śāky'|ēśvarasy' ālayam ājagāma
sad|dharma|tarṣād Asito maha"|rṣiḥ.

1.50 taṃ brahma|vid brahma|vidaṃ jvalantaṃ
brāhmyā śriyā c' âiva tapaḥ|śriyā ca
rājño gurur gaurava|sat|kriyābhyāṃ
praveśayām āsa nar'|êndra|sadma.

sa pārthiv'|ântaḥ|pura|saṃnikarṣaṃ
kumāra|janm'|āgata|harṣa|vegaḥ
viveśa dhīro vana|saṃjñay" êva
tapaḥ|prakarṣāc ca jar"|āśrayāc ca.

tato nṛpas taṃ munim āsana|sthaṃ
pādy'|ârghya|pūrvaṃ pratipūjya samyak
nimantrayām āsa yath"|ôpacāraṃ
purā Vasiṣṭhaṃ sa iv' Ântidevaḥ.

«dhanyo 'smy anugrāhyam idaṃ kulaṃ me,
yan māṃ didṛkṣur bhagavān upetaḥ.
ājñāpyatāṃ! kiṃ karavāṇi, saumya?
śiṣyo 'smi, viśrambhitum arhas' îti.»

Delighted, he honored those twice-born men,
and he gave to them rich gifts, with the wish:

"May he become a king as predicted,
And go to the forest when he is old."

Through omens and by his ascetic might,
alerted, then, to the birth of the one
who would put an end to birth, Ásita,
the great seer, thirsting for the true dharma,*
came to the abode of the Shakya king.

That knower of brahman, blazing with the splendor 1.50
of brahman and the splendor of ascetic toil,
was ushered in by the brahman-knowing
preceptor of the king with reverence and
homage into the chamber of the king.*

Feeling the thrill at the prince's birth, he entered
the vicinity of the king's seraglio,
deeming it a forest and remaining steadfast,
due to the strength of his austerities,
and the succor provided by old age.

When seated, then, the king duly honored that sage,
after he had given him water for his feet
and the water of welcome, and entreated him
with all due respect, as Anti·deva
entreated Vasíshtha in former times.*

"Fortunate am I and my household is honored,
in that Your Honor has come to see me.
Command me, gentle sire! What shall I do for you?
For I am your disciple, please have faith in me."

evaṃ nṛpeṇ' ôpanimantritaḥ san
sarveṇa bhāvena munir yathāvat
sa vismay'|ôtphulla|viśāla|dṛṣṭir
gambhīra|dhīrāṇi vacāṃsy uvāca.

1.55 «mah"|ātmani tvayy upapannam etat
priy'|âtithau tyāgini dharma|kāme
sattv'|ânvaya|jñāna|vayo|'nurūpā
snigdhā yad evaṃ mayi te matiḥ syāt.

etac ca tad yena nṛpa'|rṣayas te
dharmeṇa sūkṣmeṇa dhanāny avāpya
nityaṃ tyajanto vidhivad babhūvus
tapobhir āḍhyā vibhavair daridrāḥ.

prayojanaṃ yat tu mam'|ôpayāne
tan me śṛṇu prītim upehi ca tvam
divyā may" āditya|pathe śrutā vāg
‹bodhāya jātas tanayas tav' êti.›

śrutvā vacas tac ca manaś ca yuktvā
jñātvā nimittaiś ca tato 'smy upetaḥ
didṛkṣayā Śākya|kula|dhvajasya
Śakra|dhvajasy' êva samucchritasya.»

When he was entreated thus by the king,
in a fitting manner and full of love,
the sage uttered these words, wise and profound,
his large eyes in amazement opened wide.

"This befits you—noble, hospitable, 1.55
generous, and a lover of dharma—
That you should show me this loving regard,
fitting your character and family,
fitting your wisdom and your age.

And this is that subtle dharma by which
those royal sages, having obtained wealth,
Always ceded it according to rule,
becoming thus poor in wealth,
but rich in austerity.

But as to the reason for my visit,
listen to it and be joyful at heart;
On the sun's path I heard a voice divine:
'To you a son is born
For Awakening.'*

When I heard those words, I focused my mind,
and comprehended by means of omens;
So, I have come with the desire to see
this banner of the Shakya race,
like the banner of Shakra, raised up high."

ity etad evaṃ vacanaṃ niśamya
praharṣa|saṃbhrānta|gatir nar'|êndraḥ
ādāya dhātry|aṅka|gataṃ kumāraṃ
saṃdarśayām āsa tapo|dhanāya.

1.60 cakr'|âṅka|pādaṃ sa tato maha"|rṣir
jāl'|âvanaddh'|âṅguli|pāṇi|pādam
s'|ôrṇa|bhruvaṃ vāraṇa|vasti|kośaṃ
sa|vismayaṃ rāja|sutaṃ dadarśa.

dhātry|aṅka|saṃviṣṭam avekṣya c' âinaṃ
devy|aṅka|saṃviṣṭam iv' Âgni|sūnum
babhūva pakṣm'|ânta|vicañcit'|âśrur
niśvasya c' âiva tri|div'|ônmukho 'bhūt.

dṛṣṭv" Âsitaṃ tv aśru|pariplut'|âkṣaṃ
snehāt tanū|jasya nṛpaś cakampe;
sa|gadgadaṃ bāṣpa|kaṣāya|kaṇṭhaḥ
papraccha sa prāñjalir ānat'|âṅgaḥ.

«alp'|ântaraṃ yasya vapuḥ surebhyo
bahv|adbhutaṃ yasya ca janma dīptam
yasy' ôttamaṃ bhāvinam āttha c' ârthaṃ
taṃ prekṣya kasmāt tava, dhīra, bāṣpaḥ?

api sthir'|āyur bhagavan kumāraḥ?
kac cin na śokāya mama prasūtaḥ?
labdhā kathaṃ cit salil'|âñjalir me
na khalv imaṃ pātum upaiti kālaḥ?

Hearing these words, then, the king
with unsteady steps—
so overwhelmed was he with great delight—
took the prince lying on the lap of his nurse,
and showed him to that man rich in austerity.

With amazement, then, the great seer 1.60
gazed at the prince—
the soles of his feet with marks of a wheel,
his hands and feet with webbed fingers and toes,
a circle of hair between his eyebrows,
genitals ensheathed like an elephant's.*

Seeing him resting on his nurse's lap,
like Agni's son on the goddess's lap,*
tears danced at the edge of his eyelashes,
and, heaving a sigh, he looked up to heaven.

But seeing Ásita, his eyes drenched with tears,
the king trembled out of love for his son;
with faltering speech, his throat choked with tears,
with bent body and folded palms, he asked:

"His body differs little from that of the gods,
numerous wonders attended his dazzling birth,
And his future lot, you said, will be eminent;
seeing him, then, why do you,
a steadfast man, shed tears?

Will the prince, Lord, have a long life?
Surely he was not born to cause me grief?
This handful of water I have somehow obtained,
surely Time will not come to lap it up?*

1.65 apy a|kṣayaṃ me yaśaso nidhānaṃ?
kac cid dhruvo me kula|hasta|sāraḥ?
api prayāsyāmi sukhaṃ paratra
supto 'pi putre '|nimiṣ'|âika|cakṣuḥ?

kac cin na me jātam a|phullam eva
kula|pravālaṃ pariśoṣa|bhāgi?
kṣipraṃ, vibho, brūhi na me 'sti śāntiḥ,
snehaṃ sute vetsi hi bāndhavānām.»

ity āgat'|āvegam an|iṣṭa|bhuddhyā
buddhvā nar'|êndraṃ sa munir babhāṣe
«mā bhūn matis te, nṛpa, kā cid anyā
niḥ|saṃśayaṃ tad yad avocam asmi.

n' âsy' ânyathātvaṃ prati vikriyā me
svāṃ vañcanāṃ tu prati viklavo 'smi
kālo hi me yātum ayaṃ ca jāto
jāti|kṣayasy' â|su|labhasya boddhā.

vihāya rājyaṃ viṣayeṣv an|āsthas
tīvraiḥ prayatnair adhigamya tattvam
jagaty ayaṃ moha|tamo nihantuṃ
jvaliṣyati jñāna|mayo hi sūryaḥ.

Will the store of my fame never be depleted? 1.65
Will my family's power be ever secure?
In death, will I enter the yonder world in bliss
although asleep, with one eye open in my son?

Surely this my family shoot has not sprouted
to wither away before it has borne flowers?
Tell me quickly, My Lord, I have no peace,
for you know a father's love for his son."

When he realized that the king was distraught
by the thought of misfortune, the seer said:

"Do not let your mind be in any way perturbed;
what I said will come true, O King,
there is no doubt.

I'm perturbed not because he'll come to harm;
I have been cheated, that's why I'm distressed;
It's time for me to leave just as he's born
who will realize how to destroy birth,
a task so difficult to accomplish.

For quitting his realm, detached from pleasures,
realizing the truth through arduous efforts,
This sun of knowledge will blaze forth
in this world to dispel
the darkness of delusion.

1.70 duḥkh'|ârṇavād vyādhi|vikīrṇa|phenāj
jarā|taraṅgān maraṇ'|ôgra|vegāt
uttārayiṣyaty ayam uhyamānam
ārtaṃ jagaj jñāna|mahā|plavena.

prajñ"|âmbu|vegāṃ sthira|śīla|vaprāṃ
samādhi|śītāṃ vrata|cakravākām
asy' ôttamāṃ dharma|nadīṃ pravṛttāṃ
tṛṣṇ"|ârditaḥ pāsyati jīva|lokaḥ.

duḥkh'|ârditebhyo viṣay'|āvṛtebhyaḥ
saṃsāra|kāntāra|patha|sthitebhyaḥ
ākhyāsyati hy eṣa vimokṣa|mārgaṃ
mārga|pranaṣṭebhya iv' âdhvagebhyaḥ.

vidahyamānāya janāya loke
rāg'|âgnin" âyaṃ viṣay'|êndhanena
prahlādam ādhāsyati dharma|vṛṣṭyā
vṛṣṭyā mahā|megha iv' ātap'|ânte.

From this sea of grief, 1.70
strewn with the foam of sickness,
with waves of old age
and the fearsome tides of death,
He will rescue with the mighty boat of knowledge
this stricken world carried away by the current.

The living world that's tormented by thirst
will drink
from the lofty stream of dharma
flowing from him;
A stream that is made cool by mental trance,
a stream whose current is wisdom,
whose banks are steadfast discipline,
whose *chakra·vaka* ducks are vows.

To those who are tormented by suffering,
ensnared by the objects of sense,
roaming through samsara's wild tracks,
This one will proclaim the way to release,
as to travelers who've lost their way.

Upon men in this world who are being scorched
by the fire of passion, whose fuel
is the objects of the senses,
He'll pour relief with the rain of dharma,
like a rain cloud pouring down rain,
at the end of the summer heat.

tṛṣṇ"|ârgalaṃ moha|tamaḥ|kapāṭaṃ
dvāraṃ prajānām apayāna|hetoḥ
vipāṭayiṣyaty ayam uttamena
sad|dharma|tāḍena dur|āsadena.

1.75 svair moha|pāśaiḥ pariveṣṭitasya
duḥkh'|âbhibhūtasya nir|āśrayasya
lokasya saṃbudhya ca dharma|rājaḥ
kariṣyate bandhana|mokṣam eṣaḥ.

tan mā kṛthāḥ śokam imaṃ prati tvam
asmin sa śocyo 'sti manuṣya|loke
mohena vā kāma|sukhair madād vā
yo naiṣṭhikaṃ śroṣyati n' âsya dharmam.

bhraṣṭasya tasmāc ca guṇād ato me
dhyānāni labdhv" âpy a|kṛt'|ârthat" âiva;
dharmasya tasy' â|śravaṇād ahaṃ hi
manye vipattiṃ tri|dive 'pi vāsam.»

iti śrut'|ârthaḥ sa|suhṛt sa|dāras
tyaktvā viṣādaṃ mumude nar'|êndraḥ
«evaṃ|vidho 'yaṃ tanayo mam' êti»
mene sa hi svām api sāravattām.

With the irresistible supreme blow
of the true dharma, he will burst open
The door whose bolt is thirst and whose panels
are delusion and torpor,
so that creatures may escape.

Gaining full Awakening, this king of dharma 1.75
will release the world from bondage,
A world bound with the snares of its own delusion,
a world overcome by grief,
a world that has no refuge.

Do not grieve, therefore, on account of him;
but who through delusion or pride,
or the love of pleasures,
Listens not to his absolute dharma,
for him one should grieve
in this world of men.

Because I'm deprived of that distinction,
I have failed to attain the final goal,
although I have attained the transic states;
For, because I have not heard his dharma,
even living in the triple heaven
I consider as a calamity."

The king, when he heard that explanation,
rejoiced with his wife and his friends,
giving up his melancholy;
thinking, "Such indeed is this son of mine!"
he deemed it also his own good fortune.

«ārṣeṇa mārgeṇa tu yāsyat' îti»
cintā|vidheyaṃ hṛdayaṃ cakāra
na khalv asau na priya|dharma|pakṣaḥ
saṃtāna|nāśāt tu bhayaṃ dadarśa.

1.80 atha munir Asito nivedya tattvaṃ
suta|niyataṃ suta|viklavāya rājñe
sa|bahu|matam udīkṣyamāṇa|rūpaḥ
pavana|pathena yath"|āgataṃ jagāma.

kṛta|mitir anujā|sutaṃ ca dṛṣṭvā
muni|vacana|śravaṇe ca tan|matau ca
bahu|vidham anukampayā sa sādhuḥ
priya|sutavad viniyojayāṃ cakāra.

nara|patir api putra|janma|tuṣṭo
viṣaya|gatāni vimucya bandhanāni
kula|sa|dṛśam acīkarad yathāvat
priya|tanayas tanayasya jāta|karma.

daśasu pariṇateṣv ahaḥsu c' âiva
prayata|manāḥ parayā mudā parītaḥ
akuruta japa|homa|maṅgal'|ādyāḥ
parama|bhavāya sutasya devat"|êjyāḥ.

api ca śata|sahasra|pūrṇa|saṃkhyāḥ
sthira|balavat|tanayāḥ sa|hema|śṛṅgīḥ
an|upagata|jarāḥ payasvinīr gāḥ
svayam adadāt suta|vṛddhaye dvi|jebhyaḥ.

But his heart was still filled with anxiety,
thinking, "He will follow the path of seers;"
not that he didn't love the side of dharma;
yet he saw danger: the end of his line.

Having declared the truth about his son 1.80
to the king, much distraught about his son,
the sage Ásita then went as he came,
as they looked up with reverence at him,
along the path of the wind.

Seeing his younger sister's son, that holy man,*
having attained right knowledge, in his compassion,
instructed him in many ways, as if he were
his own dear son, to listen to the sage's words,
and to follow his advice.

The king too, delighted at his son's birth,
threw open the prisons within his realm;
he performed his son's birth rite as prescribed,
in a way befitting his family,
out of deep love for his son.

When the ten days had passed and his mind purified,*
filled with supreme joy, he offered the divine rites,
with prayers, offerings, and other auspicious rites,
for his son's supreme welfare.

For the prosperity of his son, furthermore,
he gave by himself a hundred thousand milch cows,
in the prime of their youth,
their horns gilded with gold,
cows with strong and sturdy calves.*

1.85 bahu|vidha|viṣayās tato yat'|ātmā
sva|hṛdaya|toṣa|karīḥ kriyā vidhāya
guṇavati niyate śive muhūrte
matim akaron muditaḥ pura|praveśe.

dvi|rada|rada|mayīm ath' ô mah"|ârhāṃ
sita|sitapuṣpa|bhṛtāṃ maṇi|pradīpām
abhajata śivikāṃ śivāya devī
tanayavatī praṇipatya devatābhyaḥ.

puram atha purataḥ praveśya patnīṃ
sthavira|jan'|ânugatām apatya|nāthām
nṛ|patir api jagāma paura|saṃghair
divam a|marair Maghavān iv' ârcyamānaḥ.

bhavam atha vigāhya Śākya|rājo
Bhava iva Ṣaṇ|mukha|janmanā pratītaḥ
«idam idam» iti harṣa|pūrṇa|vaktro
bahu|vidha|puṣṭi|yaśas|karaṃ vyadhatta.

iti nara|pati|putra|janma|vṛddhyā
sa|jana|padaṃ Kapil'|āhvayaṃ puraṃ tat
dhana|da|puram iv' âpsaro|'vakīrṇaṃ
muditam abhūn Nala|kūbara|prasūtau.

iti Buddhacarite mahā|kāvye Bhagavat|prasūtir nāma
prathamaḥ sargaḥ

Then, his self controlled, he carried out rites 1.85
for varied ends, bringing joy to his heart,
and, when a fine auspicious time was fixed,
gladly resolved to enter the city.

The queen paid homage to the gods and with her son
got onto a costly ivory palanquin,
with garlands made of white *sita·pushpa* flowers,
and lamps studded with precious stones.

The king then made the queen enter the city
before him,
followed by aged women, accompanied by her child;
he too entered the city, extolled by its citizens,
as Mághavan once entered heaven,
extolled by the gods.

The Shakya king then proceeded to his palace,
joyful like Bhava at the birth of Shan·mukha;
his face beaming with delight, he made arrangements
to secure manifold prosperity and fame,
saying, "Do this! Do that!"

Thus the city named Kápila and the outlying districts
rejoiced at the prosperity from the birth of the prince,
like the city of the wealth-giving god,*
thronging with *ápsaras*es,
at Nala·kúbara's birth.

Thus ends the first canto named "The Birth of the Lord"
of the great poem "Life of the Buddha."

CANTO 2
LIFE IN THE LADIES' CHAMBERS

2.1 Ā JANMANO JANMA|jar"|ânta|gasya
tasy' ātma|jasy' ātma|jitaḥ sa rājā
ahany ahany artha|gaj'|âśva|mitrair
vṛddhiṃ yayau Sindhur iv' âmbu|vegaiḥ.

dhanasya ratnasya ca tasya tasya
kṛt'|âkṛtasy' âiva ca kāñcanasya
tadā hi n' âikān sa nidhīn avāpa
mano|rathasy' âpy ati|bhāra|bhūtān.

ye Padma|kalpair api ca dvip'|êndrair
na maṇḍalaṃ śakyam ih' âbhinetum
mad'|ôtkaṭā Haimavatā gajās te
vin" âpi yatnād upatasthur enam.

nān"|âṅka|cihnair nava|hema|bhāṇḍair
vibhūṣitair lamba|saṭais tath" ânyaiḥ
saṃcukṣubhe c' âsya puraṃ turaṅgair
balena maitryā ca dhanena c' āptaiḥ.

2.5 puṣṭāś ca tuṣṭāś ca tath" âsya rājye
sādhvyo '|rajaskā guṇavat|payaskāḥ
udagra|vatsaiḥ sahitā babhūvur
bahvyo bahu|kṣīra|duhaś ca gāvaḥ.

madhya|sthatāṃ tasya ripur jagāma
madhya|stha|bhāvaḥ prayayau su|hṛttvam
viśeṣato dārḍhyam iyāya mitraṃ
dvāv asya pakṣāv a|paras tu n' āsa.

EVER SINCE THE birth of his son, 2.1
who had reached the end of birth and old age,
the self-controlled king prospered day by day,
with wealth, elephants, horses, and allies,
like the Indus with the rush of waters.*

For at that time he won untold treasures,
all sorts of wealth and gems,
gold, both wrought and unwrought;
treasures that are too much to bear even
for that chariot of the mind called desire.

Himalayan elephants, made frenzied by rut,
which even elephant kings equal to Padma,
could not steer to the stables here,
served him even without effort.

His city shook with the stomping of the horses,
some arrayed with various distinctive marks,
some bedecked with trappings made of new gold,
some adorned and others with flowing manes,
acquired by force, purchased, or given by allies.

In his realm there were large numbers of cows, 2.5
plump and content, superb and without stain,
yielding fine and abundant milk,
together with outstanding calves.

His enemies became neutrals,
the neutrals turned into allies,
allies became markedly strong;
he had two parties, the third disappeared.*

tath" âsya mand'|ânila|megha|śabdaḥ
saudāminī|kuṇḍala|maṇḍit'|âbhraḥ
vin" âśma|varṣ'|âśani|pāta|doṣaiḥ
kāle ca deśe pravavarṣa devaḥ.

ruroha sasyaṃ phalavad yatha"|rtu
tad" â|kṛten' âpi kṛṣi|śrameṇa
tā eva c' âsy' âuṣadhayo rasena
sāreṇa c' âiv' âbhyadhikā babhūvuḥ.

śarīra|saṃdeha|kare 'pi kāle
saṃgrāma|sammarda iva pravṛtte
sva|sthāḥ sukhaṃ c' âiva nir|āmayaṃ ca
prajajñire kāla|vaśena nāryaḥ.

2.10 pṛthag vratibhyo vibhave 'pi garhye
na prārthayanti sma narāḥ parebhyaḥ
abhyarthitaḥ sūkṣma|dhano 'pi c' āryas
tadā na kaś cid vimukho babhūva.

n' â|gauravo bandhuṣu n' âpy a|dātā
n' âiv' â|vrato n' ân|ṛtiko na hiṃsraḥ
āsīt tadā kaś cana tasya rājye
rājño Yayāter iva Nāhuṣasya.

udyāna|dev'|āyatan'|āśramāṇāṃ
kūpa|prapā|puṣkariṇī|vanānām
cakruḥ kriyās tatra ca dharma|kāmāḥ
pratyakṣataḥ svargam iv' ôpalabhya.

Heaven, likewise, poured down showers for him
at the proper time and the proper place,
the gentle sound of wind and thunder clouds,
and rings of lightning adorning the sky,
without the bale of hail or lightning strikes.

Grain grew fruitful then at the right season
even without laborious tilling;
those same medical herbs became for him
even richer in juice and potency.*

Even at that time of danger to the body,
as in the period of an armed conflict,
women gave birth with great ease and on the due date,
remaining healthy and free of disease.

Even in dire straits none begged from others, 2.10
except the men who had taken the vow;*
then a noble man of even small means
never turned his back on someone who begged.

At that time there was no one in his realm
who was rude to elders, not generous,
untruthful, hurtful, or non-observant,
as in that of King Yayáti, Náhusha's son.

In their love for dharma, they constructed
parks and temples, hermitages and wells,
water counters and lotus ponds and groves,
as if they had seen heaven with their own eyes.

muktaś ca dur|bhikṣa|bhay'|āmayebhyo
  hṛṣṭo janaḥ svarga iv' âbhireme;
patnīṃ patir vā mahiṣī patiṃ vā
  parasparaṃ na vyabhiceratuś ca.

kaś cit siṣeve rataye na kāmaṃ;
  kām'|ârtham arthaṃ na jugopa kaś cit;
kaś cid dhan'|ârthaṃ na cacāra dharmaṃ;
  dharmāya kaś cin na cakāra hiṃsām.

2.15 stey'|ādibhiś c' âpy aribhiś ca naṣṭaṃ
  sva|sthaṃ sva|cakraṃ para|cakra|muktam
kṣemaṃ su|bhikṣaṃ ca babhūva tasya
  pur" Ânaraṇyasya yath" âiva rāṣṭre.

tadā hi taj|janmani tasya rājño
  Manor iv' Āditya|sutasya rājye
cacāra harṣaḥ praṇanāśa pāpmā
  jajvāla dharmaḥ kaluṣaḥ śaśāma.

evaṃ|vidhā rāja|kulasya saṃpat
  sarv'|ârtha|siddhiś ca yato babhūva
tato nṛ|pas tasya sutasya nāma
  «Sarv'|ârtha|siddho 'yam iti» pracakre.

devī tu Māyā vibudha'|ṛṣi|kalpaṃ
  dṛṣṭvā viśālaṃ tanaya|prabhāvam
jātaṃ praharṣaṃ na śaśāka soḍhuṃ,
  tato nivāsāya divaṃ jagāma.

Freed from famine, from danger and disease,
people, thrilled, rejoiced as if in heaven;
husbands were never unfaithful to wives,
or wives to their husbands.

No one sought pleasure for the sake of lust;
no one protected wealth for pleasure's sake;
no one served dharma for the sake of wealth;
no one caused injury for dharma's sake.*

Independent, free of theft and such vice, 2.15
free of enemies and enemy rule,
his kingdom was prosperous and peaceful,
like Anaránya's kingdom long ago.

For, at his birth, in the realm of that king,
as in that of Manu, Adítya's son,
joy ran rampant and evil disappeared,
dharma blazed forth and sin was extinguished.

Such was the affluence of the royal house,
as also the success of all his aims;
the king, therefore, gave this name to his son:

"He is Sarvártha·siddha!
Successful in all his aims!"

But when queen Maya saw the immense might
of her son, like that of a seer divine,
she could not bear the delight it caused her;
so she departed to dwell in heaven.

tataḥ kumāraṃ sura|garbha|kalpaṃ
snehena bhāvena ca nir|viśeṣam
mātṛ|ṣvasā mātṛ|sama|prabhāvā
saṃvardhayām ātma|ja|vad babhūva.

2.20 tataḥ sa bāl'|ârka iv' ôdaya|sthaḥ
samīrito vahnir iv' ânilena
krameṇa samyag vavṛdhe kumāras
tār"|âdhipaḥ pakṣa iv' â|tamaske.

tato mah"|ârhāṇi ca candanāni
ratn'|āvalīś c' âuṣadhibhiḥ sa|garbhāḥ
mṛga|prayuktān rathakāṃś ca haimān
ācakrire 'smai su|hṛd|ālayebhyaḥ.
vayo|'nurūpāṇi ca bhūṣaṇāni
hiraṇ|mayān hasti|mṛg'|âśvakāṃś ca
rathāṃś ca go|putraka|saṃprayuktān
putrīś ca cāmīkara|rūpya|citrāḥ.

evaṃ sa tais tair viṣay'|ôpacārair
vayo|'nurūpair upacaryamāṇaḥ
bālo 'py a|bāla|pratimo babhūva
dhṛtyā ca śaucena dhiyā śriyā ca.

vayaś ca kaumāram atītya samyak
saṃprāpya kāle pratipatti|karma
alpair ahobhir bahu|varṣa|gamyā
jagrāha vidyāḥ sva|kul'|ânurūpāḥ.

Then, his mother's sister, in majesty
equal to his mother, brought up the prince,
who was equal to a son of a god,
without distinction in love and fondness,
as if he were her own son.

Then, gradually the prince grew up well, 2.20
like the young sun over the eastern hills,
like a fire that's fanned by the wind,
like the moon in the bright fortnight.

Then, they brought for him from houses of friends,
expensive sandalwood, strings of jewels
filled with medicinal herbs,
golden toy-carts drawn by deer,
ornaments appropriate for his age,
toy elephants, deer, and golden horses,
chariots yoked to toy oxen,
and dolls resplendent with silver and gold.

Entertained thus by various sensory delights
appropriate for his age, although a mere child,
he appeared unlike a child in his steadfastness,
and in purity, wisdom, and nobility.

He passed through his childhood years
    in the proper way;
he went through initiation at the proper time;
in a few days he grasped the sciences
that were suitable for his family,
that commonly take many years to grasp.

2.25 naiḥśreyasaṃ tasya tu bhavyam arthaṃ
śrutvā purastād Asitād maha'|rṣeḥ
kāmeṣu saṅgaṃ janayāṃ babhūva
vanāni yāyād iti Śākya|rājaḥ.

kulāt tato 'smai sthira|śīla|yuktāt
sādhvīṃ vapur|hrī|vinay'|ôpapannām
Yaśodharāṃ nāma yaśo|viśālāṃ
vām"|âbhidhānāṃ Śriyam ājuhāva.

vidyotamāno vapuṣā pareṇa
Sanatkumāra|pratimaḥ kumāraḥ
s'|ârdhaṃ tayā Śākya|nar'|êndra|vadhvā
Śacyā Śahasr'|âkṣa iv' âbhireme.

«kiṃ cin manaḥ|kṣobha|karaṃ pratīpaṃ
kathaṃ na paśyed» iti so 'nucintya
vāsaṃ nṛ|po vyādiśati sma tasmai
harmy'|ôdareṣv eva na bhū|pracāram.

tataḥ śarat|toyada|pāṇḍareṣu
bhūmau vimāneṣv iva rañjiteṣu
harmyeṣu sarva'|rtu|sukh'|āśrayeṣu
strīṇām udārair vijahāra tūryaiḥ.

2.30 kalair hi cāmīkara|baddha|kakṣair
nārī|kar'|âgr'|âbhihatair mṛdaṅgaiḥ
var'|âpsaro|nṛtya|samaiś ca nṛtyaiḥ
Kailāsa|vat tad|bhavanaṃ rarāja.

He had heard earlier from Ásita, the great sage, 2.25
that the highest bliss would be his son's future lot;
so the Shakya king made him attached to pleasures,
fearing that his son would repair to the forest.

Then, from a family rooted in good conduct,
he summoned for him Shri, the goddess of fortune,
in the form of a virtuous maiden of great fame,
by the name of Yasho·dhara, "the bearer of fame,"
endowed with beauty, modesty, and good bearing.

Kumára, the prince, much like Sanat·kumára,
radiant with supreme beauty, enjoyed himself
with that daughter-in-law of the Shakya king,
as with Shachi, Indra the thousand-eyed god.

"How will he not see anything evil
That would cause his mind to become distressed?"

So thinking, the king assigned him chambers
confined to the top floors of the palace,
far away from the bustle on the ground.

Then, in palaces white as autumn clouds,
like divine mansions erected on earth,
with quarters providing comfort every season,
he passed his time with women playing lofty music.

His residence sparkled like Kailása, 2.30
with soft-sounding tambourines bound with gold,
women beating them with their finger tips,
dances rivaling those of lovely *ápsaras*es.

vāgbhiḥ kalābhir lalitaiś ca hāvair
  madaiḥ sa|khelair madhuraiś ca hāsaiḥ
taṃ tatra nāryo ramayāṃ babhūvur
  bhrū|vañcitair ardha|nirīkṣitaiś ca.

tataḥ sa kām'|āśraya|paṇḍitābhiḥ
  strībhir gṛhīto rati|karkaśābhiḥ
vimāna|pṛṣṭhān na mahīṃ jagāma
  vimāna|pṛṣṭhād iva puṇya|karmā.

nṛpas tu tasy' âiva vivṛddhi|hetos
  tad|bhāvin" ârthena ca codyamānaḥ
śame 'bhireme virarāma pāpād
  bheje damaṃ saṃvibabhāja sādhūn.

n' â|dhīravat kāma|sukhe sasañje
  na saṃrarañje viṣamaṃ jananyām
dhṛty" êndriy'|âśvāṃś capalān vijigye
  bandhūṃś ca paurāṃś ca guṇair jigāya.

2.35 n' âdhyaiṣṭa duḥkhāya parasya vidyāṃ;
  jñānaṃ śivaṃ yat tu, tad adhyagīṣṭa;
svābhyaḥ prajābhyo hi yathā tath" âiva
  sarva|prajābhyaḥ śivam āśaśaṃse.

bhaṃ bhāsuraṃ c' Āṅgiras'|âdhidevaṃ
  yathāvad ānarca tad|āyuṣe saḥ;
juhāva havyāny a|kṛśe kṛśānau
  dadau dvi|jebhyaḥ kṛśanaṃ ca gāś ca.

In that palace women entertained him
with soft voices and alluring gestures,
with playful drunkenness and sweet laughter,
with curling eyebrows and sidelong glances.

Then, ensnared by women skilled in erotic arts,
who were tireless in providing sexual delights,
he did not come to earth from that heavenly mansion,
as a man of good deeds, from his heavenly mansion.

But the king to secure his son's success,
and spurred by the future foretold for him,
delighted in calm, desisted from sin,
practiced restraint, gave gifts to holy men.

He did not, like a fickle man, cling to sexual delights,
with his women he did not engage in improper love,
the unruly horses of senses he firmly controlled,
he won over by his virtues, his kin and citizens.

He did not acquire learning to hurt other men; 2.35
he mastered the knowledge that was beneficial;
as to his own people, so to all the people,
he only wished what was beneficial.

The shining constellation headed by Ángirasa,*
he duly worshipped so that his son might have
a long life;
he made offerings in a blazing fire;
on twice-born men he bestowed gold and cows.

sasnau śarīraṃ pavituṃ manaś ca
tīrth'|âmbubhiś c' âiva guṇ'|âmbubhiś ca
ved'|ôpadiṣṭaṃ samam ātma|jaṃ ca
somaṃ papau śānti|sukhaṃ ca hārdam.

sāntvaṃ babhāṣe, na ca n' ârthavad yaj;
jajalpa tattvaṃ, na ca vi|priyaṃ yat;
sāntvaṃ hy a|tattvaṃ paruṣaṃ ca tattvaṃ
hriy" âśakann ātmana eva vaktum.

iṣṭeṣv an|iṣṭeṣu ca kārya|vatsu
na rāga|doṣ'|āśrayatāṃ prapede;
śivaṃ siṣeve vyavahāra|śuddhaṃ
yajñaṃ hi mene na tathā yathā tat.

2.40 āśāvate c' âbhigatāya sadyo
dey'|âmbubhis tarṣam acechidiṣṭa;
yuddhād ṛte vṛtta|paraśvadhena
dviḍ|darpam udvṛttam abebhidiṣṭa.

ekaṃ vininye, sa jugopa sapta,
sapt' âiva tatyāja, rarakṣa pañca;
prāpa tri|vargaṃ, bubudhe tri|vargaṃ,
jajñe dvi|vargaṃ, prajahau dvi|vargam.

To cleanse his body he bathed with water
from sacred fords,
and to cleanse his mind he bathed with the waters
of virtue;
he imbibed the Soma that is prescribed by the Vedas,
along with the tranquil bliss of heart produced
by himself.

He spoke only what was pleasant,
never anything useless;
he spoke only what was true,
never anything unpleasant;
he was unable, through shame, to say even to himself,
anything pleasant but untrue,
anything harsh though true.

Toward litigants, whether friend or foe,
he never displayed either love or hate;
honesty in court he practiced as a sacred act,
for he deemed it better than a sacrificial rite.

With the waters of gifts he quenched at once 2.40
the thirst of supplicants who flocked to him;
and he squelched the swollen pride of his foes
with the battle ax of virtue, not war.

One he disciplined, seven he guarded,
seven too he gave up, five he secured;
he attained the triple set, he fathomed the triple set,
he discerned the double set, he cast off the double set.*

kṛt'|âgaso 'pi pratipādya vadhyān
n' âjīghanan n' âpi ruṣā dadarśa;
babandha sāntvena phalena c' âitāṃs
tyāgo 'pi teṣāṃ hy a|nayāya dṛṣṭaḥ.

ārṣāṇy acārīt parama|vratāni;
vairāṇy ahāsīc cira|saṃbhṛtāni;
yaśāṃsi c' āpad guṇa|gandhavanti;
rajāṃsy ahārṣīn malinī|karāṇi.

na c' âjihīrṣīd balim a|pravṛttaṃ;
na c' âcikīrṣīt para|vastv|abhidhyām;
na c' âvivakṣīd dviṣatām a|dharmaṃ;
na c' âvivakṣīdd hṛdayena manyum.

2.45 tasmiṃs tathā bhūmi|patau pravṛtte
bhṛtyāś ca paurāś ca tath" âiva ceruḥ,
śam'|ātmake cetasi viprasanne
prayukta|yogasya yath" êndriyāṇi.

kāle tataś cāru|payo|dharāyāṃ
Yaśodharāyāṃ sva|yaśo|dharāyām
Śauddhodane Rāhu|sapatna|vaktro
jajñe suto Rāhula eva nāmnā.

ath' êṣṭa|putraḥ parama|pratītaḥ
kulasya vṛddhiṃ prati bhūmi|pālaḥ
yath" âiva putra|prasave nananda
tath" âiva pautra|prasave nananda.

Even criminals judged to be worthy of death,
he did not kill or even look at them with rage;
he inflicted on them lenient punishments,
for their release too is viewed as wrong policy.

He performed severe vows that were practiced by seers;
he eliminated long-standing enmities;
he attained fame that was perfumed by his virtues;
he abandoned passions that produce defilement.

He did not wish to raise inordinate taxes,
he did not wish to take what belonged to others,
he did not wish to reveal his foes' *adhárma*,
he did not wish to carry anger in his heart.

When that lord of the earth behaved in this manner, 2.45
his servants and citizens acted the same way,
like the senses of a man engaged in Yoga,
when his mind has become fully calm and tranquil.

Then in time Yasho·dhara, the "bearer of fame,"
bearing alluring breasts and bearing her own fame,
begot a son for Shuddhódana's son,
a son who had a face like Rahu's foe,
a son who was, indeed, named Ráhula.*

Then, having obtained the son he desired,
family success being fully assured,
just as the king rejoiced at the birth of his son,
he rejoiced also at the birth of his grandson.

«putrasya me putra|gato mam' êva
  snehaḥ kathaṃ syād» iti jāta|harṣaḥ
kāle sa taṃ taṃ vidhim ālalambe
  putra|priyaḥ svargam iv' āruruksan.

sthitvā pathi prāthama|kalpikānāṃ
  rāja'|rṣabhāṇāṃ yaśas" ânvitānām
śuklāny a|muktv" âpi tapāṃsy atapta
  yajñaiś ca hiṃsā|rahitair ayaṣṭa.

2.50 ajājvaliṣṭ' âtha sa puṇya|karmā
  nṛpa|śriyā c' âiva tapaḥ|śriyā ca
kulena vṛttena dhiyā ca dīptas
  tejaḥ sahasr'|âṃśur iv' ôtsisṛkṣuḥ.

Svāyaṃbhuvaṃ c' ārcikam arcayitvā
  jajāpa putra|sthitaye sthita|śrīḥ;
cakāra karmāṇi ca duṣ|karāṇi
  prajāḥ sisṛkṣuḥ Ka iv' ādi|kāle.

"Surely, my son will love his son
just as much as I love him!
How could it be otherwise?"

So thinking, the king, overcome with joy,
carried out one rite after another
at proper times, in his love for his son,
as if longing to ascend to heaven.

Following the path of the early kings,
those mighty bulls among kings, of wide fame,
he performed ascetic toil
without casting off his white clothes,
he offered sacrifices
without injuring living beings.*

Then, that man of good deeds brightly blazed forth 2.50
with the luster of king and ascetic,
shining by reason of virtue,
wisdom and family,
as if wishing to radiate light
like the thousand-rayed sun.

With his sovereignty stable, he worshipped, softly
reciting the verses of the Self-existent
for his son's stability;
he performed most difficult deeds, like Ka, the Creator,
when in the beginning he desired
to bring forth creatures.*

tatyāja śastraṃ, vimamarśa śāstraṃ;
śamaṃ siṣeve, niyamaṃ viṣehe;
vaś" îva kaṃ cid viṣayaṃ na bheje;
pit" êva sarvān viṣayān dadarśa.

babhāra rājyaṃ sa hi putra|hetoḥ,
putraṃ kul'|ârthaṃ, yaśase kulaṃ tu,
svargāya śabdaṃ, divam ātma|hetor,
dharm'|ârtham ātma|sthitim ācakāṅkṣa.

evaṃ sa dharmaṃ vividhaṃ cakāra
sadbhir nipātaṃ śrutitaś ca siddham
«dṛṣṭvā kathaṃ putra|mukhaṃ suto me
vanaṃ na yāyād» iti nāthamānaḥ.

2.55 rirakṣiṣantaḥ śriyam ātma|saṃsthāṃ
rakṣanti putrān bhuvi bhūmi|pālāḥ;
putraṃ nar'|êndraḥ sa tu dharma|kāmo
rarakṣa dharmād viṣayeṣu muñcan.

He laid down the sword and mulled over texts;
he pursued calm and bore rules of restraint;
like a sovereign, he was not enslaved
    to the sensory realm,
like a father, he regarded all the regions of his realm.

For he fostered his realm for the sake of his son,
his son for his family, family for fame,
scriptures for heaven, heaven for the sake of self,
for dharma he sought the endurance of his self.

Thus he performed diverse acts of dharma,
followed by good men, ordained by scripture,
with the prayer:

> "Surely, once he sees the face of his son,
>   my son would not repair to the forest!
> How could it be otherwise?"

Desiring to guard their own sovereign power, 2.55
the lords of the earth guard on earth their sons;
but though he was a lover of dharma,
this king guarded his son against dharma,
letting him loose amidst sensual pleasures.

vanam an|upama|sattvā bodhi|sattvās tu sarve
viṣaya|sukha|rasa|jñā jagmur utpanna|putrāḥ;
ata upacita|karmā rūḍha|mūle 'pi hetau
sa ratim upasiṣeve bodhim āpan na yāvat.

iti Buddhacarite mahā|kāvye 'ntaḥ|pura|vihāro nāma
dvitīyaḥ sargaḥ.

But all bodhisattvas of unrivaled spirit*
went to the forest, after they'd tasted
the pleasures of the sensory objects,
and after a son had been born to them.
Although the cause had grown deep roots
by his collected good deeds,*
until he reached Awakening, therefore,
he pursued sensual pleasures.

Thus ends the second canto named "Life in the Ladies' Chambers" of the great poem "Life of the Buddha."

CANTO 3
BECOMING DEJECTED

3.1 TATAḤ KADĀ cin mṛdu|śādvalāni
puṃs|kokil'|ônnādita|pādapāni
śuśrāva padm'|ākara|maṇḍitāni
gītair nibaddhāni sa kānanāni.

śrutvā tataḥ strī|jana|vallabhānāṃ
mano|jña|bhāvaṃ pura|kānanānām
bahiḥ|prayāṇāya cakāra buddhim
antar|gṛhe nāga iv' âvaruddhaḥ.

tato nṛ|pas tasya niśamya bhāvaṃ
putr'|âbhidhānasya mano|rathasya
snehasya lakṣmyā vayasaś ca yogyām
ājñāpayām āsa vihāra|yātrām.

nivartayām āsa ca rāja|mārge
saṃpātam ārtasya pṛthag|janasya
«mā bhūt kumāraḥ su|kumāra|cittaḥ
saṃvigna|cetā iti» manyamānaḥ.

3.5 pratyaṅga|hīnān vikal'|êndriyāṃś ca
jīrṇ'|ātur'|ādīn kṛpaṇāṃś ca dikṣu
tataḥ samutsārya pareṇa sāmnā
śobhāṃ parāṃ rāja|pathasya cakruḥ.

tataḥ kṛte śrīmati rāja|mārge
śrīmān vinīt'|ânucaraḥ kumāraḥ
prāsāda|pṛṣṭhād avatīrya kāle
kṛt'|âbhyanujño nṛ|pam abhyagacchat.

Then, one day he heard songs depicting groves, 3.1
with soft fields of grass, with trees resounding
with the songs of male cuckoos,
and adorned with lotus ponds.

Then, he heard how enchanting were the city parks,
parks that were very much loved by the women folk;
so he made up his mind to visit the outdoors,
restless like an elephant confined in a house.

Then, hearing about the wish of that heart's desire
called 'son,' the king ordered a pleasure excursion
befitting his love and sovereign power,
and in keeping with the age of his son.

He prevented the common folks with afflictions
from gathering on the royal highway, thinking:

"Lest the tender mind of the prince
Thereby become perturbed."

Then, removing very gently from every side 3.5
those lacking a limb or with defective organs,
the wretched, the decrepit, the sick, and the like,
they heightened the grandeur of the royal highway.

Then, when the royal highway had been made
splendid,
the splendid prince along with his trained attendants,
came down at the right time from atop the palace,
and, when permitted, came into the king's presence.

ath' ô nar'|êndraḥ sutam āgat'|âśruḥ
śirasy upāghrāya ciraṃ nirīkṣya
«gacch' êti» c' ājñāpayati sma vācā
snehān na c' âinaṃ manasā mumoca.

tataḥ sa jāmbūnada|bhāṇḍa|bhṛdbhir
yuktaṃ caturbhir nibhṛtais turaṅ|gaiḥ
a|klība|vidvac|chuci|raśmi|dhāraṃ
hiraṇ|mayaṃ syandanam āruroha.

tataḥ prakīrṇ'|ôjjvala|puṣpa|jālaṃ
viṣakta|mālyaṃ pracalat|patākam
mārgaṃ prapede sadṛś'|ânuyātraś
candraḥ sa|nakṣatra iv' ântar|īkṣam.

3.10 kautūhalāt sphītataraiś ca netrair
nīl'|ôtpal'|ârdhair iva kīryamāṇam
śanaiḥ śanai rāja|pathaṃ jagāhe
pauraiḥ samantād abhivīkṣyamāṇaḥ.

taṃ tuṣṭuvuḥ saumya|guṇena ke cid,
vavandire dīptatayā tath" ânye,
saumukhyatas tu śriyam asya ke cid,
vaipulyam āśaṃsiṣur āyuṣaś ca.

niḥsṛtya kubjāś ca mahā|kulebhyo
vyūhāś ca Kairātaka|vāmanānām
nāryaḥ kṛśebhyaś ca niveśanebhyo
dev'|ânuyāna|dhvajavat praṇemuḥ.

Then, the king, his eyes filled with tears,
sniffed his son's head, looked at him long;*
although with the word "Go!"
he gave the command,
in his mind out of love
he did not let him go.

Then, he got into a golden carriage
drawn by four trained horses with gold trappings,
and driven by a manly charioteer,
a man both trustworthy and skilled.

Then, along that road carpeted with bright flowers,
with hanging garlands and waving banners,
he advanced surrounded by an apt retinue,
like the moon along the sky surrounded by stars.

He pressed slowly along that royal road, 3.10
as citizens from all sides gaped at him,
a road strewn with eyes like blue lotus halves,
eyes open wide with curiosity.

Some praised him for his gentleness,
others adored him for his majesty,
some, on account of his benignity,
wished him long life and sovereignty.

Humpbacks emerging from the great mansions,
throngs also of dwarfs and Kairátakas,*
and women emerging from low-class homes,
bowed down like flags carried behind a god.*

tataḥ «kumāraḥ khalu gacchat' îti»
śrutvā striyaḥ preṣya|janāt pravṛttim
didṛkṣayā harmya|talāni jagmur
janena mānyena kṛt'|âbhyanujñāḥ—

tāḥ srasta|kañcī|guṇa|vighnitāś ca
supta|prabuddh'|ākula|locanāś ca
vṛtt'|ânta|vinyasta|vibhūṣaṇāś ca
kautūhalen' â|nibhṛtāḥ parīyuḥ;

3.15 prāsāda|sopāna|tala|praṇādaiḥ
kāñcī|ravair nūpura|nisvanaiś ca
vitrāsayantyo gṛha|pakṣi|saṅghān
anyo|'nya|vegāṃś ca samākṣipantyaḥ;

kāsāṃ cid āsāṃ tu var'|âṅganānāṃ
jāta|tvarāṇām api s'|ôtsukānām
gatiṃ gurutvāj jagṛhur viśālāḥ
śroṇī|rathāḥ pīna|payo|dharāś ca;

śīghraṃ samarth" âpi tu gantum anyā
gatiṃ nijagrāha yayau na tūrṇam
hriy" â|pragalbhā vinigūhamānā
rahaḥ|prayuktāni vibhūṣaṇāni;

paras|par'|ôtpīḍana|piṇḍitānāṃ
sammarda|saṃkṣobhita|kuṇḍalānām
tāsāṃ tadā sa|svana|bhūṣaṇānāṃ
vāt'|âyaneṣv a|praśamo babhūva;

"Look, the prince is going out!"

Hearing this news from their servants,
getting their elders' permission,
the ladies, yearning for his sight,
then climbed up to the upper floors—

they gathered curious and unabashed,
hampered by the slipping of girdle strings,
eyes dazed by the sudden rousing from sleep,
ornaments slipped on at hearing the news;

frightening away the bevies of house-birds 3.15
with the clatter of steps on the stairways,
with girdles jingling and anklets tinkling,
and rebuking each other for their haste;

some of these fine women, though making haste
in their eagerness, yet were being held back
by the weight of their chariot-sized hips,
as also by their full and ample breasts;

but another, though able to move quick,
checked her steps and did not go very fast,
timid out of shame and covering up
the ornaments worn for intimacy;

commotion then reigned in those balconies,
as they thronged pressing against each other,
ornaments on their bodies jingling loud,
their earrings aflutter by the jostling;

vāt'|âyanebhyas tu viniḥsṛtāni
  paras|par'|āyāsita|kuṇḍalāni
strīṇāṃ virejur mukha|paṅkajāni
  saktāni harmyeṣv iva paṅka|jāni;

3.20 tato vimānair yuvatī|karālaiḥ
  kautūhal'|ôdghāṭita|vātayānaiḥ
śrīmat samantān nagaraṃ babhāse
  viyad vimānair iva s'|âpsarobhiḥ;

vāt'|âyanānām a|viśāla|bhāvād
  anyo|'nya|gaṇḍ'|ârpita|kuṇḍalānām
mukhāni rejuḥ pramad"|ôttamānāṃ
  baddhāḥ kalāpā iva paṅka|jānām.

taṃ tāḥ kumāraṃ pathi vīkṣamāṇāḥ
  striyo babhur gām iva gantu|kāmāḥ
ūrdhv'|ônmukhāś c' âinam udīkṣamāṇā
  narā babhur dyām iva gantu|kāmāḥ.

dṛṣṭvā ca taṃ rāja|sutaṃ striyas tā
  jājvalyamānaṃ vapuṣā śriyā ca
«dhany" âsya bhāry" êti» śanair avocañ
  śuddhair manobhiḥ khalu, n' ânya|bhāvāt.

«ayaṃ kila vyāyata|pīna|bāhū
  rūpeṇa s'|âkṣād iva Puṣpaketuḥ
tyaktvā śriyaṃ dharmam upaiṣyat' îti»
  tasmin hi tā gauravam eva cakruḥ.

and as they stretched out from the balconies,
their earrings rubbing against each other,
the lotus-faces of the women bloomed,
like lotuses hanging from the mansions;

then, with its mansions bursting with young ladies, 3.20
throwing open the windows in their excitement,
the city sparkled on all sides with splendor,
like heaven with mansions filled with *ápsaras*es;

because those balconies were not too large,
with earrings resting on each others' cheeks,
the faces of those excellent girls beamed,
like lotus bouquets tied to the windows.

As they looked down at the prince on the road,
the women, it seemed, longed to come down to earth;
as they looked up at him with their necks stretched,
the men, it seemed, longed to go up to heaven.

Seeing that prince so resplendent
with beauty and sovereign splendor,
"Blessed is his wife!" those women murmured,
with pure hearts, and for no other reason.

"This man with long and stout arms,
we have heard indeed,
in beauty like the flower-bannered god in person,*
Will give up sovereign power and follow
the dharma;"

for that reason they showed him their respect.

3.25 kīrṇaṃ tathā rāja|pathaṃ kumāraḥ
paurair vinītaiḥ śuci|dhīra|veṣaiḥ
tat pūrvam ālokya jaharṣa kiṃ cin
mene punar|bhāvam iv' ātmanaś ca.

puraṃ tu tat svargam iva prahṛṣṭaṃ
Śuddh'|âdhivāsāḥ samavekṣya devāḥ
jīrṇaṃ naraṃ nirmamire prayātuṃ
saṃcodan'|ârthaṃ kṣitip'|ātmajasya.

tataḥ kumāro jaray" âbhibhūtaṃ
dṛṣṭvā narebhyaḥ pṛthag|ākṛtiṃ tam
uvāca saṃgrāhakam āgat'|āsthas
tatr' âiva niṣkampa|niviṣṭa|dṛṣṭiḥ:

«ka eṣa, bhoḥ sūta, naro 'bhyupetaḥ
keśaiḥ sitair yaṣṭi|viṣakta|hastaḥ
bhrū|saṃvṛt'|âkṣaḥ śithil'|ānat'|âṅgaḥ?
kiṃ vikriy" âiṣā, prakṛtir, yad|ṛcchā?»

ity evam uktaḥ sa ratha|praṇetā
nivedayām āsa nṛp'|ātmajāya
saṃrakṣyam apy artham a|doṣa|darśī
tair eva devaiḥ kṛta|buddhi|mohaḥ:

Seeing for the first time the royal highway, 3.25
so crowded with respectful citizens,
dressed in clean and dignified clothes,
the prince rejoiced somewhat and thought
he was in some way born again.

But seeing that city as joyous as paradise,
gods residing in the pure realm*
created an old man in order to induce
the son of the king to go forth.*

Then, the prince saw that man overcome by old age,
with a form so different from any other man;
full of concern, he said to his driver, his gaze
unwavering directed solely on that man:

"Who is this man, dear charioteer,
hair white, and hand clasping a walking stick,
brows hiding the eyes, body slumped and bent?
Is it a transformation?
Is it his natural state?
Or is it simply chance?"

When he was addressed in this manner,
the driver revealed to the king's son
a matter he should have kept concealed,
without seeing his blunder because
his mind was confused by those same gods:

3.30 «rūpasya hantrī, vyasanaṃ balasya,
śokasya yonir, nidhanaṃ ratīnām,
nāśaḥ smṛtīnāṃ, ripur indriyāṇām—
eṣā jarā nāma yay" âiṣa bhagnaḥ.

pītaṃ hy anen' âpi payaḥ śiśutve,
kālena bhūyaḥ parisṛtam urvyām,
krameṇa bhūtvā ca yuvā vapuṣmān
krameṇa ten' âiva jarām upetaḥ.»

ity evam ukte calitaḥ sa kiṃ cid
rāj'|ātmajaḥ sūtam idaṃ babhāṣe:
«kim eṣa doṣo bhavitā mam' âp' îty?»
asmai tataḥ sārathir abhyuvāca:

«āyuṣmato 'py eṣa vayaḥ|prakarṣo
niḥ|saṃśayaṃ kāla|vaśena bhāvī;
evaṃ jarāṃ rūpa|vināśayitrīṃ
jānāti c' âiv' êcchati c' âiva lokaḥ.»

tataḥ sa pūrv'|āśaya|śuddha|buddhir
vistīrṇa|kalp'|ācita|puṇya|karmā
śrutvā jarāṃ saṃvivije mah"|ātmā
mah"|âśaner ghoṣam iv' ântike gauḥ.

3.35 niḥśvasya dīrghaṃ sva|śiraḥ prakampya
tasmiṃś ca jīrṇe viniveśya cakṣuḥ
tāṃ c' âiva dṛṣṭvā janatāṃ sa|harṣāṃ
vākyaṃ sa saṃvigna idaṃ jagāda:

"Slayer of beauty, ravager of strength, 3.30
the womb of sorrow, the end of pleasures,
Destroyer of memory, foe of sense organs—
this is called old age,
that's what has crippled this man.

For, as a baby, even he drank milk,
and in time, further, he crawled on the ground,
In due course he became a handsome youth,
that same man in due course has reached old age."

Taken aback somewhat when so informed,
the king's son said this to the charioteer:

"Will this evil affect me too?"

The charioteer then said to him:

"Though you're blessed with long life,
without a doubt,
by force of time, you too will become old;
In this manner old age destroys beauty;
people know this and still they desire it."

Then, the noble one, his mind cleansed by past intents,
who had collected good deeds through countless ages,
hearing about old age became deeply perturbed,
like a bull hearing close by a great lightning strike.

He sighed deeply and shook his head, 3.35
he fixed his eyes on that old man,
and, seeing the people full of joy,
dejected, he uttered these words:

«evaṃ jarā hanti ca nir|viśeṣaṃ
smṛtiṃ ca rūpaṃ ca parā|kramaṃ ca;
na c' âiva saṃvegam upaiti lokaḥ
praty|akṣato 'p' īdṛśam īkṣamāṇaḥ.

evaṃ gate, sūta, nivartay' âśvān,
śīghraṃ gṛhāṇy eva bhavān prayātu;
udyāna|bhūmau hi kuto ratir me
jarā|bhaye cetasi vartamāne?»

ath' ājñayā bhartṛ|sutasya tasya
nivartayām āsa rathaṃ niyantā;
tataḥ kumāro bhavanaṃ tad eva
cint"|āveśaḥ śūnyam iva prapede.

yadā tu tatr' âiva na śarma lebhe
«jarā jar" êti» praparīkṣamāṇaḥ
tato nar'|êndr'|ânumataḥ sa bhūyaḥ
krameṇa ten' âiva bahir jagāma.

3.40 ath' âparaṃ vyādhi|parīta|dehaṃ
ta eva devāḥ sasṛjur manuṣyam;
dṛṣṭvā ca taṃ sārathim ābabhāṣe
Śauddhodanis tad|gata|dṛṣṭir eva:

«sthūl'|ôdaraḥ śvāsa|calac|charīraḥ
srast'|âṃsa|bāhuḥ kṛśa|pāṇḍu|gātraḥ
‹amb" êti› vācaṃ karuṇaṃ bruvāṇaḥ
paraṃ samāśritya naraḥ ka eṣaḥ?»

"Old age thus strikes down without distinction,
memory, beauty, and manly valor;
And yet people do not become distraught,
seeing such a man with their very eyes.

Such being the case, turn around the horses,
drive back to our home quickly, charioteer;
For how can I find joy in the gardens
when fear of old age occupies my mind?"

Then, on the orders of his master's son,
the driver turned the chariot around;
to that same palace that now seemed empty,
the prince, then, retreated, engrossed in thought.

But when even there he found no relief,
lost in deep reflection: "Old age! Old age!"
in due course, then, permitted by the king,
he ventured out again with that same man.

Then, those same gods fashioned another man 3.40
with a body afflicted by disease;
when the son of Shuddhódana saw him,
he inquired of his charioteer,
his gaze riveted on that man:

"His belly swollen, his body heaves as he pants;
his arms and shoulders droop,
his limbs are thin and pale;
Leaning on someone, he cries 'Mother!' piteously;
tell me, who is this man?"

tato 'bravīt sārathir asya: «saumya,
dhātu|prakopa|prabhavaḥ pravṛddhaḥ
rog'|âbhidhānaḥ su|mahān an|arthaḥ
śakto 'pi yen' âiṣa kṛto '|svatantraḥ.»

ity ūcivān rāja|sutaḥ sa bhūyas
taṃ s'|ânukampo naram īkṣamāṇaḥ:
«asy' âiva jātaḥ pṛthag eṣa doṣaḥ,
sāmānyato roga|bhayaṃ prajānām?»

tato babhāṣe sa ratha|praṇetā:
«kumāra, sādhāraṇa eṣa doṣaḥ;
evaṃ hi rogaiḥ paripīḍyamāno
ruj" āturo harṣam upaiti lokaḥ.»

3.45 iti śrut'|ârthaḥ sa viṣaṇṇa|cetāḥ
prāvepat' âmb'|ūrmi|gataḥ śaś" îva,
idaṃ ca vākyaṃ karuṇāyamānaḥ
provāca kiṃ cin mṛdunā svareṇa:

«idaṃ ca roga|vyasanaṃ prajānāṃ
paśyaṃś ca viśrambham upaiti lokaḥ;
vistīrṇam a|jñānam, aho, narāṇāṃ!
hasanti ye roga|bhayair a|muktāḥ!

Then, his charioteer responded:

"The great evil called sickness, much advanced,
rising, dear sir, from the clash of humors;
That is what makes this man, though once able,
now no longer self-reliant."

Looking at that man with great compassion,
the king's son once again asked this question:

"Is this an evil that's specific to this man?
Or is sickness a danger common to all men?"

The charioteer then responded:

"This is an evil, prince, common to all;
for though they are by sickness thus oppressed,
And although they are tormented by pain,
people continue to enjoy themselves."

Hearing this truth, he trembled, despondent, 3.45
like the moon shining in rippling waters;
and he said these words with deep compassion,
in a voice that was somewhat enfeebled:

"This evil of sickness striking mankind,
people notice, yet they remain content;
O how widespread the ignorance of men!
Though not freed from the danger of sickness,
yet they continue to laugh!

nivartyatāṃ, sūta, bahiḥ|prayāṇān
  nar'|êndra|sadm' âiva rathaḥ prayātu;
śrutvā ca me roga|bhayaṃ ratibhyaḥ
  pratyāhataṃ saṃkucat' îva cetaḥ.»

tato nivṛttaḥ sa nivṛtta|harṣaḥ
  pradhyāna|yuktaḥ praviveśa veśma;
taṃ dvis tathā prekṣya ca saṃnivṛttaṃ
  paryeṣaṇaṃ bhūmi|patiś cakāra.

śrutvā nimittaṃ tu nivartanasya
  saṃtyaktam ātmānam anena mene;
mārgasya śauc'|âdhikṛtāya c' âiva
  cukrośa ruṣṭo 'pi ca n' ôgra|daṇḍaḥ.

3.50 bhūyaś ca tasmai vidadhe sutāya
  viśeṣa|yuktaṃ viṣaya|pracāram
«cal'|êndriyatvād api nāma sakto
  n' âsmān vijahyād» iti nāthamānaḥ.

yadā ca śabd'|ādibhir indriy'|ârthair
  antaḥ|pure n' âiva suto 'sya reme,
tato bahir vyādiśati sma yātrāṃ
  «ras'|ântaraṃ syād» iti manyamānaḥ.

snehāc ca bhāvaṃ tanayasya buddhvā
  sa rāga|doṣān a|vicintya kāṃś cit
yogyāḥ samājñāpayati sma tatra
  kalāsv abhijñā iti vāra|mukhyāḥ.

Turn back, charioteer, from our excursion,
drive the carriage back to the king's palace;
Learning the danger of sickness, my mind
is repelled by pleasures
and seems, as if, to recoil."

Then, his joy disappeared and he returned
and entered his dwelling, brooding deeply;
seeing him return twice in this fashion,
the king proceeded to make inquiries.

When he heard the reason for his return,
he felt forsaken by him already;
he raged at the man in charge of clearing the road,
but, though angry, he imposed no harsh punishment.

And once again he arranged for his son 3.50
the most exquisite of sensual delights,
with the hope that,

"Perhaps, when his senses are excited,
He'll become attached and not forsake us."

But when within the seraglio his son found
no delight in sounds and other objects of sense,
he then ordered another excursion outdoors,
thinking that it might produce a different affect.

Out of love, knowing his son's state of mind,
disregarding any evils of lust,
he assigned to it skillful courtesans,
known to be accomplished in the fine arts.

tato viśeṣeṇa nar'|êndra|mārge
sv|alaṃkṛte c' âiva parīkṣite ca
vyatyasya sūtaṃ ca rathaṃ ca rājā
prasthāpayām āsa bahiḥ kumāram.

tatas tathā gacchati rāja|putre
tair eva devair vihito gat'|âsuḥ;
taṃ c' âiva mārge mṛtam uhyamānaṃ
sūtaḥ kumāraś ca dadarśa, n' ânyaḥ.

3.55 ath' âbravīd rāja|sutaḥ sa sūtaṃ:
«naraiś caturbhir hriyate ka eṣaḥ
dīnair manuṣyair anugamyamāno
[vi]bhūṣitaś c' âpy avarudyate ca?»

tataḥ sa śuddh'|ātmabhir eva devaiḥ
Śuddh'|âdhivāsair abhibhūta|cetāḥ
a|vācyam apy artham imaṃ niyantā
pravyājahār' ârthavad īśvarāya:

«buddh'|îndriya|prāṇa|guṇair viyuktaḥ
supto vi|saṃjñas tṛṇa|kāṣṭha|bhūtaḥ
saṃvardhya saṃrakṣya ca yatnavadbhiḥ
priya|priyais tyajyata eṣa ko 'pi.»

iti praṇetuḥ sa niśamya vākyaṃ
saṃcukṣubhe kiṃ cid uvāca c' âinam:
«kiṃ kevalo 'sy' âiva janasya dharmaḥ,
sarva|prajānām ayam īdṛśo 'ntaḥ?»

Then, he had the royal road inspected
and festooned superbly with special care;
he changed the driver and the chariot,
and sent the prince off on his trip outdoors.

Then, as the prince was traveling in this way,
those very gods contrived a lifeless man;
only the prince and driver, none other,
saw the dead man being carried on the road.

Then, the king's son said to the charioteer: 3.55

"Who is this man being carried by four men
and followed by people who are downcast?
He is well adorned, yet they weep for him?"

Then, the driver, whose mind was bewildered
by those same pure deities of the pure realm,
explained the matter frankly to his lord,
a matter that he should have kept concealed.

"Lying here unconscious, like straw or a log,
bereft of mind, sense, breath, or qualities,
This is someone his dearest ones discard,
though they nurtured and guarded him
with care."

When he heard these words of the charioteer,
he was shaken a bit and said to him:

"Is this dharma peculiar to this man?
Or is such the end that awaits all men?"

tataḥ praṇetā vadati sma tasmai:
«sarva|prajānām idam anta|karma;
hīnasya madhyasya mah"|ātmano vā
sarvasya loke niyato vināśaḥ.»

3.60 tataḥ sa dhīro 'pi nar'|êndra|sūnuḥ
śrutv" âiva mṛtyuṃ viṣasāda sadyaḥ;
aṃsena saṃśliṣya ca kūbar'|âgraṃ
provāca nihrādavatā svareṇa:

«iyaṃ ca niṣṭhā niyatā prajānāṃ,
pramādyati tyakta|bhayaś ca lokaḥ.
manāṃsi śaṅke kaṭhināni nṝṇāṃ
sva|sthās tathā hy adhvani vartamānāḥ.

tasmād rathaḥ, sūta, nivartyatāṃ no,
vihāra|bhūmer na hi deśa|kālaḥ;
jānan vināśaṃ katham ārti|kāle
sa|cetanaḥ syād iha hi pramattaḥ.»

iti bruvāṇe 'pi nar'|âdhip'|ātmaje
nivartayām āsa sa n' âiva taṃ ratham;
viśeṣa|yuktaṃ tu nar'|êndra|śāsanāt
sa Padma|ṣaṇḍaṃ vanam eva niryayau.

tataḥ śivaṃ kusumita|bāla|pādapaṃ
paribhramat|pramudita|matta|kokilam
vimānavat sa kamala|cāru|dīrghikaṃ
dadarśa tad vanam iva Nandanaṃ vanam.

Then, the charioteer said to him:

> "This is the final act of every man;
> whether one is low, middling, or noble,
> In this world for all men death is certain."

Then, the king's son, as he learned about death, 3.60
although steadfast, soon became despondent;
leaning his shoulder against the railing,
he said in a voice that was resonant:

> "This is the inevitable end of all men;
> yet the world rashly revels,* casting fears aside;
> The hearts of men, I suspect, must indeed be hard,
> that they journey along this road so unperturbed.
>
> Let us turn back our carriage, therefore, charioteer;
> for this is not the time or place for pleasure groves;
> For, perceiving death, how can a sensible* man,
> keep on reveling* here rashly at a time of pain."

Though he was so ordered by the son of the king,
yet he did not turn the chariot around; instead
to the specially prepared Padma·shanda park
he drove directly, on the orders of the king.

Then, with young trees in full bloom
and with cuckoo birds
flying around excited and intoxicated,
with pavilions and ponds lovely with lotuses,
he saw that park resembling the Nándana park.

3.65 var'|âṅganā|gaṇa|kalilaṃ nṛp'|ātmajas
tato balād vanam atinīyate sma tat
var'|âpsaro|vṛtam Alak"|âdhip'|ālayaṃ
nava|vrato munir iva vighna|kātaraḥ.

iti Buddhacarite mahā|kāvye Saṃveg'|ôtpattir nāma
tṛtīyaḥ sargaḥ.

Then, the king's son was led into that park by force, 3.65
a park that was crowded with throngs of lovely girls,
like a novice hermit fearful of obstacles
led by force to the palace of Álaka's king,
a palace crowded with lovely *ápsaras*es.

Thus ends the third canto named "Becoming Dejected"
of the great poem "Life of the Buddha."

CANTO 4
REBUFFING THE WOMEN

4.1 TATAS TASMĀT pur'|ôdyānāt
kautūhala|cal'|êkṣaṇāḥ
pratyujjagmur nṛpa|sutaṃ
prāptaṃ varam iva striyaḥ.

abhigamya ca tās tasmai
vismay'|ôtphulla|locanāḥ
cakrire samudācāraṃ
padma|kośa|nibhaiḥ karaiḥ.

tasthuś ca parivāry' âinaṃ
manmath'|ākṣipta|cetasaḥ
niścalaiḥ prīti|vikacaiḥ
pibanty iva locanaiḥ.

taṃ hi tā menire nāryaḥ:
«Kāmo vigrahavān» iti
śobhitaṃ lakṣaṇair dīptaiḥ
saha|jair bhūṣaṇair iva.

4.5 saumyatvāc c' âiva dhairyāc ca
kāś cid enaṃ prajajñire:
«avatīrṇo mahīṃ sākṣād
gūḍh'|âṃśuś candramā iti.»

tasya tā vapuṣ" ākṣiptā
nigṛhītaṃ jajṛmbhire
anyo|'nyaṃ dṛṣṭibhir hatvā
śanaiś ca viniśaśvasuḥ.

THEN, WOMEN from that city park 4.1
went out to receive the king's son,
their eyes darting in excitement,
as if going to receive
an approaching bridegroom.

When the women came up to him,
their eyes open wide in wonder,
they greeted him with due respect,
their hands folded like lotus buds.

And they stood there surrounding him,
minds surrendered to the god of love,
drinking him, as if, with their eyes,
unblinking, open wide with joy.

For those women imagined him to be
Kama, god of love, in bodily form;
for he was resplendent with brilliant marks,
as if with adornments that were inborn.

Because he was both so gentle and firm,* 4.5
some of those women came to this surmise:

"He is Moon himself in a bodily form,
Come down to earth here with his beams
concealed."

Smitten by his beauty,
they gaped, trying to hold back;
striking each other with
glances, they softly sighed.

evaṃ tā dṛṣṭi|mātreṇa
  nāryo dadṛśur eva tam;
na vyājahrur na jahasuḥ
  prabhāveṇ' âsya yantritāḥ.

tās tathā tu nir|ārambhā
  dṛṣṭvā praṇaya|viklavāḥ
purohita|suto dhīmān
  Udāyī vākyam abravīt:

«sarvāḥ sarva|kalā|jñāḥ stha
  bhāva|grahaṇa|paṇḍitāḥ
rūpa|cāturya|sampannāḥ
  sva|guṇair mukhyatāṃ gatāḥ.

4.10 śobhayeta guṇair ebhir
  api tān uttarān Kurūn
Kuberasy' âpi c' ākrīḍaṃ
  prāg eva vasu|dhām imām.

śaktāś cālayituṃ yūyaṃ
  vīta|rāgān ṛṣīn api
apsarobhiś ca kalitāṇ
  grahītuṃ vibudhān api.

bhāva|jñānena hāvena
  rūpa|cāturya|sampadā
strīṇām eva ca śaktāḥ stha
  saṃrāge, kiṃ punar nṛṇām?

Thus those women did nothing else,
but look at him with just their eyes;
they did not speak, they did not laugh,
so captivated by his might.

Wise Udáyin, the chaplain's son,
seeing them this way so paralyzed,
timid in their display of love,*
spoke, however, to those women:

"You are all skilled in all fine arts,
experts at capturing the heart;
You are all lovely and artful,
your qualities make you excel.

With these qualities you'd adorn 4.10
even the Kurus of the north,*
Even Kubéra's pleasure grove!
How much more then this lowly earth?

And you are able to arouse
even seers who are freed of lust;
You can capture even the gods,
who are charmed by *ápsaras*es.

With your flirtatious dalliance,
with your knowledge of emotions,
the wealth of your beauty and charm,
You can even excite passion
in women, how much more in men?

tāsām evaṃ|vidhānāṃ vo
niyuktānāṃ sva|gocare
iyam evaṃ|vidhā ceṣṭā
na tuṣṭo 'smy ārjavena vaḥ.

idaṃ nava|vadhūnāṃ vo
hrī|nikuñcita|cakṣuṣām
sa|dṛśaṃ ceṣṭitaṃ hi syād,
api vā gopa|yoṣitām!

4.15 yad api syād ayaṃ dhīraḥ
śrī|prabhāvān mahān iti*
strīṇām api mahat teja
iti* kāryo 'tra niścayaḥ.

purā hi Kāśisundaryā
veśa|vadhvā mahān ṛṣiḥ
taḍito 'bhūt padā Vyāso
dur|dharṣo devatair api.

Manthāla|Gautamo bhikṣur
Jaṅghayā vāra|mukhyayā
piprīṣuś ca tad|arth'|ârthaṃ
vyasūn niraharat purā.

Gautamaṃ Dīrghatapasaṃ
maha"|ṛṣiṃ dīrgha|jīvinam
yoṣit saṃtoṣayām āsa
varṇa|sthān'|âvarā satī.

When you are like that, appointed
each to your own specific task,*
Yet you conduct yourselves like this!
Your artlessness pleases me not.

For the way you conduct yourself
is only proper for new brides,
Who blushingly avert their eyes,
or else for the wives of cowherds!

Though he may be steadfast and great, 4.15
by the power of his majesty,
Yet women's verve is also great!
So should you conclude in this case.*

Long ago Kashi·súndari,
the prostitute, kicked with her foot
Vyasa, the great seer, whom even
the gods found it hard to assail.*

Once when Manthála Gáutama
lusted after Jangha,
the lovely courtesan,
He carried bodies of dead men,
desiring to please her with wealth.*

And Gáutama Dirgha·tapas,
the great seer, advanced in age,
Was pleasured by a young woman,
though she was low in rank and caste.*

Ṛṣyaśṛṅgaṃ muni|sutaṃ
  tath" âiva strīṣv a|paṇḍitam
upāyair vividhaiḥ Śāntā
  jagrāha ca jahāra ca.

4.20 Viśvāmitro maha"|rṣiś ca
  vigaḍho 'pi mahat tapaḥ
daśa varṣāṇy ahar mene
  Ghṛtācy" âpsarasā hṛtaḥ.

evam|ādīn ṛṣīṃs tāṃs tān
  anayan vikriyāṃ striyaḥ;
lalitaṃ pūrva|vayasaṃ
  kiṃ punar nṛ|pateḥ sutam?

tad evaṃ sati viśrabdhaṃ
  prayatadhvaṃ tathā yathā
iyaṃ nṛpasya vaṃśa|śrīr
  ito na syāt parāṅ|mukhī.

yā hi kāś cid yuvatayo
  haranti sa|dṛśaṃ janam;
nikṛṣṭ'|ôtkṛṣṭayor bhāvaṃ
  yā gṛhṇanti tu, tāḥ striyaḥ.»

ity Udāyi|vacaḥ śrutvā
  tā viddhā iva yoṣitaḥ
samāruruhur ātmānaṃ
  kumāra|grahaṇaṃ prati.

Rishya·shringa, son of a sage,
with no experience of women,
Was likewise entrapped and dragged off
by Shanta with manifold wiles.*

To Vishva·mitra, the great seer, 4.20
seeped in potent austerities,
Ten years seemed a day under the
spell of *ápsaras* Ghritáchi.*

Women have caused the arousal
of various seers such as these;
How much more then the king's son here,
gentle, in the flower of his youth?

Such being the case you should, therefore,
strive boldly in such a way that
This royal heir of the king's line
not turn his face away from here.

For any girl can captivate
the hearts of men of equal class;
But true women capture the love
of both the high-born and the low."

And when they heard these words of Udáyin,
those women were, as if, cut to the quick;
with determination they set their minds,
on captivating the prince.

4.25 tā bhrūbhiḥ prekṣitair hāvair
hasitair laḍitair gataiḥ
cakrur ākṣepikāś ceṣṭā
bhīta|bhītā iv' âṅganāḥ.

rājñas tu viniyogena
kumārasya ca mārdavāt
jahuḥ kṣipram a|viśrambhaṃ
madena madanena ca.

atha nārī|jana|vṛtaḥ
kumāro vyacarad vanam
vāsitā|yūtha|sahitaḥ
kar" îva Himavad|vanam.

sa tasmin kānane ramye
jajvāla strī|puraḥsaraḥ
ākrīḍa iva Vibhrāje
Vivasvān apsaro|vṛtaḥ—

maden' āvarjitā nāma
taṃ kāś cit tatra yoṣitaḥ
kaṭhinaiḥ pasprśuḥ pīnaiḥ
saṃhatair valgubhiḥ stanaiḥ;

4.30 srast'|âṃsa|komal'|ālamba|
mṛdu|bāhu|lat" âbalā
an|ṛtaṃ skhalitaṃ kā cit
kṛtv" âinaṃ sasvaje balāt;

Somewhat timidly, then, those damsels 4.25
made gestures aimed at arousing love;
with eyebrows, glances, and flirtations,
and with laughter, frolicking, and gait.

But on account of the king's command,
and the gentle nature of the prince,
they quickly dropped their timidity,
under the spell of liquor and love.

Surrounded, then, by those women,
the prince strolled about in the grove,
like an elephant with a female herd,
in a Himalayan grove.

In that lovely grove he sparkled,
escorted by the women folk,
like Vivásvat surrounded by *ápsaras*es,*
in the Vibhrája pleasure grove—

Some of the women who were there,
under the pretense of being drunk,
touched him with their firm and full breasts,
that were charming and closely set.

One of the girls feigned to stumble, 4.30
and with tender tendril-like arms,
hanging loosely from her drooping
shoulders, embraced him by force.

kā cit tāmr'|âdhar'|oṣṭhena
mukhen' āsava|gandhinā
viniśaśvāsa karṇe 'sya:
«rahasyaṃ śrūyatām» iti;

kā cid ājñāpayant" îva
provāc' ārdr'|ânulepanā:
«iha bhaktiṃ kuruṣv' êti»
hasta|saṃśleṣa|lipsayā;

muhur muhur mada|vyāja|
srasta|nīl'|âṃśuk" âparā
ālakṣya|raśanā reje
sphurad|vidyud iva kṣapā;

kāś cit kanaka|kāñcībhir
mukharābhir itas tataḥ
babhramur darśayantyo 'sya
śroṇīs tanv|aṃśuk'|āvṛtāḥ;

4.35 cūta|śākhāṃ kusumitāṃ
pragṛhy' ânyā lalambire
su|varṇa|kalaśa|prakhyān
darśayantyaḥ payo|dharān;

kā cit padma|vanād etya
sa|padmā padma|locanā
padma|vaktrasya pārśve 'sya
Padmaśrīr iva tasthuṣī;

One girl whispered in his ear,
her mouth smelling of liquor,
her lower lip coppery red:

"Listen to a secret!"

One girl, still wet with unguents,
said, as if she were commanding:

"Make a line here!"*

longing to be touched by his hand.

Another, pretending that she was drunk,
repeatedly let her blue dress slip down.
Flashing her girdle, she gleamed,
like the night with lightning streaks.

Some rambled hither and thither,
with their golden girdles tinkling,
displaying to him their hips,
covered with fine see-through cloth.

Others, grasping branches 4.35
of mango in full bloom,
bent down to expose breasts
resembling golden pots.

Another lotus-eyed girl came out
with a lotus from the lotus-grove,
and stood next to the lotus-faced prince,
like Padma·shri, the Lotus-Fortune.*

madhuraṃ gītam anv|arthaṃ
  kā cit s'|âbhinayaṃ jagau
taṃ sva|sthaṃ codayant" îva
  «vañcito 's' îty» avekṣitaiḥ;

śubhena vadanen' ânyā
  bhrū|kārmuka|vikarṣiṇā
prāvṛty' ânucakār' âsya
  ceṣṭitaṃ dhīra|līlayā;

pīna|valgu|stanī kā cid
  ghās'|āghūrṇita|kuṇḍalā
uccair avajahās' âinaṃ:
  «sa m" āpnotu bhavān» iti;*

4.40 apayāntaṃ tath" âiv' ânyā
  babandhur mālya|dāmabhiḥ,
kāś cit s'|ākṣepa|madhurair
  jagṛhur vacan'|âṅkuśaiḥ;

pratiyog'|ârthinī kā cid
  gṛhītvā cūta|vallarīm
«idaṃ puṣpaṃ tu kasy' êti»
  papraccha mada|viklavā;

kā cit puruṣavat kṛtvā
  gatiṃ saṃsthānam eva ca
uvāc' âinaṃ: «jitaḥ strībhir!
  jaya, bho, pṛthivīm imām!»

Another girl sang a sweet song,
with gestures that brought out its sense,
as if prodding the composed prince
with glances that appeared to say:

"You are cheating yourself!"

Another parodied his bearing
by stretching the bow of her brows
upon her beautiful countenance,
mimicking his resolute mien.

One girl with full and charming breasts,
her earrings shaking with her laugh,
made fun of him loudly, saying:

"Catch me, sir!"*

As he was running off, likewise, 4.40
others bound him with garland chains,
some restrained him with goads of words,
sweetened with seductive hints.

One girl, wanting to start a fight,
grabbed a branch of a mango tree
and inquired, her speech slurred by drink:

"Whose flower is this?"

One girl, mimicking the gait
and the bearing of a man,
said to him:

"Women have conquered you!
Now, sir, conquer this earth!"

atha lol'|êkṣaṇā kā cij
  jighrantī nīlam utpalam
kiṃ|cin|mada|kalair vākyair
  nṛp'|ātmajam abhāṣata:

«paśya, bhartaś, citaṃ cūtaṃ
  kusumair madhu|gandhibhiḥ
hema|pañjara|ruddho vā
  kokilo yatra kūjati.

4.45 aśoko dṛśyatām eṣa
  kāmi|śoka|vivardhanaḥ,
ruvanti bhramarā yatra
  dahyamānā iv' âgninā.

cūta|yaṣṭyā samāśliṣṭo
  dṛśyatāṃ tilaka|drumaḥ,
śukla|vāsā iva naraḥ
  striyā pīt'|âṅga|rāgayā.

phullaṃ kurubakaṃ paśya
  nirbhukt'|âlaktaka|prabham,
yo nakha|prabhayā strīṇāṃ
  nirbhartsita iv' ānataḥ.

bāl'|âśokaś ca nicito
  dṛśyatām eṣa pallavaiḥ,
yo 'smākaṃ hasta|śobhābhir
  lajjamāna iva sthitaḥ.

Then, one girl, her eyes rolling,
smelling a blue lotus bloom,
spoke to the king's son with words
that were somewhat slurred by drink:

"Look, Lord, at this mango tree,
full of honey-scented blooms;
A cuckoo cries there, as if
locked up in a golden cage.*

Look at this *ashóka* tree, 4.45
increasing a lover's grief;
Bees are buzzing there, as if
by a fire they are being scorched.*

Look at this *tílaka* tree
embraced by a mango branch,
Like a man dressed in white clothes
being embraced by a woman
with her body painted gold.*

Look at this *kúrubaka* tree in bloom,
shining like lac that has been just squeezed out,
Bent low, as if it has been put to shame,
by the brilliance of the women's nails.*

Look at this *ashóka* tree,
young and covered with young shoots,
That appears to stand abashed,
at the dazzle of our hands.*

dīrghikāṃ prāvṛtāṃ paśya
  tīra|jaiḥ sinduvārakaiḥ
pāṇḍur'|âṃśuka|saṃvītāṃ
  śayānāṃ pramadām iva.

4.50 dṛśyatāṃ strīṣu māh"|ātmyaṃ
  cakravāko hy asau jale
pṛṣṭhataḥ preṣyavad bhāryām
  anuvarty anugacchati.

mattasya para|puṣṭasya
  ruvataḥ śrūyatāṃ dhvaniḥ
a|paraḥ kokilo 'nvakṣaṃ
  pratiśrutk" êva kūjati.

api nāma vihaṅ|gānāṃ
  vasanten' āhṛto madaḥ
na tu cintayato '|cintyaṃ
  janasya prājña|māninaḥ.»

ity evaṃ tā yuvatayo
  manmath'|ôddāma|cetasaḥ
kumāraṃ vividhais tais tair
  upacakramire nayaiḥ.

evam ākṣipyamāṇo 'pi
  sa tu dhairy'|āvṛt'|êndriyaḥ
«martavyam» iti s'|ôdvego
  na jaharṣa na vivyathe.

Look at this pond surrounded by
sindu·várakas on its banks,
Like a young woman lying down,
decked out in her silky white clothes.*

Look at the greatness of women! 4.50
That *chakra·vaka* in the lake
Obediently follows its wife,
trailing behind her like a slave.

Listen to the sound of the cuckoo
maddened by passion, as it cries out;
At once like an echo,
another cuckoo coos.

How could it be that spring has brought
the passion of love to the birds;
Not to this man who thinks he's wise,
thinking what is beyond all thought?"*

In this manner those young girls,
their minds elated by love,
assailed the prince with intrigues
of many and diverse kinds.

Although seduced in this way,
he wavered not, nor rejoiced,
firmly guarding his senses,
and perturbed at the thought:

"One must die."*

4.55 tāsāṃ tattve 'n|avasthānaṃ
dṛṣṭvā sa puruṣ'|ôttamaḥ
samaṃ vignena dhīreṇa
cintayāmāsa cetasā:

«kiṃ v imā n' âvagacchanti
capalaṃ yauvanaṃ striyaḥ
yato rūpeṇa saṃmattaṃ
jarā yan nāśayiṣyati?

nūnam etā na paśyanti
kasya cid roga|saṃplavam;
tathā hṛṣṭā bhayaṃ tyaktvā
jagati vyādhi|dharmiṇi.

an|abhijñāś ca su|vyaktaṃ
mṛtyoḥ sarv'|âpahāriṇaḥ;
tataḥ sva|sthā nir|udvignāḥ
krīḍanti ca hasanti ca.

jarāṃ vyādhiṃ ca mṛtyuṃ ca
ko hi jānan sa|cetanaḥ
sva|sthas tiṣṭhen niṣīded vā
śayed vā kiṃ punar haset?

4.60 yas tu dṛṣṭvā paraṃ jīrṇaṃ
vyādhitaṃ mṛtam eva ca
sva|stho bhavati n' ôdvigno
yath" â|cetās tath" âiva saḥ.

When he saw that those women 4.55
had no firm grasp of the truth,
his mind both perturbed and firm,
that supreme man pondered thus:

"Do these women not understand
the transient nature of youth,
That they are drunk with their beauty,
which old age will surely destroy?

Surely they have never seen
a man by sickness oppressed,
That, without fear, they rejoice thus,
in this world subject to disease.

Quite clearly they are ignorant
of death that snatches away all;
Therefore, they have fun and they laugh,
at total ease and unperturbed.

For what sensible man who knows*
about old age, sickness, and death,
Would stand, sit, or lie down at ease?
How much less would he laugh, indeed?

But when a man happens to see 4.60
someone who is old, sick, or dead,
And remains at ease, unperturbed,
he's the same as a senseless man.*

viyujyamāne hi tarau
  puṣpair api phalair api
patati chidyamāne vā
  tarur anyo na śocate.»

iti dhyāna|paraṃ dṛṣṭvā
  viṣayebhyo gata|spṛham
Udāyī nīti|śāstra|jñas
  tam uvāca su|hṛttayā:

«ahaṃ nṛ|patinā dattaḥ
  sakhā tubhyaṃ kṣamaḥ kila
yasmāt, tvayi vivakṣā me
  tayā paṇayavattayā.

a|hitāt pratiṣedhaś ca
  hite c' ânupravartanam
vyasane c' â|parityāgas—
  tri|vidhaṃ mitra|lakṣaṇam.

4.65 so 'haṃ maitrīṃ pratijñāya
  puruṣ'|ârthāt parāṅ|mukham*
yadi tvā samupekṣeya,
  na bhaven mitratā mayi.

tad bravīmi suhṛd bhūtvā
  taruṇasya vapuṣmataḥ:
idaṃ na pratirūpaṃ te
  strīṣv a|dākṣiṇyam īdṛśam.

For when one tree is stripped
of its flowers or fruits;
Or when it's cut down or falls,
another tree does not grieve."

Seeing him in this way absorbed in deep thought,
without desire for any sensual things,
that expert in the science of polity,
Udáyin, out of friendship said to him:

"The king assigned me as your friend,
thinking I was up to the task;
Therefore, I want to speak to you,
because he placed his trust in me.

To curb him from what's undesirable,
to press him to do what's desirable,
Not to desert him in difficult times—
these, indeed, are the three marks of a friend.

After I have pledged my friendship to you, 4.65
should I be disinterested in you,
Who have turned your back on the goals of man,*
there would, indeed, be no friendship in me.

So, I speak as a friend of yours,
you who are so handsome and young;
This lack of courtesy to women;
it is unbecoming of you.

an|ṛten' âpi nārīṇāṃ
  yuktaṃ samanuvartanam
tad|vrīḍā|parihār'|ârtham
  ātma|raty|artham eva ca.

saṃnatiś c' ânuvṛttiś ca
  strīṇāṃ hṛdaya|bandhanam;
snehasya hi guṇā yonir
  māna|kāmāś ca yoṣitaḥ.

tad arhasi, viśāl'|âkṣa,
  hṛdaye 'pi parāṅ|mukhe
rūpasy' âsy' ânurūpeṇa
  dākṣiṇyen' ânuvartitum.

4.70 dākṣiṇyam auṣadhaṃ strīṇāṃ,
  dākṣiṇyaṃ bhūṣaṇaṃ param;
dākṣiṇya|rahitaṃ rūpaṃ
  niṣ|puṣpam iva kānanam.

kiṃ vā dākṣiṇya|mātreṇa?
  bhāven' âstu parigrahaḥ.
viṣayān dur|labhāl labdhvā
  na hy avajñātum arhasi.

‹kāmaṃ param› iti jñātvā
  devo 'pi hi Puraṃdaraḥ
Gautamasya muneḥ patnīm
  Ahalyāṃ cakame purā.

It's fit to pander to women
even by telling a falsehood,
To rid them of their bashfulness,
to gratify oneself as well.

To submit and pander to them,
that's what binds the hearts of women;
For virtues are the womb of love,
and women long to be admired.

So, O large-eyed one, though your heart
is turned away, deign to pander
With a gallantry that befits
the true beauty of your body.

Gallantry is the medicine 4.70
and chief ornament for women;
For beauty without gallantry
is like a park without flowers.

Or what good is just gallantry?
Embrace them with feeling that's true.
For, finding pleasures hard to find,
you should not treat them with contempt.*

Knowing pleasure to be the best,
even god Indra long ago
Made love to Ahálya,
the sage Gáutama's wife.*

Agastyaḥ prārthayām āsa
soma|bhāryāṃ ca Rohiṇīm
tasmāt tat|sadṛśīṃ lebhe
Lopāmudrām—iti śrutiḥ.

Utathyasya ca bhāryāyāṃ
Mamatāyāṃ mahā|tapaḥ
Mārutyāṃ janayām āsa
Bharadvājaṃ Bṛhaspatiḥ.

4.75 Bṛhas|pater mahiṣyāṃ ca
juhvatyāṃ juhvatāṃ varaḥ
Budhaṃ vibudha|karmāṇaṃ
janayām āsa Candramāḥ.

Kālīṃ c' âiva purā kanyāṃ
jala|prabhava|saṃbhavām
jagāma Yamunā|tīre
jāta|rāgaḥ Parāśaraḥ.

Mātaṅgyām Akṣamālāyāṃ
garhitāyāṃ riraṃsayā
Kapiñjalādaṃ tanayaṃ
Vasiṣṭho 'janayan muniḥ.

Yayātiś c' âiva rāja'|rṣir
vayasy api vinirgate
Viśvācy" âpsarasā s'|ârdhaṃ
reme Caitrarathe vane.

Though Pandu of the Kuru line knew
 that sex indeed would lead to his death,
Seduced by the beauty of Madri,
 he gave in to the pleasure of sex.*

And Karála·jánaka as well, 4.80
 who abducted a brahmin girl,
Never stopped holding fast to his love,
 although he came to ruin thereby.*

Men of eminence such as these,
 to satisfy their carnal lust,
Enjoyed pleasures even abject,
 how much more, then, excellent ones?

Yet you, youthful, handsome, and strong,
 treat pleasures with utter contempt,
Pleasures you have rightly obtained,
 pleasures to which the whole world clings."

When he heard this smooth speech of his,
supported by scriptural texts,
the prince answered back in a voice,
like the thunder clap of a cloud:

"Your words are becoming of you,
 disclosing your friendship for me;
But I'll convince you point by point
 every place you have judged me wrong.

4.85 n' âvajānāmi viṣayān,
jāne lokaṃ tad|ātmakam;
a|nityaṃ tu jagan matvā
n' âtra me ramate manaḥ.

jarā vyādhiś ca mṛtyuś ca
yadi na syād idaṃ trayam
mam' âpi hi manojñeṣu
viṣayeṣu ratir bhavet.

nityaṃ yady api hi strīṇām
etad eva vapur bhavet
doṣavatsv api kāmeṣu
kāmaṃ rajyeta me manaḥ.

yadā tu jarayā pītaṃ
rūpam āsāṃ bhaviṣyati,
ātmano 'py an|abhipretaṃ
mohāt tatra ratir bhavet.

mṛtyu|vyādhi|jarā|dharmā
mṛtyu|vyādhi|jar"|ātmabhiḥ
ramamāṇo hy a|saṃvignaḥ
samāno mṛga|pakṣibhiḥ.

4.90 yad apy āttha ‹mah"|ātmānas
te 'pi kām'|ātmakā iti›
saṃvego 'tr' âiva kartavyo,
yadā teṣām api kṣayaḥ.

I show no contempt for pleasures of sense, 4.85
I know that people are obsessed with them;
But knowing that the world is transient,
my heart finds no delight in them at all.

For if old age, sickness, and death,
these three things were not to exist,
I would also have found delight
in delightful pleasures of sense.

For if women could just maintain
these same bodies for evermore,
My heart may well have found delight,
even in these sinful pleasures.

But when these lovely forms of theirs
will have been consumed by old age,
They'll be repulsive even to themselves;
it is delusion to delight in them.

For when a man who's subject to
death, sickness, and old age as well,
Dallies unperturbed with women
gripped by death, sickness, and old age,
he's no better than beasts or birds.

What you say about those eminent men, 4.90
that they were also given to pleasures;
It should indeed cause us all anxiety,
that these men also have succumbed to death!

māh"|ātmyaṃ na ca tan manye
   yatra sāmānyataḥ kṣayaḥ
viṣayeṣu prasaktir vā
   yuktir vā n' ātmavattayā.

yad apy ātth' ‹ân|ṛten' âpi
   strī|jane vartyatām› iti
an|ṛtaṃ n' âvagacchāmi
   dākṣiṇyen' âpi kiṃ cana.

na c' ânuvartanaṃ tan me
   rucitaṃ yatra n' ârjavam;
sarva|bhāvena saṃparko
   yadi n' âsti, dhig astu tat.

a|dhṛteḥ śrad|dadhānasya
   saktasy' â|doṣa|darśinaḥ
kiṃ hi vañcayitavyaṃ syāj
   jāta|rāgasya cetasaḥ.

4.95 vañcayanti ca yady evaṃ
   jāta|rāgāḥ paras|param
nanu n' âiva kṣamaṃ draṣṭuṃ
   narāḥ strīṇāṃ nṛṇāṃ striyaḥ.

tad evaṃ sati duḥkh'|ārtaṃ
   jarā|maraṇa|bhāginam
na māṃ kāmeṣv an|āryeṣu
   pratārayitum arhasi.

No true eminence exists in my view,
where death exists as a general trait,
Where attachment to sense objects persists,
or where self-possession is not attained.

As to what you say that one should pander
to women by speaking even falsehoods;
I cannot condone anything that's false,
even when it is linked to gallantry.

I do not relish pandering
that's devoid of sincerity;
I deplore sexual union
that is without full commitment.

For is it proper to deceive someone
who is unsteady and is full of trust,
Who is attached and is blind to perils,
whose mind is caught in the grip of passion?

If those in the grip of passion, 4.95
were to deceive each other thus,
Surely, it would not be proper,
then, for men to look at women,
or for women to look at men.

So, that being the case, it behooves you not
to lure me into ignoble pleasures,
I, who am afflicted with suffering,
under the power of old age and death.

aho 'ti|dhīraṃ balavac ca te manaś
 caleṣu kāmeṣu ca sāra|darśinaḥ
bhaye 'ti|tīvre viṣayeṣu sajjase
 nirīkṣamāṇo maraṇ'|âdhvani prajāḥ.

ahaṃ punar bhīrur at' îva viklavo
 jarā|vipad|vyādhi|bhayaṃ vicintayan
labhe na śāntiṃ na dhṛtiṃ, kuto ratiṃ,
 niśāmayan dīptam iv' âgninā jagat.

‹a|saṃśayaṃ mṛtyur› iti prajānato
 narasya rāgo hṛdi yasya jāyate,
ayo|mayīṃ tasya paraimi cetanāṃ
 mahā|bhaye rajyati yo na roditi.»

4.100 ath' ô kumāraś ca viniścay'|ātmikāṃ
 cakāra kām'|āśraya|ghātinīṃ kathām
janasya cakṣur|gamanīya|maṇḍalo
 mahī|dharaṃ c' âstam iyāya bhās|karaḥ.

tato vṛthā|dhārita|bhūṣaṇa|srajaḥ
 kalā|guṇaiś ca praṇayaiś ca niṣ|phalaiḥ
sva eva bhāve vinigṛhya manmathaṃ
 puraṃ yayur bhagna|mano|rathāḥ striyaḥ.

tataḥ pur'|ôdyāna|gatāṃ jana|śriyaṃ
 nirīkṣya sāyaṃ pratisaṃhṛtāṃ punaḥ
a|nityatāṃ sarva|gatāṃ vicintayan
 viveśa dhiṣṇyaṃ kṣiti|pālak'|ātmajaḥ.

O how steady and strong your mind must be
that you see substance in fleeting pleasures,
That, seeing these creatures on the path of death,
you are attached to sensual pleasures
in the midst of the most frightful dangers.

I, however, am timid, much perturbed,
as I think of the dangers
of old age, sickness, and death;
I find no peace or content, much less joy,
seeing the world with fire as if ablaze.

When passion arises in a man's heart
who understands the certainty of death,
His heart, I reckon, must be made of steel,
when in the face of such a great danger
he makes merry and does not weep."

Then, as the prince made this resolute speech, 4.100
that wiped out any resort to pleasure,
the sun, upon whose orb people could gaze,
proceeded to the mountains of the west.

Then, the women went back to the city,
locking love within their hearts, their hopes dashed—
vain the ornaments and garlands they wore,
fruitless their fine arts and displays of love.*

Then, seeing the beauty of the women folk
in the city park withdrawn at sunset,
pondering the transience of everything,
the ruler's son entered his dwelling place.

tataḥ śrutvā rājā
    viṣaya|vimukhaṃ tasya tu mano,
  na śiśye tāṃ rātriṃ
    hṛdaya|gata|śalyo gaja iva;
atha śrānto mantre
    bahu|vividha|mārge sa|sacivo
  na so 'nyat kāmebhyo
    niyamanam apaśyat suta|mateḥ.

iti Buddhacarite mahā|kāvye Strī|vighātano nāma caturthaḥ sargaḥ.

Then, hearing that his son's mind was averse
to objects of sense, the king did not sleep
that night, like an elephant with a dart
  buried in its heart.

Then, he toiled hard with his counsels
on the diverse paths of counsel;
but besides pleasures he did not
see another path to restrain
  the mind of his son.

Thus ends the fourth canto named "Rebuffing the Women"
of the great poem "Life of the Buddha."

CANTO 5
THE DEPARTURE

5.1 Sa tathā viṣayair vilobhyamānaḥ
param'|ârhair api Śākya|rāja|sūnuḥ
na jagāma dhṛtiṃ na śarma lebhe,
hṛdaye siṃha iv' âti|digdha|viddhaḥ.

atha mantri|sutaiḥ kṣamaiḥ kadā cit
sakhibhiś citra|kathaiḥ kṛt'|ânuyātraḥ
vana|bhūmi|didṛkṣayā śam'|êpsur
nara|dev'|ânumato bahiḥ pratasthe.

nava|rukma|khalīna|kiṅkiṇīkaṃ
pracalac|cāmara|cāru|hema|bhāṇḍam
abhiruhya sa Kanthakaṃ sad|aśvaṃ
prayayau ketum iva drum'|âbja|ketuḥ.

sa vikṛṣṭatarāṃ van'|ânta|bhūmiṃ
vana|lobhāc ca yayau mahī|guṇāc ca;
salil'|ōrmi|vikāra|sīra|mārgāṃ
vasu|dhāṃ c' âiva dadarśa kṛṣyamāṇām.

5.5 hala|bhinna|vikīrṇa|śaṣpa|darbhāṃ
hata|sūkṣma|krimi|kīṭa|jantu|kīrṇām
samavekṣya rasāṃ tathā|vidhāṃ tāṃ
sva|janasy' êva vadhe bhṛśaṃ śuśoca.

ALTHOUGH, IN this way, the Shakya king's son 5.1
was enticed with priceless objects of sense,
yet he got no content, found no relief,
like a lion shot in the heart
with a poison-tipped arrow.

Then one day, with the consent of the king,
he went outside to see the wooded groves,
along with able sons of ministers
and friends good at narrating vivid tales,
yearning to find peace.

He set out mounted on the good horse Kánthaka—
the bells hanging from its bit were made of new gold,
its gold trappings made charming with
flowing chowries—
like the glint of *drumábja* mounted on a flag.*

Love of the woods and the exquisite land
drew him deep into the distant forest;
there he saw the earth being plowed, with furrows
resembling the rippling waves on water.

Clumps of grass dug up by the plow littered the earth, 5.5
covered with tiny dead creatures, insects and worms;
as he beheld the earth with all these strewn about,
he grieved greatly, as if a kinsman had been killed.

kṛṣataḥ puruṣāṃś ca vīkṣamāṇaḥ
pavan'|ârk'|âṃśu|rajo|vibhinna|varṇān
vahana|klama|viklavāṃś ca dhuryān
param'|āryaḥ paramāṃ kṛpāṃ cakāra.

avatīrya tatas turaṅga|pṛṣṭāc
chanakair gāṃ vyacarac chucā parītaḥ
jagato janana|vyayaṃ vicinvan
«kṛpaṇaṃ khalv idam» ity uvāca c' ārtaḥ.

manasā ca viviktatām abhīpsuḥ
su|hṛdas tān anuyāyino nivārya
abhitaś cala|cāru|parṇavatyā
vijane mūlam upeyivān sa jambvāḥ.

niṣasāda sa yatra śaucavatyāṃ
bhuvi vaiḍūrya|nikāśa|śādvalāyām
jagataḥ prabhava|vyayau vicinvan
manasaś ca sthiti|mārgam ālalambe.

5.10 samavāpta|manaḥ|sthitiś ca sadyo
viṣay'|êcch''|ādibhir ādhibhiś ca muktaḥ
sa|vitarka|vicāram āpa śāntaṃ
prathamaṃ dhyānam an|āsrava|prakāram.

Seeing the men plowing the fields,
their bodies discolored
by the wind, the dust, the scorching
rays of the sun,
oxen wearied by the toil of pulling the plows,
great compassion overwhelmed that great noble man.

Getting down from the horse, then, he began to pace
slowly across that land, deeply engulfed by grief,
reflecting on the birth and death of all creatures;
and deeply anguished, he cried out:

"How wretched, indeed, is this world!"

Getting rid of those friends who accompanied him,
wishing to reach some clarity in his own mind,
he reached the foot of a rose apple tree in a
lonely spot with charming leaves rustling all around.

On that pure ground with grass the color of beryl,
he sat down, and as he began to contemplate
the origin and destruction of all creatures,
he embarked upon the path of mental stillness.

Achieving at once the state of mental stillness, 5.10
and freedom from worries, such as sensual desire,
he attained the first trance—
with thought and reflection,
tranquil, uninfluenced by the evil inflows.*

adhigamya tato viveka|jaṃ tu
paramā|prīti|sukhaṃ manaḥ|samādhim
idam eva tataḥ paraṃ pradadhyau
manasā loka|gatiṃ niśāmya samyak:

«kṛpaṇaṃ, bata, yaj|janaḥ svayaṃ sann
a|vaśo vyādhi|jarā|vināśa|dharmā
jaray" ârditam āturaṃ mṛtaṃ vā
param a|jño vijugupsate mad'|ândhaḥ.

iha ced aham īdṛśaḥ svayaṃ san
vijugupseya paraṃ tathā|svabhāvam,
na bhavet sa|dṛśaṃ hi tat kṣamaṃ vā
paramaṃ dharmam imaṃ vijānato me.»

iti tasya vipaśyato yathāvaj
jagato vyādhi|jarā|vipatti|doṣān
bala|yauvana|jīvita|pravṛtto
vijagām' ātma|gato madaḥ kṣaṇena.

5.15 na jaharṣa na c' âpi c' ânutepe;
vicikitsāṃ na yayau na tandri|nidre;
na ca kāma|guṇeṣu saṃrarañje;
na vididveṣa paraṃ na c' âvamene.

Thereupon, he attained absorption of the mind,
born of discernment, with the joy of supreme bliss;
knowing rightly in his mind the course of the world,
thereafter he pondered over this very thing:

"How wretched that ignorant man,
blinded by pride,
who, though himself powerless
and subject to the law
Of disease, old age, and death,
should treat with contempt*
another who's sick, dead, or oppressed by old age!

If I, being myself like that,
should treat with contempt*
another man here with a nature just like that,
It would not befit me, and it would not be right,
I who have come to fathom
this supreme dharma."

As he thus saw rightly the evils of the world,
the evils of disease, old age, and death,
pride of self in an instant departed from him,
pride resulting from his strength, youth, and life.

He did not give in to dejection or delight; 5.15
he did not give in to doubt, or to sloth or sleep;
he felt no attachment to sensual delights;
he did not hate others or treat them with contempt.

iti buddhir iyaṃ ca nī|rajaskā
vavṛdhe tasya mah"|ātmano viśuddhā
puruṣair a|parair a|dṛśyamānaḥ
puruṣaś c' ôpasasarpa bhikṣu|veṣaḥ.

nara|deva|sutas tam abhyapṛcchad:
«vada, ko 's' îti?» śaśaṃsa so 'tha tasmai:
«nara|puṃgava, janma|mṛtyu|bhītaḥ
śramaṇaḥ pravrajito 'smi mokṣa|hetoḥ.

jagati kṣaya|dharmake mumukṣur
mṛgaye 'haṃ śivam a|kṣayaṃ padaṃ tat
sva|jane 'nya|jane ca tulya|buddhir
viṣayebhyo vinivṛtta|rāga|doṣaḥ.

nivasan kva cid eva vṛkṣa|mūle
vijane v" āyatane girau vane vā
vicarāmy a|parigraho nir|āśaḥ
param'|ârthāya yath"|ôpapanna|bhaikṣaḥ.»

5.20 iti paśyata eva rāja|sūnor
idaṃ uktvā sa nabhaḥ samutpapāta;
sa hi tad|vapur anya|buddha|darśī
smṛtaye tasya sameyivān div'|âukāḥ.

As this awareness, stainless and free of passion,
began to wax strong in that noble man,
a man approached him wearing a mendicant's garb,
unseen by any of the other men.

The son of the king then questioned that man:

"Tell me. Who are you?"

And the man gave him this reply:

"Frightened by birth and death, bull among men,
I have gone forth as a recluse,
for the sake of release.

I seek release within this perishable world,
I seek that holy and imperishable state,
I regard my own people and others alike,
love and hate of sensual things
have been extinguished in me.

Dwelling anywhere at all—under trees,
a deserted temple, forest or hill—
I wander without possessions or wants,
living on almsfood I happen to get,
in search of the supreme goal."

Having said this, he flew into the sky, 5.20
even as the son of the king looked on;
for he was a deity who in that form
had seen other Buddhas and had come down
to arouse the attention of the prince.

gaganaṃ kha|gavad gate ca tasmin
  nṛ|varaḥ saṃjahṛṣe visismiye ca;
upalabhya tataś ca dharma|saṃjñām*
  abhiniryāṇa|vidhau matiṃ cakāra.

tata Indra|samo jit'|êndriy'|âśvaḥ
  pravivikṣuḥ puram aśvam āruroha;
parivāra|janaṃ tv avekṣamāṇas
  tata ev' âbhimataṃ vanaṃ na bheje.

sa jarā|maraṇa|kṣayaṃ cikīrṣur
  vana|vāsāya matiṃ smṛtau nidhāya
praviveśa punaḥ puraṃ na kāmād
  vana|bhūmer iva maṇḍalaṃ dvip'|êndraḥ.

«sukhitā, bata, nirvṛtā ca sā strī
  patir īdṛkṣa ih' āyat'|âkṣa yasyāḥ!»
iti taṃ samudīkṣya rāja|kanyā
  praviśantaṃ pathi s'|âñjalir jagāda.

5.25 atha ghoṣam imaṃ mah"|âbhra|ghoṣaḥ
  pariśuśrāva śamaṃ paraṃ ca lebhe;
śrutavān sa hi «nirvṛt" êti» śabdaṃ
  parinirvāṇa|vidhau matiṃ cakāra.

When he had flown to the sky like a bird,
that foremost of men was thrilled and amazed;
then, perceiving that emblem of dharma,*
he set his mind on how he might leave home.

Then, that Indra's equal,
who had controlled the horses of senses,
  mounted his horse to enter the city;
out of concern for his men he did not
go directly to the forest he loved.

Intending to destroy old age and death,
his mind set on living the forest life,
  he entered the city again
unwillingly, like an elephant king
from the forest entering a corral.

On seeing him entering along the road,
a royal maiden, her palms joined, exclaimed:

  "Happy, indeed, and fulfilled is the wife,
    O Long-eyed One,
  Who has for her husband here such a man!"

Then, as he heard this voice, 5.25
  he obtained supreme calm,
he whose voice was like that of a great thunder cloud;
for, as he heard the word "fulfilled," he set his mind
on the means to final Nirvanic fulfillment.

atha kāñcana|śaila|śṛṅga|varṣmā
gaja|megha|ṛṣabha|bāhu|nisvan'|âkṣaḥ
kṣayam a|kṣaya|dharma|jāta|rāgaḥ
śaśi|siṃh'|ânana|vikramaḥ prapede.

mṛga|rāja|gatis tato 'bhyagacchan
nṛ|patiṃ mantri|gaṇair upāsyamānam
samitau Marutām iva jvalantaṃ
Maghavantaṃ tri|dive Sanatkumāraḥ.

praṇipatya ca s'|âñjalir babhāṣe:
«diśa mahyaṃ, nara|deva, sādhv anujñām;
parivivrajiṣāmi mokṣa|hetor,
niyato hy asya janasya viprayogaḥ.»

iti tasya vaco niśamya rājā
kariṇ" êv' âbhihato drumaś cacāla
kamala|pratime 'ñjalau gṛhītvā
vacanaṃ c' êdam uvāca bāṣpa|kaṇṭhaḥ:

5.30 «pratisaṃhara, tāta, buddhim etāṃ,
na hi kālas tava dharma|saṃśrayasya;
vayasi prathame matau calāyāṃ
bahu|doṣāṃ hi vadanti dharma|caryām.

Then, in stature like the peak of the golden mount,
arms of an elephant, voice of a thunder cloud,
eyes of a bull, gait of a lion, face like the moon,
he reached the dwelling place
    with his yearning aroused
for the dharma that's imperishable.

Then he, with the gait of the king of beasts, approached
the king attended by the group of ministers,
as Sanat·kumára in the third heaven approached
Indra shining in the council of the Maruts.

He prostrated himself with his palms joined and said:

  "Kindly grant me permission, O god among men;
    to gain release, I desire the wandering life,
  For separation is appointed for this man."

Hearing his words, the king began to shake,
like a tree struck down by an elephant;
grasping his hands that looked like lotus buds,
the king uttered these words, choking with tears:

  "Turn back, my son, from this resolution, 5.30
    for it's not the time for you
    to give yourself to dharma;
  For, when you're young and your mind is fickle,
    there're many dangers, they say,
    in the practice of dharma.

viṣayeṣu kutūhal'|êndriyasya
  vrata|khedeṣv a|samartha|niścayasya
taruṇasya manaś calaty araṇyād
  an|abhijñasya viśeṣato viveke.

mama tu, priya|dharma, dharma|kālas
  tvayi lakṣmīm avasṛjya lakṣma|bhūte;
sthira|vikrama, vikrameṇa dharmas
  tava hitvā tu guruṃ bhaved a|dharmaḥ.

tad imaṃ vyavasāyam utsṛja tvaṃ,
  bhava tāvan nirato gṛha|stha|dharme;
puruṣasya vayaḥ|sukhāni bhuktvā
  ramaṇīyo hi tapo|vana|praveśaḥ.»

iti vākyam idaṃ niśamya rājñaḥ
  kalaviṅka|svara uttaraṃ babhāṣe:
«yadi me pratibhūś caturṣu rājan
  bhavasi tvaṃ na tapo|vanaṃ śrayiṣye.

5.35 na bhaven maraṇāya jīvitaṃ me,
  viharet svāsthyam idam ca me na rogaḥ,
na ca yauvanam ākṣipej jarā me,
  na ca saṃpattim imāṃ hared vipattiḥ.»

As objects of sense tend to excite his senses,
  as he can't be firm facing the hardships of vows,
A young man's mind turns away
    from the wilderness,
  above all as he is not used to solitude.

But for me it is the time for dharma,
  after conferring on you sovereignty,
  you who possess the marks of sovereignty
  O lover of dharma;
But if you leave your father by violating
  the right order, you whose courage is firm,*
  your dharma will turn into *adhárma*.

So, give up this resolution of yours,
  give yourself for now to household dharma;
For, when one goes to the ascetic grove
  after he has enjoyed the joys of youth,
  it's truly a wonderful sight!"

Hearing these words of the king, he gave this reply, in a voice like that of a *kalavínka* bird:

"If you will become a surety for me
  in four things, O King,
I will not go to the ascetic grove.

My life shall never be subject to death, 5.35
  disease shall not steal this good health of mine,
Old age shall never overtake my youth,
  no mishap shall rob this fortune of mine."

iti dur|labham artham ūcivāṃsaṃ
  tanayaṃ vākyam uvāca Śākya|rājaḥ:
«tyaja buddhim imām ati|pravṛttām
  avahāsyo 'ti|mano|ratho '|kramaś ca.»

atha Meru|gurur guruṃ babhāṣe:
  «yadi n' âsti krama eṣa, n' âsmi vāryaḥ;
śaraṇāj jvalanena dahyamānān
  na hi niścikramiṣuḥ kṣamaṃ grahītum.

jagataś ca yadā dhruvo viyogo,
  nanu dharmāya varaṃ svayaṃ|viyogaḥ;
a|vaśaṃ nanu viprayojayen mām
  a|kṛta|sv'|ârtham a|tṛptam eva mṛtyuḥ.»

iti bhūmi|patir niśamya tasya
  vyavasāyaṃ tanayasya nirmumukṣoḥ
abhidhāya «na yāsyat' îti» bhūyo
  vidadhe rakṣaṇam uttamāṃś ca kāmān.

5.40 sacivais tu nidarśito yathāvad
  bahu|mānāt praṇayāc ca śāstra|pūrvam
guruṇā ca nivārito 'śru|pātaiḥ
  praviveś' āvasathaṃ tataḥ sa śocan—

To his son making such a hard request,
the king of the Shakyas made this response:

"Withdraw this your request, it is inordinate;
An extravagant wish is improper and extreme."*

Then that one, mighty as Meru, told his father:

"If that's not possible, don't hold me back;
for it is not right to obstruct a man,
Who's trying to escape from a burning house.

When separation is the fixed rule for this world,
is it not far better for dharma's sake
to make that separation on my own?
Will death not separate me as I stand
helpless and unfulfilled,
without reaching my goal?"

When the king thus ascertained the resolve
of his son in search of final release,
he exclaimed, "He shall not leave!"
and made arrangements for security,
and provided him with choicest pleasures.

But when the ministers had duly counseled him, 5.40
according to scriptures, with deep respect and love;
and his father had stopped him,
shedding copious tears,
sorrowfully, then, he entered his residence—

cala|kuṇḍala|cumbit'|ânanābhir
ghana|niśvāsa|vikampita|stanībhiḥ
vanitābhir a|dhīra|locanābhir
mṛga|śāvābhir iv' âbhyudīkṣyamāṇaḥ.

sa hi kāñcana|parvat'|âvadāto
hṛday'|ônmāda|karo var'|âṅganānām
śravaṇ'|âṅga|vilocan'|ātma|bhāvān
vacana|sparśa|vapur|guṇair jahāra.

vigate divase tato vimānaṃ
vapuṣā sūrya iva pradīpyamānaḥ
timiraṃ vijighāṃsur ātma|bhāsā
ravir udyann iva Merum āruroha.

kanak'|ôjjvala|dīpta|dīpa|vṛkṣaṃ
vara|kāl'|âguru|dhūpa|pūrṇa|garbham
adhiruhya sa vajra|bhakti|citraṃ
pravaraṃ kāñcanam āsanaṃ siṣeve.

5.45 tata uttamam uttam'|âṅganās taṃ
niśi tūryair upatasthur Indra|kalpam
Himavac|chiras' îva candra|gaure
Draviṇ'|êndr'|ātmajam apsaro|gaṇ'|âughāḥ.

while young women, their faces kissed by their
dangling earrings, their breasts throbbing with deep
and constant sighs, their eyes darting hither
and thither, gazed up at him like young does.

For he, as bright as the golden mountain
bewitching the hearts of those peerless girls,
enthralled their ears and limbs, their eyes and selves,
with his speech and touch, beauty and virtues.

Then, as the day came to an end,
his body shining like the sun,
he climbed up to the high palace,
like the rising sun Mount Meru,
so as to dispel the darkness
with the light of his self.

Going up to his inner chamber
filled with incense of the best black aloe,
lit by candelabra glistening with gold,
he sat on a splendid seat made of gold
and bespeckled with streaks of diamonds.

Then, during that night, splendid girls 5.45
playing their musical instruments
entertained that equal of Indra, that splendid man,
as on the Himalayan peak as white as the moon,
large throngs of *ápsaras*es entertained
the son of the Lord of Wealth.*

paramair api divya|tūrya|kalpaiḥ
sa tu tair n' âiva ratiṃ yayau na harṣam;
param'|ârtha|sukhāya tasya sādhor
abhiniścikramiṣā yato na reme.

atha tatra surais tapo|variṣṭhair
Akaniṣṭhair vyavasāyam asya buddhvā
yugapat pramadā|janasya nidrā
vihit" āsīd vikṛtāś ca gātra|ceṣṭāḥ—

abhavac chayitā hi tatra kā cid
viniveśya pracale kare kapolam
dayitām api rukma|pattra|citrāṃ
kupit" êv' âṅka|gatāṃ vihāya vīṇām;

vibabhau kara|lagna|veṇur anyā
stana|visrasta|sit'|âṃśukā śayānā
ṛju|ṣaṭ|pada|paṅkti|juṣṭa|padmā
jala|phena|prahasat|taṭā nad" îva;

5.50 nava|puṣkara|garbha|komalābhyāṃ
tapanīy'|ôjjvala|saṃgat'|âṅgadābhyām
svapiti sma tath" â|parā bhujābhyāṃ
parirabhya priyavan mṛdaṅgam eva;

But even that music of the finest instruments,
rivaling those of heaven,
did not bring him mirth or joy;
the sole desire of that good man was to leave his home
in search of ultimate joy;
therefore, he did not rejoice.

Then, Akaníshtha deities, who
practiced the best austerities,
became aware of his resolve;
at once they made those young women succumb
to sleep,
and in unsightly postures positioned their limbs—

one was reclining there resting her cheek
on her unsteady hand, tossing her lute
adorned with gold leaf resting on her lap
as if in anger, though she loved it much;

another sparkled, a flute in her hand,
lying down, her white gown slipping
from her breasts,
looking like a river, its banks laughing with foam,
its lotuses relished by a straight row of bees;*

another slept embracing her tambour, 5.50
as if it were her lover, with her hands
tender as the hearts of new lotuses,
glistening gold armlets linked to each other;

nava|hāṭaka|bhūṣaṇās tath" ânyā
vasanaṃ pītam an|uttamaṃ vasānāḥ
a|vaśā ghana|nidrayā nipetur
gaja|bhagnā iva karṇikāra|śākhāḥ;

avalambya gav'|âkṣa|pārśvam anyā
śayitā cāpa|vibhugna|gātra|yaṣṭiḥ
virarāja vilambi|cāru|hārā
racitā toraṇa|śāla|bhañjik" êva;

maṇi|kuṇḍala|daṣṭa|pattra|lekhaṃ
mukha|padmaṃ vinataṃ tath" âparasyāḥ
śata|pattram iv' ârdha|vakra|nāḍaṃ
sthita|kāraṇḍava|ghaṭṭitaṃ cakāśe;

aparāḥ śayitā yath" ôpaviṣṭāḥ
stana|bhārair avanamyamāna|gātrāḥ
upaguhya paras|paraṃ virejur
bhuja|pāśais tapanīya|pārihāryaiḥ;

5.55 mahatīṃ parivādinīṃ ca kā cid
vanit" āliṅgya sakhīm iva prasuptā
vijughūrṇa calat|suvarṇa|sūtrā
vadanen' ākula|yoktrakeṇa;

others too, decked with jewelry of new gold,
dressed in peerless yellow clothes,
fell down helpless overcome by deep sleep,
like a *karnikára* branch
torn down by an elephant;*

another slept leaning on a window,
her slender body was bent like a bow;
she sparkled, her lovely necklace dangling,
looking like a *shala* plucker
carved upon a gateway;*

another had her lotus-face bent down,
her jeweled earrings scraping
the decorative lines on her face,
looking like a lotus with its stalk half bent down,
pushed by the perching of a *karándava* coot;*

others were resplendent—
lying down where they sat,
bodies bent down by the weight of their breasts,
embracing each other with entwined arms
adorned with golden bracelets;

one girl in deep sleep embraced her large lute 5.55
as if it were her girl-friend,
as she rolled, her gold chains shook,
her earrings in disarray on her face;

paṇavaṃ yuvatir bhuj'|âṃsa|deśād
avavisraṃsita|cāru|pāśam anyā
sa|vilāsa|rat'|ânta|tāntam ūrvor
vivare kāntam iv' âbhinīya śiśye;

aparā na babhur* nimīlit'|âkṣyo
vipul'|âkṣyo 'pi śubha|bhruvo 'pi satyaḥ
pratisaṃkucit'|âravinda|kośāḥ
savitary astam ite yathā nalinyaḥ;

śithil'|ākula|mūrdhajā tath" ânyā
jaghana|srasta|vibhūṣaṇ'|âṃśu|kāntā
aśayiṣṭa vikīrṇa|kaṇṭha|sūtrā
gaja|bhagnā pratiyātan'|âṅgan" êva;

aparās tv a|vaśā hriyā viyuktā
dhṛti|matyo 'pi vapur|guṇair upetāḥ
viniśaśvasur ulbaṇaṃ śayānā
vikṛtāḥ kṣipta|bhujā jajṛmbhire ca;

5.60 vyapaviddha|vibhūṣaṇa|srajo 'nyā
visṛt'|āgranthana|vāsaso vi|saṃjñāḥ
a|nimīlita|śukla|niścal'|âkṣyo
na virejuḥ śayitā gat'|âsu|kalpāḥ;

another girl was lying down
laying her drum between her thighs—
the drum's beautiful cord
slipping from her shoulder—
like a lover lying exhausted
after making passionate love;

but others, though their brows were pretty,
and their eyes were large,
displayed no beauty with their eyes closed,
like lotuses with their flower-buds closed
after the setting of the sun;

another girl likewise was lying there,
her hair disheveled and hanging loose,
her clothes and ornaments slipping down
from her waist, her necklaces scattered,
like a statue of a girl
trampled by an elephant;

although genteel and endowed with beauty,
others were snoring with their mouths agape,
without any shame and out of control,
with limbs distorted and arms extended,
sleeping in immodest pose;

others looked revolting, lying as if dead, 5.60
their jewelry and their garlands fallen down,
unconscious, with eyes unblinking,
the whites gazing in a fixed stare;

vivṛt'|āsya|puṭā vivṛddha|gātrī
   prapatad|vaktra|jalā prakāśa|guhyā
aparā mada|ghūrṇit" êva śiśye
   na babhāse vikṛtaṃ vapuḥ pupoṣa.

iti sattva|kul'|ânvay'|ânurūpaṃ
   vividhaṃ sa pramadā|janaḥ śayānaḥ
sarasaḥ sadṛśaṃ babhāra rūpaṃ
   pavan'|āvarjita|rugna|puṣkarasya.

samavekṣya tathā tathā śayānā
   vikṛtās tā yuvatīr a|dhīra|ceṣṭāḥ
guṇavad|vapuṣo 'pi valgu|bhāṣā
   nṛpa|sūnuḥ sa vigarhayāṃ babhūva:

«a|śucir vikṛtaś ca jīva|loke
   vanitānām ayam īdṛśaḥ sva|bhāvaḥ;
vasan'|ābharaṇais tu vañcyamānaḥ
   puruṣaḥ strī|viṣayeṣu rāgam eti.

5.65 vimṛśed yadi yoṣitāṃ manuṣyaḥ
   prakṛtiṃ svapna|vikāram īdṛśaṃ ca,
dhruvam atra na vardhayet pramādaṃ
   guṇa|saṃkalpa|hatas tu rāgam eti.»

iti tasya tad|antaraṃ viditvā
   niśi niścikramiṣā samudbabhūva;
avagamya manas tato 'sya devair
   bhavana|dvāram apāvṛtaṃ babhūva.

another was lying as if she was drunk,
mouth wide open and saliva oozing,
legs wide open and genitals exposed,
body distorted, looking repulsive.

Thus, in diverse postures those enticing girls slept,
each in keeping with her nature,
her family and pedigree;
in appearance they resembled a pond,
with its lilies knocked down, crushed by the wind.

When he saw those girls sleeping in such poses,
their bodies distorted, movements unrestrained,
the king's son gave vent to his utter contempt—
though their bodies were exquisite,
and the way they spoke was so sweet:

"Dirty and distorted lies here exposed
the true nature of women in this world;
Deluded by their nice clothes and jewelry,
men become infatuated with them.

If men reflect on women's true nature 5.65
and this mutation brought about by sleep,
Surely their passion for them would not wax;
yet, struck by the thought of their elegance,
they become infatuated with them."

When he understood thus their difference,
the urge to depart surged in him that night;
when the gods discerned his intention, then,
they opened the door of his residence.

atha so 'vatatāra harmya|pṛṣṭhād
yuvatīs tāḥ śayitā vigarhamāṇaḥ;
avatīrya tataś ca nir|viśaṅko
gṛha|kakṣyāṃ prathamāṃ vinirjagāma.

turag'|âvacaraṃ sa bodhayitvā
javinaṃ Chandakam ittham ity uvāca:
«hayam ānaya Kanthakaṃ tvarāvān!
a|mṛtaṃ prāptum ito 'dya me yiyāsā.

hṛdi yā mama tuṣṭir adya jātā
vyavasāyaś ca yathā matau niviṣṭaḥ
vijane 'pi ca nāthavān iv' âsmi,
dhruvam artho 'bhimukhaḥ sameta iṣṭaḥ.

5.70 hriyam eva ca saṃnatiṃ ca hitvā
śayitā mat|pramukhe yathā yuvatyaḥ
vivṛte ca yathā svayaṃ kapāṭe
niyataṃ yātum ato mam' âdya kālaḥ.»

pratigṛhya tataḥ sa bhartur ājñāṃ
vidit'|ârtho 'pi nar'|êndra|śāsanasya
manas' îva pareṇa codyamānas
tura|gasy' ānayane matiṃ cakāra.

Then, he came down from the palace roof-top,
in utter contempt of those sleeping girls;
having come down, then, resolute,
he went out to the first courtyard.

He woke up Chándaka and told
that quick-footed groom of his horse:

"Quickly bring the horse Kánthaka!
I want to leave this place today,
To arrive at the deathless state.

Contentment has arisen in my heart,
and resolve has taken hold of my mind;
Even in a deserted place
I do have some sort of a guide;
The goal I yearn for has appeared
before my eyes, that is certain.

Abandoning modesty and deference, 5.70
the girls slept right in front of me;
And the doors were thrown open on their own—
so today is the time I must
depart from this place, that's certain."

Then, although he knew well the king's decree,
he acceded to his master's command;
and he made up his mind to bring the horse,
his mind as if goaded by someone else.

atha hema|khalīna|pūrṇa|vaktraṃ
 laghu|śayy"|āstaraṇ'|ôpagūḍha|pṛṣṭham
bala|sattva|jav'|ânvay'|ôpapannaṃ
 sa var'|âśvaṃ tam upāninābhartre,
pratata|trika|puccha|mūla|pārṣṇiṃ
 nibhṛta|hrasva|tanūja|puccha|karṇam
vinat'|ônnata|pṛṣṭha|kukṣi|pārśvaṃ
 vipula|protha|lalāṭa|katy|uraskam.

upagṛhya sa taṃ viśāla|vakṣāḥ
 kamal'|ābhena ca sāntvayan kareṇa
madhur'|âkṣarayā girā śaśāsa
 dhvajinī|madhyam iva praveṣṭu|kāmaḥ:

5.75 «bahuśaḥ kila śatravo nirastāḥ
 samare tvām adhiruhya pārthivena;
aham apy a|mṛtaṃ padaṃ yathāvat,
 turaga|śreṣṭha, labheya tat kuruṣva.

su|labhāḥ khalu saṃyuge sahāyā
 viṣay'|âvāpta|sukhe dhan'|ârjane vā;
puruṣasya tu dur|labhāḥ sahāyāḥ
 patitasy' āpadi dharma|saṃśraye vā.

iha c' âiva bhavanti ye sahāyāḥ
 kaluṣe karmaṇi dharma|saṃśraye vā,
avagacchati me yath" ântar|ātmā
 niyataṃ te 'pi janās tad|aṃśa|bhājaḥ.

Then, he brought to his lord that sterling steed,
a horse endowed with strength, heart, speed,
  and breed—
 its mouth was furnished with a golden bit,
 its back was covered with a soft bedspread,
 its chine, rump, and fetlocks were long,
 hair, tail, and ears were short and still,
 with sunken back, bulging belly and flanks,
 and with wide nostrils, forehead, hips and chest.

The wide-chested prince then embraced that horse,
caressing it with his lotus-like hand;
he ordered it in a sweet voice, as if
wishing to charge into enemy lines:

"Many a time did the sovereign mount you, 5.75
  and vanquish in battle his foes;
  that is well known;
So act in such a way, O best of steeds,
  that I too may obtain the deathless state.

Companions are easy to find to fight a war,
  to win riches or to enjoy sensual delights;
But they are hard to find when one is in dire straits,
  or when one takes to the path of dharma.

The companions of a man in this world
  in foul acts or in the path of dharma,
They too will doubtless partake of the fruits,
  this is what I'm told by my inner self.

tad idaṃ parigamya dharma|yuktaṃ
mama niryāṇam ito jagadd|hitāya,
turag'|ôttama, vega|vikramābhyāṃ
prayatasv' ātma|hite jagadd|hite ca.»

iti su|hṛdam iv' ânuśiṣya kṛtye
turaga|varaṃ nṛ|varo vanaṃ yiyāsuḥ
sitam a|sita|gati|dyutir vapuṣmān
ravir iva śāradam abhram āruroha.

5.80 atha sa pariharan niśītha|caṇḍaṃ
parijana|bodha|karaṃ dhvaniṃ sad|aśvaḥ
vigata|hanu|ravaḥ praśānta|heṣaś
cakita|vimukta|pada|kramo jagāma.

kanaka|valaya|bhūṣita|prakoṣṭhaiḥ
kamala|nibhaiḥ kamalān iva pravidhya
avanata|tanavas tato 'sya yakṣāś
cakita|gatair dadhire khurān kar'|âgraiḥ.

guru|parigha|kapāṭa|saṃvṛtā yā
na sukham api dvi|radair apāvriyante,
vrajati nṛpa|sute gata|svanās tāḥ
svayam abhavan vivṛtāḥ puraḥ pratolyaḥ.

Knowing, therefore, that my exit from here
is connected with dharma
and for the good of the world,
Strive, you best of horses, with speed and dare,
for your own welfare
and that of the world."

Wishing to enter the forest, that finest king
thus instructed in his duty that finest horse,
as if he were a friend;
and that handsome prince, who was blazing like a fire,
mounted the white horse, like the sun
an autumn cloud.

Then, the good horse went without making any sound 5.80
that would cause alarm in the night
or awaken the attendants;
his jaws made no noise and his neighing
was suppressed;
he walked with unwavering steps.

Yakshas, then, bending their bodies low, supported
the horse's hooves with the tips of their
trembling hands,
hands that resembled lotus buds,
forearms adorned with golden bands,
so that it seemed they were scattering lotuses.

As the prince made his way, the city's gates
opened noiselessly on their own,
gates that were closed with heavy iron bars,
gates not easily burst open
even by elephants.

pitaram abhimukhaṃ sutaṃ ca bālaṃ
janam anuraktam an|uttamāṃ ca lakṣmīm
kṛta|matir apahāya nir|vyapekṣaḥ
pitṛ|nagarāt sa tato vinirjagāma.

atha sa vimala|paṅkaj'|āyat'|âkṣaḥ
puram avalokya nanāda siṃha|nādam:
«janana|maraṇayor a|dṛṣṭa|pāro
na puram ahaṃ Kapil'|āhvayaṃ praveṣṭā.»

5.85 iti vacanam idaṃ niśamya tasya
Draviṇa|pateḥ pariṣad|gaṇā nananduḥ
pramudita|manasaś ca deva|saṅghā
vyavasita|pāraṇam āśaśaṃsire 'smai.

huta|vaha|vapuṣo div'|âukaso 'nye
vyavasitam asya su|duṣ|karaṃ viditvā
akṛṣata tuhine pathi prakāśaṃ
ghana|vivara|prasṛtā iv' êndu|pādāḥ.

hari|turaga|turaṅgavat turaṅgaḥ
sa tu vicaran manas' îva codyamānaḥ
aruṇa|paruṣa|tāram antar|ikṣaṃ
sa ca su|bahūni jagāma yojanāni.

iti Buddhacarite mahā|kāvye 'bhiniṣkramaṇo nāma
pañcamaḥ sargaḥ.

He then left the city of his father,
firm in his resolve and unwavering,
leaving his loving father and young son,
his devout subjects and highest fortune.

Then he, with long eyes like white lotuses,
caught sight of the city
and roared this lion-roar:

> "I will not enter this city called Kápila,
> Before I've seen the farther shore of birth and death."

Hearing these words of his, the retinue 5.85
of the court of the Lord of Wealth rejoiced,
and hosts of deities, their minds filled with joy,
announced to him the success of his vow.

Other fiery-bodied denizens of heaven,
knowing his vow was exceedingly hard to keep,
shined a light on his frosty path,
like moonbeams coming down through
an opening in a cloud.

As that steed sped along like the steed of the sun,
its mind as if spurred on, he traveled many leagues,
before the stars became faint in the sky
at the coming of the dawn.

Thus ends the fifth canto named "The Departure"
of the great poem "Life of the Buddha."

CANTO 6
CHÁNDAKA IS SENT BACK

6.1 TATO MUHŪRT'|âbhyudite
jagac|cakṣuṣi bhās|kare
Bhārgavasy' āśrama|padaṃ
sa dadarśa nṛṇāṃ varaḥ.

supta|viśvasta|hariṇaṃ
sva|stha|sthita|vihaṅgamam
viśrānta iva yad dṛṣṭvā
kṛt'|ârtha iva c' âbhavat.

sa vismaya|nivṛtty|arthaṃ
tapaḥ|pūj"|ârtham eva ca
svāṃ c' ânuvartitāṃ rakṣann
aśva|pṛṣṭhād avātarat.

avatīrya ca pasparśa
«nistīrṇam» iti vājinam
Chandakaṃ c' âbravīt prītaḥ
snāpayann iva cakṣuṣā:

6.5 «imaṃ Tārkṣy'|ôpama|javaṃ
turaṅ|gam anugacchatā
darśitā saumya mad|bhaktir
vikramaś c' âyam ātmanaḥ.

sarvath" âsmy anya|kāryo 'pi
gṛhīto bhavatā hṛdi,
bhartṛ|snehaś ca yasy' âyam
īdṛśaḥ śaktir eva ca.

Then, at the moment when the sun, 6.1
the eye of the world, rose,
that best of men beheld
Bhárgava's hermitage.*

When he saw that hermitage,
with deer sleeping full of trust,
birds resting in perfect ease,
he felt as if he was refreshed,
as if he had attained his goal.

To remove any arrogance,
and to respect ascetic toil,
to guard his own subservience,*
he got down from the horse.

Having got down, he stroked the horse,
saying: "You have fulfilled your task;"
he spoke to Chándaka, full of joy,
as if bathing him with his eyes:

"By following this steed, 6.5
as fast as Gáruda,
You have shown devotion to me,
as well as this prowess of yours.

I'm given wholly to other pursuits,
yet you have clasped me to your heart;
Your devotion to your master
is paralleled by such ability.

a|snigdho 'pi samartho 'sti
  niḥ|sāmarthyo 'pi bhaktimān;
bhaktimāṃś c' âiva śaktaś ca
  dur|labhas tvad|vidho bhuvi.

tat prīto 'smi tav' ânena
  mahā|bhāgena karmaṇā;
yasya te mayi bhāvo 'yaṃ
  phalebhyo 'pi parāṅ|mukhaḥ.

ko janasya phala|sthasya
  na syād abhimukho janaḥ;
janī|bhavati bhūyiṣṭhaṃ
  sva|jano 'pi viparyaye.

6.10 kul'|ârthaṃ dhāryate putraḥ,
  poṣ'|ârthaṃ sevyate pitā,
āśayāc chliśyati jagan;
  n' âsti niṣ|kāraṇā svatā.

kim uktvā bahu? saṃkṣepāt,
  kṛtaṃ me su|mahat priyam;
nivartasv' âśvam ādāya
  saṃprāpto 'sm' īpsitaṃ padam.»

ity uktvā sa mahā|bāhur
  anuśaṃsa|cikīrṣayā
bhūṣaṇāny avamucy' âsmai
  saṃtapta|manase dadau.

One may be capable without being devoted,
  one may be devoted without being capable;
But one who is both capable and devoted,
  such as you, is difficult to find in this world.

I am delighted, therefore,
  at this lofty deed of yours;
This love of yours toward me,
  has no regard for rewards.

What man will not fawn upon
  someone bestowing rewards;
When the tide turns, for the most part,
  even kinsfolk act like strangers.

One supports a son for family's sake, 6.10
  one serves the father to get sustenance;
The world shows affection for a motive;
  kinship cannot endure without a cause.

What is the use of saying more? In short,
  it's a great favor you have done for me;
Take the horse with you and return,
  I've arrived at the desired spot."

After saying this, the mighty-armed prince,
wishing to render an act of kindness,
took off his jewelry and gave it
to that broken-hearted man.

mukuṭād dīpa|karmāṇaṃ
  maṇim ādāya bhāsvaram
bruvan vākyam idaṃ tasthau
  s'|āditya iva Mandaraḥ:

«anena maṇinā, Chanda,
  praṇamya bahuśo nṛpaḥ
vijñāpyo '|mukta|viśrambhaṃ
  saṃtāpa|vinivṛttaye:

6.15 ‹jarā|maraṇa|nāś'|ârthaṃ
  praviṣṭo 'smi tapo|vanam,
na khalu svarga|tarṣeṇa
  n' â|snehen' êha na manyunā.

tad evam abhiniṣkrāntaṃ
  na māṃ śocitum arhasi;
bhūtv" âpi hi ciraṃ śleṣaḥ,
  kālena na bhaviṣyati.

dhruvo yasmāc ca viśleṣas
  tasmān mokṣāya me matiḥ—
«viprayogaḥ kathaṃ na syād
  bhūyo 'pi sva|janād» iti.

śoka|tyāgāya niṣkrāntaṃ
  na māṃ śocitum arhasi;
śoka|hetuṣu kāmeṣu
  saktāḥ śocyās tu rāgiṇaḥ.

Taking the shining gem from his head-dress,
a gem that performed the task of a lamp,
he stood there as he made this oration,
like Mount Mándara holding up the sun:

"With this gem, Chanda, you must pay
repeated homage to the king,
And beseech him without being diffident,
to relieve his anguish, using these words:

'I've entered the ascetic grove 6.15
not because I long for heaven,
am angry, or lack affection,
but to destroy old age and death.

Therefore, please do not grieve for me,
who have departed in this way;
for a union however long
will in due course come to an end.

Since separation is certain,
I have turned my mind to release
with the thought—"How may I never again
be separated from my relatives?"

Therefore, please do not grieve for me,
who have departed to end grief;
grieve rather for passionate men,
attached to pleasures that cause grief.

ayaṃ ca kila pūrveṣām
asmākaṃ niścayaḥ sthiraḥ
iti dāy'|ādya|bhūtena
na śocyo 'smi pathā vrajan.

6.20 bhavanti hy artha|dāy'|ādāḥ
puruṣasya viparyaye;
pṛthivyāṃ dharma|dāy'|ādāḥ
dur|labhās tu, na santi vā.

yad api syād «a|samaye
yāto vanam asāv» iti,
a|kālo n' âsti dharmasya
jīvite cañcale sati.

tasmād «ady' âiva me śreyaś
cetavyam» iti niścayaḥ;
jīvite ko hi viśrambho
mṛtyau praty|arthini sthite?›

evam|ādi tvayā, saumya,
vijñāpyo vasudh"|âdhipaḥ;
prayatethās tathā c' âiva
yathā māṃ na smared api.

api nairguṇyam asmākaṃ
vācyaṃ nara|patau tvayā;
nairguṇyāt tyajyate snehaḥ,
sneha|tyāgān na śocyate.»

This was the firm resolution,
as you know, of our ancestors;
do not grieve for me as I walk
on this path, my patrimony.

For when a man passes away, 6.20
there are here heirs to his wealth;
but heirs to dharma on this earth
are absent or hard to find.

Should you argue that I have departed
to the forest at an improper time;
for pursuing dharma there is no time
that's improper when life's so insecure.

Therefore, I have resolved, I must
this very day seek final bliss;
for what trust can one place in life,
when death, its foe, is standing by?'

With words such as these, my dear man,
you should beseech the Lord of Earth;
Try your best, likewise, to ensure
that he won't even think of me.

Even tell the king that I lack virtue;
he will stop loving me
Because I lack virtue;
when he stops loving me,
his grief will surely cease."

6.25 iti vākyam idaṃ śrutvā
Chandaḥ saṃtāpa|viklavaḥ
bāṣpa|grathitayā vācā
pratyuvāca kṛt'|âñjaliḥ:

«anena tava bhāvena
bāndhav'|āyāsa|dāyinā,
bhartaḥ, sīdati me ceto
nadī|paṅka iva dvi|paḥ.

kasya n' ôtpādayed bāṣpaṃ
niścayas te 'yam īdṛśaḥ
ayo|maye 'pi hṛdaye,
kiṃ punaḥ sneha|viklave?

vimāna|śayan'|ârhaṃ hi
saukumāryam idaṃ kva ca!
khara|darbh'|âṅkuravatī
tapo|vana|mahī kva ca!

śrutvā tu vyavasāyaṃ te
yad aśvo 'yaṃ may" āhṛtaḥ
balāt|kāreṇa tan, nātha,
daiven' âiv' âsmi kāritaḥ.

6.30 kathaṃ hy ātma|vaśo jānan
vyavasāyam imaṃ tava
upānayeyaṃ tura|gaṃ
śokaṃ Kapilavāstunaḥ?

When he heard these words of his, 6.25
Chanda, overcome by grief,
folded his hands and replied
in a voice choking with tears:

"Seeing you in this frame of mind,
causing anguish to your kinsfolk,
My mind sinks, O my Lord, just like
an elephant in river mud.

Who indeed would not be reduced to tears
at the kind of resolve that you have made,
Even if his heart was carved out of steel?
How much more when it is throbbing with love?

Look at this delicate body of yours,
fit to lie on a palace bed!
Look at the ground of the ascetic grove,
strewn with harsh blades of *darbha* grass!

But after hearing your resolve,
when I brought to you the horse,
I was forced to do it, My Lord,
clearly by some divine force.

For knowing this resolve of yours, 6.30
would I have brought to you the horse,
To make Kápila·vastu grieve,
had I been master of myself?

tan n' ârhasi, mahā|bāho,
vihātuṃ putra|lālasam
snigdhaṃ vṛddhaṃ ca rājānaṃ
sad|dharmam iva n'|âstikaḥ.

saṃvardhana|pariśrāntāṃ
dvitīyāṃ tāṃ ca mātaram
devīṃ n' ârhasi vismartuṃ
kṛta|ghna iva sat|kriyām.

bāla|putrāṃ guṇavatīṃ
kula|ślāghyāṃ pati|vratām
devīm arhasi na tyaktuṃ
klībaḥ prāptām iva śriyam.

putraṃ Yāśodharaṃ ślāghyaṃ
yaśo|dharma|bhṛtāṃ varam
bālam arhasi na tyaktuṃ
vyasan' îv' ôttamaṃ yaśaḥ.

6.35 atha bandhuṃ ca rājyaṃ ca
tyaktum eva kṛtā matiḥ,
māṃ n' ârhasi, vibho, tyaktuṃ
tvat|pādau hi gatir mama.

n' âsmi yātuṃ puraṃ śakto
dahyamānena cetasā
tvām araṇye parityajya
Sumantra iva Rāghavam.

Please do not, therefore, O mighty-armed prince,
forsake the king who so longs for his son;
Like infidels forsaking true dharma,
please do not forsake that tender old king.

Please do not forget that
second mother of yours,
The queen exhausted by bringing you up,
like an ingrate who forgets a good deed.

Please do not abandon that virtuous queen,
faithful to her lord, with an infant son,
The queen who's born in an illustrious line,
like a sissy his inherited crown.

Please don't abandon your young son,
Yasho·dhara's illustrious child,
Best bearer of dharma and fame,*
like a villain the highest fame.

If, however, you have made up your mind 6.35
to abandon your father and kingdom,
Please don't abandon me, My Lord,
for your feet are my sole refuge.

I cannot go to the city
with a heart smoldering with grief
Abandoning you in the wild,
like Sumántra did Rághava.*

kiṃ hi vakṣyati māṃ rājā
tvad|ṛte nagaraṃ gatam?
vakṣyāmy ucita|darśitvāt
kiṃ tav' ântaḥ|purāṇi vā?

yad apy ātth' ‹âpi nairguṇyaṃ
vācyaṃ nara|patāv› iti,
kiṃ tad vakṣyāmy a|bhūtaṃ te
nir|doṣasya muner iva?

hṛdayena sa|lajjena
jihvayā sajjamānayā
ahaṃ yady api vā brūyāṃ,
kas tac chrad|dhātum arhati?

6.40 yo hi candramasas taikṣṇyaṃ
kathayec chrad|dadhīta vā,
sa doṣāṃs tava, doṣajña,
kathayec chrad|dadhīta vā.

s'|ânukrośasya satataṃ
nityaṃ karuṇa|vedinaḥ
snigdha|tyāgo na sadṛśo;
nivartasva, prasīda me.»

iti śok'|âbhibhūtasya
śrutvā Chandasya bhāṣitam
sva|sthaḥ paramayā dhṛtyā
jagāda vadatāṃ varaḥ:

For what will the king say to me
when I come to the city without you?
What will I, because I'm used to seeing them,
say to women in the seraglio?*

You say that I should even tell the king
that you lack any virtue;
But how can I tell a lie about you,
as about a faultless sage?

Even if I did say that
with a heart laden with shame
And with a stuttering tongue,
who will ever believe that?

For if a man believes in and declares 6.40
the scorching power of the moon,
Such a man may, indeed, you who know faults,
believe in and declare your faults.

To forsake loved one does not befit you,
you who are at all times tender at heart;
You who are compassionate at all times,
have pity on me and turn back."

Having heard these words of Chanda,
who was overcome by grief,
that best of speakers, self-composed,
spoke with the utmost resolve:

«mad|viyogaṃ prati, Chanda,
saṃtāpas tyajyatām ayam;
nānā|bhāvo hi niyataṃ
pṛthag|jātiṣu dehiṣu.

sva|janaṃ yady api snehān
na tyajeyam ahaṃ svayam,
mṛtyur anyo|'nyam a|vaśān
asmān saṃtyājayiṣyati.

6.45 mahatyā tṛṣṇayā duḥkhair
garbheṇ' âsmi yayā dhṛtaḥ,
tasyā niṣphala|yatnāyāḥ
kv' âhaṃ mātuḥ, kva sā mama?

vāsa|vṛkṣe samāgamya
vigacchanti yath" âṇḍa|jāḥ,
niyataṃ viprayog'|ântas
tathā bhūta|samāgamaḥ.

sametya ca yathā bhūyo
vyapayānti balāhakāḥ,
saṃyogo viprayogaś ca
tathā me prāṇināṃ mataḥ.

yasmād yāti ca loko 'yaṃ
vipralabhya paraṃ|param
mamatvaṃ na kṣamaṃ tasmāt
svapna|bhūte samāgame.

"Abandon, Chanda, this anguish
at your separation from me;
Embodied beings in diverse births
are bound to part from each other.

Even if out of love I forsake not
my kinsmen on my own,
Death will make us abandon each other
even against our will.

She bore me in her womb 6.45
with great yearning and pain;
Yet her efforts are vain:
What am I to my mother?
What is she to me?

As birds come to a tree to roost
and then go their separate ways,
So the union of beings is bound
to conclude in dissolution.

As clouds gather together
only to scatter apart,
So, I reckon, is the union
and disunion of living beings.

As this world continues to roll
sundering one from another,
So it's wrong to invest yourself
in this coming together
that's as fleeting as a dream.

sahajena viyujyante
  parṇa|rāgeṇa pāda|pāḥ;
anyen' ânyasya viśleṣaḥ
  kiṃ punar na bhaviṣyati?

6.50 tad evaṃ sati saṃtāpaṃ
  mā kārṣīḥ, saumya! gamyatām!
lambate yadi tu sneho
  gatv" âpi punar āvraja.

brūyāś c' âsmat|kṛt'|âpekṣaṃ
  janaṃ Kapilavāstuni:
‹tyajyatāṃ tad|gataḥ snehaḥ!
  śrūyatāṃ c' âsya niścayaḥ!

kṣipram eṣyati vā kṛtvā
  janma|mṛtyu|kṣayaṃ kila;
a|kṛt'|ârtho nir|ārambho
  nidhanaṃ yāsyat' îti vā.› »

iti tasya vacaḥ śrutvā
  Kanthakas turag'|ôttamaḥ
jihvayā lilihe pādau
  bāṣpam uṣṇaṃ mumoca ca.

jālinā svastik'|âṅkena
  cakra|madhyena pāṇinā
āmamarśa kumāras taṃ
  babhāṣe ca vayasyavat:

If innate leaves fall from trees
as their color turns;*
Why surely will not one being
be severed from another?

So, that being the case, my dear man, 6.50
do not grieve! Be on your way!
If, however, your love endures,
leave now, but return again.

And tell the folks of Kápila·vastu,
who have affection for me:

'Give up your love for him!
Listen to his resolve!

After destroying birth and death,
he will return quickly, I'm told;
or lacking initiative
and failing to reach the goal,
he will proceed to his death.'"

After hearing these words of his,
Kánthaka, the best of steeds,
licked with his tongue the prince's feet,
and began to shed warm tears.

With his webbed hand, swastika-marked,
having the wheel-mark on its palm,
the prince stroked the horse soothingly,
and he spoke to him like a friend:

6.55 «muñca, Kanthaka, mā bāṣpaṃ
darśit" êyaṃ sad|aśvatā;
mṛṣyatāṃ, sa|phalaḥ śīghraṃ
śramas te 'yaṃ bhaviṣyati!»

maṇi|tsaruṃ Chandaka|hasta|saṃsthaṃ
tataḥ sa dhīro niśitaṃ gṛhītvā
kośād asiṃ kāñcana|bhakti|citraṃ
bilād iv' âśī|viṣam udbabarha.

niṣkāsya taṃ c' ôtpala|pattra|nīlaṃ
ciccheda citraṃ mukuṭaṃ sa|keśam
vikīryamāṇ'|âṃśukam antar|īkṣe
cikṣepa c' âinaṃ saras' îva haṃsam.

pūj"|âbhilāṣeṇa ca bāhu|mānyād
div'|âukasas taṃ jagṛhuḥ praviddham
yathāvad enaṃ divi deva|saṅghā
divyair viśeṣair mahayāṃ ca cakruḥ.

muktvā tv alaṃkāra|kalatravattāṃ
śrī|vipravāsaṃ śirasaś ca kṛtvā
dṛṣṭv" âṃśukaṃ kāñcana|haṃsa|cihnaṃ
vanyaṃ sa dhīro 'bhicakāṅkṣa vāsaḥ.

6.60 tato mṛga|vyādha|vapur div'|âukā
bhāvaṃ viditv" âsya viśuddha|bhāvaḥ
kāṣāya|vastro 'bhiyayau samīpaṃ
taṃ Śākya|rāja|prabhavo 'bhyuvāca:

"Please, Kánthaka, do not shed tears, 6.55
you've been a good horse;
Be patient, and this toil of yours
will quickly bear fruit!"

Then, from Chándaka's hand the resolute prince
took the sword with the hilt inlaid with gems;
he then drew out the sword from its scabbard,
with its blade streaked with gold,
like a snake from its hole.

Unsheathing the sword, dark as a lotus petal,
he cut his ornate head-dress along with the hair,
and threw it in the air, the cloth trailing behind—
it seemed he was throwing
a swan into a lake.

As it was thrown up, heavenly beings caught it
out of reverence so they may worship it;
throngs of gods in heaven paid it homage
with divine honors according to rule.

Freeing himself from beloved adornments,
exiling royal splendor from his head,
seeing the cloth band resembling a gold swan,
he steadfastly longed for the sylvan robe.

Then, a pure heavenly being, knowing his wish, 6.60
took on the appearance of a hunter
and came near him wearing an ochre robe;
the son of the Shakya king said to him:

«śivaṃ ca kāṣāyam ṛṣi|dhvajas te
na yujyate hiṃsram idaṃ dhanuś ca;
tat, saumya, yady asti na saktir atra
mahyaṃ prayacch' êdam idaṃ gṛhāṇa.»

vyādho 'bravīt: «kāmada, kāmam ārād
anena viśvāsya mṛgān nihanmi;
arthas tu Śakr'|ôpama yady anena,
hanta, pratīcch' ānaya śuklam etat.»

pareṇa harṣeṇa tataḥ sa vanyaṃ
jagrāha vāso 'ṃśukam utsasarja;
vyādhas tu divyaṃ vapur eva bibhrat
tac chuklam ādāya divaṃ jagāma.

tataḥ kumāraś ca sa c' âśva|gopas
tasmiṃs tathā yāti visismiyāte
āraṇyake vāsasi c' âiva bhūyas
tasminn akārṣṭāṃ bahu|mānam āśu.

6.65 Chandaṃ tataḥ s'|âśru|mukhaṃ visṛjya
kāṣāya|saṃbhṛd dhṛti|kīrti|bhṛt saḥ
yen' āśramas tena yayau mah"|ātmā,
saṃdhy"|âbhra|saṃvīta iv' ôḍu|rājaḥ.

tatas tathā bhartari rājya|niḥ|spṛhe
tapo|vanaṃ yāti vivarṇa|vāsasi
bhujau samutkṣipya tataḥ sa vāji|bhṛd
bhṛśaṃ vicukrośa papāta ca kṣitau.

"This deadly bow of yours does not go with
your holy ochre robe that's the seer's badge;
So, good man, if you're not attached to it,
give me the robe and take this in exchange."

The hunter replied:

"Dispenser of desires, although with this
I inspire trust from afar and kill deer;
If you, Shakra's equal, have need for it,
however, take it and give me the white."*

Then, with great joy he took the sylvan robe
and cast away the garment of fine cloth;
but the hunter, assuming his own divine form,
went up to heaven taking with him the white clothes.

Then, the prince and the keeper of the horse
marveled as he departed in that wise,
and forthwith regarded that sylvan robe
with a reverence all the more great.

Then, having dismissed the tearful Chanda, 6.65
the noble one went to the hermitage
wearing the ochre robe
and the fame of resolve,
like the king of stars wrapped in twilight clouds.*

Then, as his master went to the ascetic grove,
with no longing for kingdom, wearing dirty clothes,
the keeper of the horse threw up his arms
and, weeping bitterly, fell on the ground.

vilokya bhūyaś ca ruroda sa|svaraṃ
　hayaṃ bhujābhyām upaguhya Kanthakam;
tato nir|āśo vilapan muhur muhur
　yayau śarīreṇa puraṃ, na cetasā.

kva cit pradadhyau, vilalāpa ca kva cit,
　kva cit pracaskhāla, papāta ca kva cit;
ato vrajan bhakti|vaśena duḥkhitaś
　cacāra bahvīr a|vaśaḥ* pathi kriyāḥ.

iti Buddhacarite mahā|kāvye Chandaka|nivartano nāma ṣaṣṭhaḥ sargaḥ.

Looking at him again he wept aloud,
clasping the horse, Kánthaka, with his arms;
then, in despair, lamenting over and over again,
he returned to the city with his body, not his mind.

Sometimes he brooded, sometimes he wept,
sometimes he staggered, sometimes he fell;
  so, driven by his devotion,
  sorrowfully he went,
  doing many things along the road,
  in complete abandon.

Thus ends the sixth canto named "Chándaka is Sent Back"
of the great poem "Life of the Buddha."

CANTO 7

ENTERING THE ASCETIC GROVE

7.1 TATO VISṚJY' âśru|mukhaṃ rudantaṃ
Chandaṃ vana|cchandatayā nir|āsthaḥ
Sarvārthasiddho vapuṣ" âbhibhūya
tam āśramaṃ siddha iva prapede.

sa rāja|sūnur mṛga|rāja|gāmī
mṛg'|âjiraṃ tan mṛgavat praviṣṭaḥ
lakṣmī|viyukto 'pi śarīra|lakṣmyā
cakṣūṃṣi sarv'|āśramiṇāṃ jahāra.

sthitā hi hasta|stha|yugās tath" âiva
kautūhalāc cakra|dharāḥ sa|dārāḥ
tam Indra|kalpaṃ dadṛśur, na jagmur,
dhuryā iv' ârdh'|âvanataiḥ śirobhiḥ.

viprāś ca gatvā bahir idhma|hetoḥ
prāptāḥ samit|puṣpa|pavitra|hastāḥ
tapaḥ|pradhānāḥ kṛta|buddhayo 'pi
taṃ draṣṭum īyur na maṭhān abhīyuḥ—

7.5 hṛṣṭāś ca kekā mumucur mayūrā
dṛṣṭv" âmbu|daṃ nīlam iv' ônnamantaḥ;
śaṣpāṇi hitv" âbhimukhāś ca tasthur
mṛgāś cal'|âkṣā mṛga|cāriṇaś ca.

THEN, BEING detached through his longing 7.1
for the forest
and dismissing Chanda, teary-eyed and weeping,
Sarvártha·siddha went into that hermitage,
like a *siddha*, engulfing it with his beauty.*

The king's son, walking like the king of beasts,
like a deer, entered that abode of deer;
though stripped of royal majesty,
the majesty of his body
gripped the eyes of all in that hermitage.

For ascetics stood with their wives,
holding the yoke poles in their hands;
and they looked in wonder at him,
who looked like Indra;
they did not move but just stood there
with their heads bowed like yoked oxen.*

And brahmins who had gone out for firewood,
coming with wood, flowers, and sacred grass,
though they were intent on ascetic toil,
though their minds were well trained,
went to see him without going to their huts—

And, necks upturned, as if seeing a dark cloud, 7.5
the peacocks, thrilled, burst into song;
and, leaving the grass, these stood facing him—
ascetics keeping the deer-vow,
and the deer with their darting eyes.*

dṛṣṭvā tam Ikṣvāku|kula|pradīpaṃ
  jvalantam udyantam iv' âṃśumantam
kṛte 'pi dohe janita|pramodāḥ
  prasusruvur homa|duhaś ca gāvaḥ.

«kac cid Vasūnām ayam aṣṭamaḥ syāt?
  syād Aśvinor anyataraś cyuto vā?»
uccerur uccair iti tatra vācas
  tad|darśanād vismaya|jā munīnām.

lekha'|rṣabhasy' êva vapur dvitīyaṃ
  dhām' êva lokasya car'|âcarasya
sa dyotayām āsa vanaṃ hi kṛtsnaṃ
  yad|ṛcchayā sūrya iv' âvatīrṇaḥ.

tataḥ sa tair āśramibhir yathāvad
  abhyarcitaś c' ôpanimantritaś ca
pratyarcayāṃ dharma|bhṛto babhūva
  svareṇa s'|âmbho|'mbu|dhar'|ôpamena.

7.10 kīrṇaṃ tathā puṇya|kṛtā janena
  svarg'|âbhikāmena vimokṣa|kāmaḥ
tam āśramaṃ so 'nucacāra dhīras
  tapāṃsi citrāṇi nirīkṣamāṇaḥ.

tapo|vikārāṃś ca nirīkṣya saumyas
  tapo|vane tatra tapo|dhanānām
tapasvinaṃ kaṃ cid anuvrajantaṃ
  tattvaṃ vijijñāsur idaṃ babhāṣe:

And from the cows that gave ritual milk,
milk flowed, although they were already milked,
when they saw that lamp of the Ikshváku race,
blazing like the rising sun.

The sages living there, when they saw him,
exclaimed loudly these words of amazement:

"Is he, perhaps, an eighth Vasu?
Or one of the Ashvins fallen to earth?"*

For, like a second form of the king of the gods,*
like the light of the mobile and immobile world,
he lit up that entire forest,
like the sun perchance come to earth.

Then, those hermits duly paid him homage
and bade him welcome; and he in return
paid homage to those bearers of dharma
in a voice that resembled
the roar of a thunder cloud.

Steadfast, then, he walked through that hermitage 7.10
filled with men longing for heaven
and performing good deeds,
observing the diverse forms of ascetic toil,
he who was filled with longing for release.

And, as he observed the varieties of ascetic toil
of men rich in ascetic toil in that ascetic grove,
wishing to discover the truth, that gentle sage said this
to an ascetic who was following him:

«tat|pūrvam ady' âśrama|darśanam me
yasmād imaṃ dharma|vidhiṃ na jāne,
tasmād bhavān arhati bhāṣituṃ me—
yo niścayo yat prati vaḥ pravṛttaḥ.»

tato dvi|jātiḥ sa tapo|vihāraḥ
Śākya'|rṣabhāya' rṣabha|vikramāya
krameṇa tasmai kathayāṃ cakāra
tapo|viśeṣāṃs tapasaḥ phalaṃ ca:

«a|grāmyam annaṃ salile prarūḍhaṃ
parṇāni toyaṃ phala|mūlam eva—
yath" |āgamaṃ vṛttir iyaṃ munīnāṃ,
bhinnās tu te te tapasāṃ vikalpāḥ:

7.15 uñchena jīvanti kha|gā iv' ânye,
tṛṇāni ke cin mṛgavac caranti,
ke cid bhujaṅ|gaiḥ saha vartayanti
valmīka|bhūtā vana|mārutena;

aśma|prayatn'|ârjita|vṛttayo 'nye,
ke cit sva|dant'|âpahat'|ânna|bhakṣāḥ,
kṛtvā par'|ârthaṃ śrapaṇaṃ tath" ânye,
kurvanti kāryaṃ yadi śeṣam asti;

ke cij jala|klinna|jaṭā|kalāpā
dviḥ pāvakaṃ juhvati mantra|pūrvam,
mīnaiḥ samaṃ ke cid apo vigāhya
vasanti kūrm'|ôllikhitaiḥ śarīraiḥ;

"As I have not seen a hermitage till today,
I do not know this method of dharma;
So be kind enough to explain to me—
what is your resolve?
What do you seek to achieve?"

Then that brahmin delighting in ascetic toil
explained step by step to that bull of the Shakyas,
who had the valor of a bull,
the varieties and rewards of ascetic toil:

"food not grown in a village,
whatever grows in water,
leaves and water, fruits and roots—
according to scriptural texts
that's the livelihood of a sage;
there are, however, numerous
alternative ascetic paths;

some live by gleaning like the birds, 7.15
some, like the deer, subsist on grass,
others live in the company of snakes,
turned into anthills by the forest winds;*

some procure their food by pounding with stones,
others eat food that's been ground with their teeth,
some cook for others and if there's some left,
with that they do take care of their own needs;

some offer oblations twice a day in the fire
with mantras, their matted hair dripping with water;
plunging into water, some live among the fish,
their bodies scored by turtles;

evaṃ|vidhaiḥ kāla|citais tapobhiḥ
parair divaṃ yānty, aparair nṛ|lokam;
duḥkhena mārgeṇa sukhaṃ hy upaiti,
sukhaṃ hi dharmasya vadanti mūlam.»

ity evam|ādi dvipad'|êndra|vatsaḥ
śrutvā vacas tasya tapo|dhanasya
a|dṛṣṭa|tattvo 'pi na saṃtutoṣa,
śanair idaṃ c' ātma|gataṃ babhāṣe:

7.20 «duḥkh'|ātmakaṃ n' âika|vidhaṃ tapaś ca,
svarga|pradhānaṃ tapasaḥ phalaṃ ca;
lokāś ca sarve pariṇāmavantaḥ
sv|alpe śramaḥ khalv ayam āśramāṇām!

priyāṃś ca bandhūn viṣayāṃś ca hitvā
ye svarga|hetor niyamaṃ caranti,
te viprayuktāḥ khalu gantu|kāmā
mahattaraṃ bandhanam eva bhūyaḥ.

kāya|klamair yaś ca tapo|'bhidhānaiḥ
pravṛttim ākāṅkṣati kāma|hetoḥ
saṃsāra|doṣān a|parīkṣamāṇo,
duḥkhena so 'nvicchati duḥkham eva.

trāsaś ca nityaṃ maraṇāt prajānāṃ,
yatnena c' êcchanti punaḥ|prasūtim;
satyāṃ pravṛttau niyataś ca mṛtyus,
tatr' âiva magnā yata eva bhītāḥ.

when such ascetic toil is amassed over time,
through the higher kind they go to heaven,
through the lower kind, to the world of men,
for it's the path of pain that leads to bliss,
for the root of dharma, they say, is bliss."

The king's son heard this and like orations
from that man whose wealth was ascetic toil;
yet, even though he did not know the truth,
he was not pleased and whispered to himself:

"Pain is basic to the many types of ascetic toil, 7.20
while heaven is the highest reward of ascetic toil;
And yet, all the worlds are subject to change;
such toil in hermitages
only to gain so little!

They forsake their dear kin and objects of sense
and for the sake of heaven practice restraint;
Yet parted from that, they are destined to go
only to states of bondage even more dire.

When someone seeks continued life
for pleasure's sake
through bodily pains that are named ascetic toil,
Without grasping the evils of samsaric life,
by means of pain he is seeking nothing but pain.

Creatures are always mortally afraid of death,
and yet they strenuously seek repeated birth;
Death is certain where there is active existence;
creatures wallow in the very thing they most fear.

ih'|ârtham eke praviśanti khedaṃ,
svarg'|ârtham anye śramam āpnuvanti;
sukh'|ârtham āśā|kṛpaṇo '|kṛt'|ârthaḥ
pataty an|arthe khalu jīva|lokaḥ.

7.25 na khalv ayaṃ garhita eva yatno
yo hīnam utsṛjya viśeṣa|gāmī;
prājñaiḥ samānena pariśrameṇa
kāryaṃ tu tad, yatra punar na kāryam.

śarīra|pīḍā tu yad' îha dharmaḥ
sukhaṃ śarīrasya bhavaty a|dharmaḥ;
dharmeṇa c' āpnoti sukhaṃ paratra
tasmād a|dharmaṃ phalat' îha dharmaḥ.

yataḥ śarīraṃ manaso vaśena
pravartate c' âpi nivartate ca,
yukto damaś cetasa eva tasmāc;
cittād ṛte kāṣṭha|samaṃ śarīram.

āhāra|śuddhyā yadi puṇyam iṣṭaṃ,
tasmān mṛgāṇām api puṇyam asti!
ye c' âpi bāhyāḥ puruṣāḥ phalebhyo
bhāgy'|âparādhena parāṅ|mukh'|ârthāḥ.

duḥkhe 'bhisaṃdhis tv atha puṇya|hetuḥ,
sukhe 'pi kāryo nanu so 'bhisaṃdhiḥ;
atha pramāṇaṃ na sukhe 'bhisaṃdhir
duḥkhe pramāṇaṃ nanu n' âbhisaṃdhiḥ.

Some take on pain with this world as their end,
 others endure toil with heaven as their end;
Forlorn in their hope, with bliss as their end,
 these living beings, with their ends unattained,
 only reach a disastrous end.

Not that this effort is totally vile, 7.25
 which seeks the noble, forsaking the base;
But wise people with the same kind of toil
 ought to attain that state in which
 nothing needs to be done again.

But, if dharma here consists of bodily pain,
 then bodily bliss should be *adhárma*;
So when by dharma one attains bliss hereafter,
 dharma here bears the fruit of *adharma*!

Because the body acts and ceases from action
 under the control of the mind,
It is the mind, therefore, that requires to be tamed;
 body without the mind
 is like a piece of wood.

If you seek merit through the purity of food,
 then even by the deer merit should be acquired!
So also should men excluded from such rewards,
 who, due to some misfortune,
 are bereft of wealth.*

But, if in pain the cause of merit is intent,
 surely, also in pleasure intent should hold good;
But, if in pleasure the basis is not intent,
 surely, it is not a basis even in pain.

7.30 tath" âiva ye karma|viśuddhi|hetoḥ
spṛśanty apas ‹tīrtham› iti pravṛttāḥ,
tatr' âpi toṣo hṛdi kevalo 'yaṃ
na pāvayiṣyanti hi pāpam āpaḥ.

spṛṣṭaṃ hi yad yad guṇavadbhir ambhas
tat tat pṛthivyāṃ yadi tīrtham iṣṭam,
tasmād guṇān eva paraimi tīrtham
āpas tu niḥ|saṃśayam āpa eva.»

iti sma tat tad bahu|yukti|yuktaṃ
jagāda c' âstaṃ ca yayau Vivasvān
tato havir|dhūma|vivarṇa|vṛkṣaṃ
tapaḥ|praśāntaṃ sa vanaṃ viveśa,

abhyuddhṛta|prajvalit'|âgni|hotraṃ
kṛt'|âbhiṣeka'|rṣi|jan'|âvakīrṇam
jāpya|svan'|ākūjita|deva|koṣṭhaṃ
dharmasya karm'|ântam iva pravṛttam.

kāś cin niśās tatra niśā|kar'|ābhaḥ
parīkṣamāṇaś ca tapāṃsy uvāsa;
sarvaṃ parikṣepya tapaś ca matvā
tasmāt tapaḥ|kṣetra|talāj jagāma.

7.35 anvavrajann āśramiṇas tatas taṃ
tad|rūpa|māhātmya|gatair manobhiḥ,
deśād an|āryair abhibhūyamānān
maha"|rṣayo dharmam iv' âpayāntam.

And likewise when they touch water, 7.30
  thinking it is a sacred ford,*
  so as to purify their deeds,
That too just brings joy to the heart,
  for water will not cleanse one's sins.

For, if whatever water touched by virtuous men
  is thought to be a sacred ford on earth,
Then I consider virtues alone as the ford;
  water is just water without a doubt."

As he made these various points buttressed
by numerous arguments, the sun set;
then, he entered that forest—
  with trees darkened by the smoke of fire oblations,
  a forest rendered tranquil by ascetic toil,

  a forest that was like the workshop of dharma,
  and crowded with seers who had just taken
    their baths,
  with blazing sacred fires being taken out,
  and its divine shrines humming with the sound
  of the hushed recitation of mantras.

There, probing those austerities, he spent some nights,
he who resembled the moon, maker of the night;
deciding to abandon all austerities,*
he departed from that field of austerities.

Then, the hermits began to follow after him, 7.35
their minds drawn by his beauty and his majesty,
as great seers follow after dharma departing
from a land that's overrun by barbarous men.

tato jaṭā|valkala|cīra|khelāṃs
tapo|dhanāṃś c' âiva sa tān dadarśa,
tapāṃsi c' âiṣām anurudhyamānas
tasthau śive śrīmati vṛkṣa|mūle.

ath' ôpasṛty' āśrama|vāsinas taṃ
manuṣya|varyaṃ parivārya tasthuḥ;
vṛddhaś ca teṣāṃ bahu|māna|pūrvaṃ
kalena sāmnā giram ity uvāca:

«tvayy āgate pūrṇa iv' āśramo 'bhūt,
saṃpadyate śūnya iva prayāte;
tasmād imaṃ n' ârhasi, tāta, hātuṃ
jijīviṣor deham iv' êṣṭam āyuḥ.

brahma'|rṣi|rāja'|rṣi|sura'|rṣi|juṣṭaḥ
puṇyaḥ samīpe Himavān hi śailaḥ,
tapāṃsi tāny eva tapo|dhanānāṃ
yat|saṃnikarṣād bahulī bhavanti.

7.40 tīrthāni puṇyāny abhitas tath" âiva
sopāna|bhūtāni nabhas|talasya
juṣṭāni dharm'|ātmabhir ātmavadbhir
deva'|rṣibhiś c' âiva maha"|rṣibhiś ca.

itaś ca bhūyaḥ kṣamam uttar" âiva
dik sevituṃ dharma|viśeṣa|hetoḥ,
na tu kṣamaṃ dakṣiṇato budhena
padaṃ bhaved ekam api prayātum.

Then, he saw those hermits rich in austerities,
with matted hair, wearing garments of bark and grass,
and in deference to their austerities, he stopped
at the foot of a lovely and auspicious tree.

Then, the residents of the hermitage
approached that best of men and stood around;
the oldest addressed him with reverence,
with these kind and conciliatory words:

"When you arrived the hermitage became, as if, full,
now that you have left, it has become, as if, empty;
Therefore, son, you should not leave it,
as life that's cherished, the body
of a man longing to live.

For nearby stands the holy Himálaya mount,
frequented by seers—brahmin, royal, and divine;
Because it is near, these very austerities
of men rich in austerity are amplified.

All around, likewise, there are sacred fords, 7.40
which are true stairways to the heavenly plane,
Visited by seers, both great and divine,
devoted to dharma and self-controlled.

And from here again it is proper to proceed
only to the northern quarter
to pursue a special dharma;
But it is not proper for a wise man to take
even one step toward the south.*

tapo|vane 'sminn atha niṣ|kriyo vā
  saṃkīrṇa|dharm'|āpatito '|śucir vā
dṛṣṭas tvayā yena na te vivatsā,
  tad brūhi, yāvad rucito 'stu vāsaḥ.

ime hi vāñchanti tapaḥ|sahāyaṃ
  tapo|nidhāna|pratimaṃ bhavantam
vāsas tvayā h' Îndra|samena s'|ârdhaṃ
  Bṛhaspater abhyuday'|āvahaḥ syāt.»

ity evam ukte sa tapasvi|madhye
  tapasvi|mukhyena manīṣi|mukhyaḥ
bhava|praṇāśāya kṛta|pratijñaḥ
  svaṃ bhāvam antar|gatam ācacakṣe:

7.45 «ṛjv|ātmanāṃ dharmabhṛtāṃ munīnām
  iṣṭ'|âtithitvāt sva|jan'|ôpamānām
evaṃ|vidhair māṃ prati bhāva|jātaiḥ
  prītiḥ parā me janitaś ca mānaḥ.

snigdhābhir ābhir hṛdayaṃ|gamābhiḥ
  samāsataḥ snāta iv' âsmi vāgbhiḥ;
ratiś ca me dharma|nava|grahasya
  vispanditā taṃ prati* bhūya eva.

evaṃ pravṛttān bhavataḥ śaraṇyān
  at'|îva saṃdarśita|pakṣapātān
yāsyāmi hitv" êti mam' âpi duḥkhaṃ
  yath" âiva bandhūṃs tyajatas tath" âiva.

If, however, you've seen in this ascetic grove
someone who neglects rites, or is impure,
Or has fallen into a corrupted dharma,
for which reason you do not wish to stay,
report it; so you'd be pleased to dwell here.

For these here desire to have you
as a companion in ascetic toil,
you who are the store of ascetic toil;
For to dwell with you, the equal of Indra,
will bring success even to Brihas·pati."

So addressed by the chief of the hermits
amid the hermits, the chief of the wise
revealed his inner feeling, he who had
resolved to destroy the rebirth process:

"At such a display of love toward me by these 7.45
upright sages, upholders of dharma,
Whom, because of their love of hospitality,
I consider my own kinsfolk,
I feel honored, and my joy overflows.

In brief, I am as if bathed by these words,
full of love and gripping the heart;
Although in dharma I'm still a novice,
they double my passion for it.*

The thought of leaving you all thus engaged,
so hospitable, so kind toward me,
The thought of leaving you grieves me as much
as when I first left my own relatives.

svargāya yuṣmākam ayaṃ tu dharmo,
mam' âbhilāṣas tv a|punar|bhavāya;
asmin vane yena na me vivatsā
bhinnaḥ pravṛttyā hi nivṛtti|dharmaḥ.

tan n' â|ratir me na par'|âpacāro
vanād ito yena parivrajāmi;
dharme sthitāḥ pūrva|yug'|ânurūpe
sarve bhavanto hi maha"|rṣi|kalpāḥ.»

7.50 tato vacaḥ sūnṛtam arthavac ca
su|ślakṣṇam ojasvi ca garvitaṃ ca
śrutvā kumārasya tapasvinas te
viśeṣa|yuktaṃ bahu|mānam īyuḥ.

kaś cid dvijas tatra tu bhasma|śāyī
prāṃśuḥ śikhī dārava|cīra|vāsāḥ
ā|piṅgal'|âkṣas tanu|dīrgha|ghoṇaḥ
kuṇḍ'|âika|hasto giram ity uvāca:

«dhīmann, udāraḥ khalu niścayas te
yas tvaṃ yuvā janmani dṛṣṭa|doṣaḥ;
svarg'|âpavargau hi vicārya samyag
yasy' âpavarge matir asti, so 'sti!

But your dharma aims at attaining heaven,
and my desire is to be free from rebirth.
So, I have no wish to live in this forest,
for the dharma of cessation is opposed
to the dharma of continued existence.

The reason, therefore, for my leaving this forest
is not dislike or an offense by another;
For all of you are equal to the great sages,
you who follow a dharma
conforming to the first age."*

Then, when they had heard those words of the prince, 7.50
words that were kind and pregnant with meaning,
so gentle, yet spirited and powerful,
those ascetics paid him special homage.

But a certain tall brahmin among them,
used to lying on ash, wearing a topknot,
with reddish eyes, wearing a bark garment,
with a thin long nose and a water pot,
made this oration:

"Wise one, your resolve is truly magnificent,
in that, still young, you have seen
the peril of birth;
For, having examined well heaven and release,
one who sets his mind on release,
he alone does truly exist!

yajñais tapobhir niyamaiś ca tais taiḥ
svargaṃ yiyāsanti hi rāgavantaḥ;
rāgeṇa s'|ârdhaṃ ripuṇ" êva yuddhvā
mokṣaṃ parīpsanti tu sattvavantaḥ.

tad buddhir eṣā yadi niścitā te,
tūrṇaṃ bhavān gacchatu Vindhya|koṣṭham;
asau munis tatra vasaty Arāḍo,
yo naiṣṭhike śreyasi labdha|cakṣuḥ.

7.55 tasmād bhavāñ chroṣyati tattva|mārgaṃ,
satyāṃ rucau saṃpratipatsyate ca;
yathā tu paśyāmi matis tath" âiṣā,
tasy' âpi yāsyaty avadhūya buddhim.

spaṣṭ'|ôcca|ghoṇaṃ vipul'|āyat'|âkṣaṃ
tāmr'|âdhar'|âuṣṭhaṃ sita|tīkṣṇa|daṃṣṭram
idaṃ hi vaktraṃ tanu|rakta|jihvaṃ
jñey'|ârṇavaṃ pāsyati kṛtsnam eva.

gambhīratā yā bhavatas tv a|gādhā
yā dīptatā yāni ca lakṣaṇāni,
ācāryakaṃ prāpsyasi tat pṛthivyāṃ
yan na' rṣibhiḥ pūrva|yuge 'py avāptam.»

For men of passion seek to attain heaven
by various sacrifices, austerities, and restraints;
Men of spirit, however, yearn for release,
waging war against passion as against an enemy.

Therefore, if this resolve of yours is firm,
go quickly then to the Vindhya·koshtha;*
A sage lives there by the name Aráda,
who has gained insight into final bliss.

From him you will learn 7.55
the path of the ultimate principles;*
if that pleases you, you may follow it;
But as I perceive this resolve of yours,
you will leave him too, rejecting his view.

For this face of yours with nose straight and high,
eyes large and long, and a red lower lip,
teeth white and sharp,
and tongue narrow and red,
Will drink up the entire ocean
of all that can be known.

Look at your unfathomable profundity,
your mighty effulgence and the auspicious signs!
Clearly you'll become on earth the kind of teacher
that even seers of the first age could not become."

«paramam» iti tato nṛp'|ātmajas tam
ṛṣi|janaṃ pratinandya niryayau;
vidhivad anuvidhāya te 'pi taṃ
praviviśur āśramiṇas tapo|vanam.

iti Buddhacarite mahā|kāvye Tapo|vana|praveśo nāma saptamaḥ sargaḥ.

Then, the son of the king said, "Very well,"
bid farewell to those seers, and departed;
the hermits too duly saluted him
and entered the ascetic grove.

Thus ends the seventh canto named "Entering the Ascetic Grove"
of the great poem "Life of the Buddha."

CANTO 8
LAMENTING IN THE SERAGLIO

8.1 TATAS TURAṄG'|âvacaraḥ sa dur|manās
tathā vanaṃ bhartari nir|mame gate
cakāra yatnaṃ pathi śoka|nigrahe
tath" âpi c' âiv' âśru na tasya cikṣiye.

yam eka|rātreṇa tu bhartur ājñayā
jagāma mārgaṃ saha tena vājinā,
iyāya bhartur virahaṃ vicintayaṃs
tam eva panthānam ahobhir aṣṭabhiḥ.

hayaś ca s'|âujā vicacāra Kanthakas
tatāma bhāvena babhūva nir|madaḥ;
alaṃ|kṛtaś c' âpi tath" âiva bhūṣaṇair
abhūd gata|śrīr iva tena varjitaḥ.

nivṛtya c' âiv' âbhimukhas tapo|vanaṃ
bhṛśaṃ jiheṣe karuṇaṃ muhur muhuḥ;
kṣudh"|ânvito 'py adhvani śaṣpam ambu vā
yathā purā n' âbhinananda, n' ādade.

8.5 tato vihīnaṃ Kapil'|āhvayaṃ puraṃ
mah"|ātmanā tena jagadd|hit'|ātmanā
krameṇa tau śūnyam iv' ôpajagmatur
divā|kareṇ' êva vinā|kṛtaṃ nabhaḥ.

sa|puṇḍarīkair api śobhitaṃ jalair
alaṃ|kṛtaṃ puṣpa|dharair nagair api
tad eva tasy' ôpavanaṃ van'|ôpamaṃ
gata|praharṣair na rarāja nāgaraiḥ.

THEN, AS HIS master entered the forest, 8.1
selfless, the steed's groom became despondent;
on the road he tried to suppress his grief,
yet his tears did not cease to flow.

But the road he had traversed along with his horse
in just a single night at his master's command,
that same road took him eight days,
as he mused over his separation from his lord.

And Kánthaka, the powerful horse, walked on;
his spirits were low, his ardor was gone;
though adorned with ornaments as before,
yet without his master he was,
as if, bereft of majesty.

And, turning back and facing the ascetic grove,
he neighed aloud piteously again and again;
although hungry, he did not welcome as before,
or consume, the grass or the water on the path.

Then, in due course the two approached 8.5
the city named Kápila that now seemed empty
without that noble man who was dedicated
to the welfare of the world,
like the sky without the sun.

Although adorned with lotus ponds
and festooned with flowering trees,
the same city park with forlorn city folks
did not sparkle, looking more like a jungle.

tato bhramadbhir diśi dīna|mānasair
anujjvalair bāṣpa|hat'|êkṣaṇair naraiḥ
nivāryamāṇāv iva tāv ubhau puraṃ
śanair apasnātam iv' âbhijagmatuḥ.

niśāmya ca srasta|śarīra|gāminau
vin" āgatau Śākya|kula'|rṣabheṇa tau,
mumoca bāṣpaṃ pathi nāgaro janaḥ
purā rathe Dāśarather iv' āgate.

atha bruvantaḥ samupeta|manyavo
janāḥ pathi Chandakam āgat'|āśravaḥ:
«kva rāja|putraḥ pura|rāṣṭra|nandano
hṛtas tvay" âsāv» iti pṛṣṭhato 'nvayuḥ.

8.10 tataḥ sa tān bhaktimato 'bravīj janān:
«nar'|êndra|putraṃ na parityajāmy aham,
rudann ahaṃ tena tu nirjane vane
gṛha|stha|veśaś ca visarjitāv» iti.

idaṃ vacas tasya niśamya te janāḥ
«su|duṣ|karaṃ khalv» iti niścayaṃ yayuḥ
patadd hi jahruḥ salilaṃ na netra|jaṃ
mano nininduś ca phal'|ôttham ātmanaḥ.

Then, the two slowly went to the city,
as if they were going to a funeral bath,
hindered as if by men rambling around,
eyes filled with tears, dejected and downcast.

When the townsfolk saw the two return
without that bull of the Shakya race
and walking with their bodies drooping,
they shed tears along the path, as when
long ago the chariot
of Dásharatha returned.*

Then, the people followed behind them
filled with anger, shedding copious tears,
telling Chándaka along the road:

"Where is the king's son, the joy
of the town and kingdom?
Where have you carried him away?"

Then, he said to those devoted people: 8.10

"I've not forsaken the son of the king.
It is he who in the lonely forest
forsook me, as I wept,
and the householder's garb."

Hearing these words of his,
the people concluded:

"It was truly a most difficult act!"

for they did not restrain the tears that flowed,
blaming their mind rising from their own fruit.*

ath' ōcur: «ady' âiva viśāma tad vanaṃ,
gataḥ sa yatra dvipa|rāja|vikramaḥ;
jijīviṣā n' âsti hi tena no vinā
yath" êndriyāṇāṃ vigame śarīriṇām.

idaṃ puraṃ tena vivarjitaṃ vanaṃ
vanaṃ ca tat tena samanvitaṃ puram
na śobhate tena hi no vinā puraṃ
Marutvatā Vṛtra|vadhe yathā divam.»

punaḥ «kumāro vinivṛtta ity» ath' ô
gav'|âkṣa|mālāḥ pratipedire 'ṅganāḥ;
vivikta|pṛṣṭhaṃ ca niśāmya vājinaṃ
punar gav'|âkṣāṇi pidhāya cukruśuḥ.

8.15 praviṣṭa|dīkṣas tu sut'|ôpalabdhaye
vratena śokena ca khinna|mānasaḥ
jajāpa dev'|āyatane nar'|âdhipaś,
cakāra tās tāś ca yath"|āśayāḥ kriyāḥ.

tataḥ sa bāṣpa|pratipūrṇa|locanas
turaṅ|gam ādāya turaṅgam'|ânugaḥ
viveśa śok'|âbhihato nṛpa|kṣayaṃ
yudh" âpinīte ripuṇ" êva bhartari.

vigāhamānaś ca nar'|êndra|mandiraṃ
vilokayann aśru|vahena cakṣuṣā
svareṇa puṣṭena rurāva Kanthako
janāya duḥkhaṃ prativedayann iva.

Then, they declared:

"We shall then go this very day to the forest
where he with an elephant king's valor has gone;
For without that one we have no desire to live,
like embodied beings when vital organs are gone.

Without him this city is a forest,
and with him that forest is a city;
For without him our city does not shine,
like heaven without Indra
at the time Vritra was slain."*

Then, believing that the prince had returned,
to the rows of windows the women rushed;
but seeing the horse with its back empty,
they closed the windows once again and wept.

Undertaking vows to get back his son, 8.15
his mind beleaguered by penance and grief,
the king muttered mantras in the temple
and performed various rites as he desired.

Then, the horse's groom, his eyes filled with tears,
taking the horse and overcome with grief,
went into the residence of the king,
as if an enemy soldier
had carried away his lord.

Going deep into the king's palace,
looking around with tearful eyes,
Kánthaka neighed in a loud voice,
as if he was announcing
his anguish to the people.

tataḥ kha|gāś ca kṣaya|madhya|gocarāḥ
samīpa|baddhās tura|gāś ca sat|kṛtāḥ
hayasya tasya pratisasvanuḥ svanaṃ
nar'|êndra|sūnor upayāna|śaṅkinaḥ.

janāś ca harṣ'|âtiśayena vañcitā
jan'|âdhip'|ântaḥ|pura|saṃnikarṣa|gāḥ
«yathā hayaḥ Kanthaka eṣa heṣate
dhruvaṃ kumāro viśat' îti» menire.

8.20 ati|praharṣād atha śoka|mūrchitāḥ
kumāra|saṃdarśana|lola|locanāḥ
gṛhād viniścakramur āśayā striyaḥ
śarat|payo|dād iva vidyutaś calāḥ.

vilamba|keśyo malin'|âṃśuk'|âmbarā
nir|añjanair bāṣpa|hat'|êkṣaṇair mukhaiḥ
striyo na rejur mṛjayā vinā|kṛtā
div' îva tārā rajanī|kṣay'|âruṇāḥ—

a|rakta|tāmraiś caraṇair a|nūpurair
a|kuṇḍalair ārjava|kandharair mukhaiḥ
sva|bhāva|pīnair jaghanair a|mekhalair
a|hāray'|ôktrair muṣitair iva stanaiḥ.

nirīkṣya tā bāṣpa|parīta|locanā
nir|āśrayaṃ Chandakam aśvam eva ca,
viṣaṇṇa|vaktrā rurudur var'|âṅganā
van'|ântare gāva iva' ṛṣabh'|ôjjhitāḥ.

Then, the birds living within the palace
and the pampered horses tied up nearby,
thinking that the prince had returned,
echoed that horse's cry.

Those living near the king's seraglio
believed, fooled by the excess of their joy:

"Since this horse Kánthaka is neighing,
The prince, for sure, must be entering!"

Then, the women who had swooned out of grief 8.20
rushed with hope from their houses in great joy,
eyes darting to gain a glimpse of the prince,
like streaks of lightning from an autumn cloud.*

Their hair was hanging loose,
and their fine clothes were soiled,
their faces without makeup, their eyes filled with tears,
their toilet left undone, the women did not shine,
like stars in the sky dimmed at the end of the night—

their feet were without anklets or red dye,
their faces without earrings, with bare necks,
naturally plump hips without girdles,
their breasts seemingly robbed of their pearl strings.

Seeing with tearful eyes just the horse
and Chándaka, without their lord,
those splendid women wept, faces downcast,
like cows abandoned by their bull
in the middle of a forest.

tataḥ sa|bāṣpā mahiṣī mahī|pateḥ
pranaṣṭa|vatsā mahiṣ" îva vatsalā
pragṛhya bāhū nipapāta Gautamī
vilola|parṇā kadal" îva kāñcanī.

8.25 hata|tviṣo 'nyāḥ śithil'|âṃsa|bāhavaḥ
striyo viṣādena vicetanā iva
na cukruśur, n' âśru jahur, na śaśvasur,
na celur, āsur likhitā iva sthitāḥ.

a|dhīram anyāḥ pati|śoka|mūrchitā
vilocana|prasravaṇair mukhaiḥ striyaḥ
siṣiñcire proṣita|candanān stanān
dharā|dharaḥ prasravaṇair iv' ôpalān.

mukhaiś ca tāsāṃ nayan'|âmbu|taḍitai
rarāja tad|rāja|niveśanaṃ tadā
nav'|âmbu|kāle 'mbu|da|vṛṣṭi|taḍitaiḥ
sravaj|jalais tāmarasair yathā saraḥ.

su|vṛtta|pīn'|âṅgulibhir nir|antarair
a|bhūṣaṇair gūḍha|sirair var'|âṅganāḥ
urāṃsi jaghnuḥ kamal'|ôpamaiḥ karaiḥ
sva|pallavair vāta|calā latā iva.

Then, Gáutami, the chief queen of the king,
like a kind she-buffalo that has lost her calf,
eyes filled with tears, fell on the ground
flinging her arms,
like a gold plantain-tree with fluttering leaves.

Other women, their luster gone, 8.25
and their shoulders and arms sagging,
almost blacked out out of despair;
they did not wail, they did not weep,
they did not sigh, they did not stir,
they looked like shapes in a drawing.

Other women, losing all self-control,
passing out out of anguish for their lord,
sprinkled their breasts deprived of sandalwood,
with cascades from their eyes gushing down their faces,
as a mountain sprinkles the rocks with its cascades.

At that time the residence of the king,
with the women's faces battered by tears,
looked like a lake with lotuses dripping
with water and battered by the rain from
the rain clouds at the time of the first rains.

Those exquisite women beat their breasts
with hands that resembled lotus buds,
whose fingers touched each other, full and plump,
whose unadorned fingers revealed no veins,
like creepers swaying in the wind
beating themselves with their own tendrils.

kara|prahāra|pracalaiś ca tā babhus
  tath" âpi nāryaḥ sahit'|ônnataiḥ stanaiḥ,
van'|ânil'|āghūrṇita|padma|kampitai
  rath'|âṅga|nāmnāṃ mithunair iv' âpagāḥ.

8.30 yathā ca vakṣāṃsi karair apīḍayaṃs
  tath" âiva vakṣobhir apīḍayan karān
akārayaṃs tatra paras|paraṃ vyathāḥ
  kar'|âgra|vakṣāṃsy abalā day"|âlasāḥ.

tatas tu roṣa|pravirakta|locanā
  viṣāda|saṃbandhi|kaṣāya|gadgadam
uvāca niśvāsa|calat|payo|dharā
  vigaḍha|śok'|âśru|dharā Yaśodharā:

«niśi prasuptām a|vaśāṃ vihāya māṃ
  gataḥ kva sa, Chandaka, man|mano|rathaḥ?
upāgate ca tvayi Kanthake ca me
  samaṃ gateṣu triṣu kampate manaḥ.

an|āryam a|snigdham a|mitra|karma me
  nṛśaṃsa kṛtvā, kim ih' âdya rodiṣi?
niyaccha bāṣpaṃ! bhava tuṣṭa|mānaso!
  na saṃvadaty aśru ca tac ca karma te!

priyeṇa vaśyena hitena sādhunā
  tvayā sahāyena yath"|ârtha|kāriṇā
gato 'rya|putro hy a|punar|nivṛttaye!
  ramasva! diṣṭyā sa|phalaḥ śramas tava!

Yet those women, with their breasts close-set and erect
swaying as they beat them with their hands,
were radiant,
like rivers with pairs of ruddy geese tossed about
by lotuses buffeted by a forest wind.

As they hurt their chests with their hands, 8.30
so they hurt their hands with their chests;
the women there, bereft of compassion,
made their hands and their chests hurt each other.

Then Yasho·dhara spoke up, eyes red with anger,
her voice choking by the bitterness of despair,
and her breasts heaving along with her sighs,
tears streaming due to the depth of her grief:

"Where did he go, Chándaka, the joy of my heart,
leaving me as I slept helpless at night?
As I see you and Kánthaka return,
whereas three had departed,
my heart begins to tremble.

You have done me an unfriendly act,
ignoble and cruel, you heartless man!
So why do you weep here today?
Contain your tears, be of good cheer!
Your tears don't accord with your deed!

For that noble man went with you, his aide,
loving, loyal, trustworthy, and upright,
always doing what's appropriate,
Never to return again! Be happy!
By good fortune your toil has produced fruit!

8.35 varaṃ manuṣyasya vicakṣaṇo ripur,
na mitram a|prājñam a|yoga|peśalam;
suhṛd|bruveṇa hy a|vipaścitā tvayā
kṛtaḥ kulasy' âsya mahān upaplavaḥ.

imā hi śocyā vyavamukta|bhūṣaṇāḥ
prasakta|bāṣp'|āvila|rakta|locanāḥ
sthite 'pi patyau Himavan|mahī|same
pranaṣṭa|śobhā vidhavā iva striyaḥ.

imāś ca vikṣipta|viṭaṅka|bāhavaḥ
prasakta|pārāvata|dīrgha|nisvanāḥ
vinā|kṛtās tena sah' âvarodhanair
bhṛśaṃ rudant' îva vimāna|paṅktayaḥ.

an|artha|kāmo 'sya janasya sarvathā
turaṅ|gamo 'pi dhruvam eṣa Kanthakaḥ;
jahāra sarvasvam itas tathā hi me
jane prasupte niśi ratna|cauravat.

yadā samarthaḥ khalu soḍhum āgatān
iṣu|prahārān api, kiṃ punaḥ kaśāḥ;
gataḥ kaśā|pāta|bhayāt kathaṃ nv ayaṃ
śriyaṃ gṛhītvā hṛdayaṃ ca me samam?

8.40 an|ārya|karmā bhṛśam adya heṣate
nar'|êndra|dhiṣṇyaṃ pratipūrayann iva;
yadā tu nirvāhayati sma me priyaṃ
tadā hi mūkas turag'|âdhamo 'bhavat.

It's better for a man to have a prudent foe, 8.35
than a foolish friend, skilled in doing
what is unfit;
For calling yourself a friend, you dimwitted man,
you have brought this family to utter ruin.

It's for these women, surely, we should grieve,
their jewelry cast aside, their eyes
stained and reddened by constant tears;
They are like widows, their splendor erased,
though their husband remains alive,
like the earth or Himalayas.*

And these rows of castles, separated from him,
weep profusely, as if, along with the women,
With soaring turrets for their arms,
sighing deeply through their cuddling doves.

This horse, Kánthaka, it's clear, must always
wish me ill, for like a burglar of gems,
He carried off from here my all,
while people were asleep at night.

When he could withstand even the lash of arrows,
how much more could he the lash of the whip;
Why then did he leave for fear of the whip,
taking my fortune along with my heart?

Given to ignoble deeds, he neighs loud today, 8.40
filling up, as it were, the abode of the king;
But when he took away my love,
this vile horse in fact remained mute.

yadi hy aheṣiṣyata bodhayan janaṃ
khuraiḥ kṣitau v" âpy akariṣyata dhvanim
hanu|svanaṃ v" âjaniṣyad uttamaṃ,
na c' âbhaviṣyan mama duḥkham īdṛśam.»

it' îha devyāḥ paridevit'|āśrayaṃ
niśamya bāṣpa|grathit'|âkṣaraṃ vacaḥ
adho|mukhaḥ s'|âśru|kalaḥ kṛt'|âñjaliḥ
śanair idaṃ Chandaka uttaraṃ jagau:

«vigarhituṃ n' ârhasi devi Kanthakaṃ;
na c' âpi roṣaṃ mayi kartum arhasi;
an|āgasau svaḥ samavehi sarvaśo,
gato nṛ|devaḥ sa hi devi devavat.

ahaṃ hi jānann api rāja|śāsanaṃ
balāt kṛtaḥ kair api daivatair iva
upānayaṃ tūrṇam imaṃ turaṅ|gamaṃ
tath" ânvagacchaṃ vigata|śramo 'dhvani.

8.45 vrajann ayaṃ vāji|varo 'pi n' âspṛśan
mahīṃ khur'|âgrair vidhṛtair iv' ântarā;
tath" âiva daivād iva saṃyat'|ânano
hanu|svanaṃ n' âkṛta n' âpy aheṣata.

yato bahir gacchati pārthiv'|ātmaje
tad" âbhavad dvāram apāvṛtaṃ svayam
tamaś ca naiśaṃ ravin" êva pāṭitaṃ—
tato 'pi daivo vidhir eṣa gṛhyatām.

For had he neighed waking up the people,
  or made a noise on the ground with his hooves,
Or had he made a loud noise with his jaws,
  I'd not be enduring this kind of grief."

After listening to these words of the queen, pregnant with reproach, stammering amidst tears, Chándaka bowed his head, folded his hands, and responded slowly, choking with tears:

"Please do not reproach Kánthaka, my queen;
  please do not be angry also with me;
Know that we are completely without blame,
  for that god among men, my queen,
  departed like a god.

For even though I knew the king's decree,
  I brought this horse quickly, as if coerced
By some god, and likewise along the road
  as I followed him I felt no fatigue.

As it galloped, this fine steed did not touch the ground, 8.45
  with the tips of his hooves, as it were, borne aloft;
Its mouth too was sealed as if by a divine force;
  and it did not neigh or make a sound with its jaws.

The gate opened on its own
  as the king's son departed,
The night's dark was cleaved as if by the sun—
  because of this too we must conclude,
  this was a divine disposition.

yad a|pramatto 'pi nar'|êndra|śāsanād
  gṛhe pure c' âiva sahasraśo janaḥ
tadā sa n' âbudhyata nidrayā hṛtas—
  tato 'pi daivo vidhir eṣa gṛhyatām.

yataś ca vāso vana|vāsa|saṃmataṃ
  nisṛṣṭam asmai samaye div'|âukasā
divi praviddhaṃ mukuṭaṃ ca tadd hṛtaṃ—
  tato 'pi daivo vidhir eṣa gṛhyatām.

tad evam āvāṃ, nara|devi, doṣato
  na tat|prayātaṃ prati gantum arhasi;
na kāma|kāro mama, n' âsya vājinaḥ;
  kṛt'|ânuyātraḥ sa hi daivatair gataḥ.»

8.50 iti prayāṇaṃ bahu|devam adbhutaṃ
  niśamya tās tasya mah"|ātmanaḥ striyaḥ
pranaṣṭa|śokā iva vismayaṃ yayur
  mano|jvaraṃ pravrajanāt tu lebhire.

viṣāda|pāriplava|locanā tataḥ
  pranaṣṭa|potā kurar" îva duḥkhitā
vihāya dhairyaṃ virurāva Gautamī,
  tatāma c' âiv' âśru|mukhī jagāda ca:

Thousands of people in palace and town,
mindful though they were of the king's decree,
Succumbed to sleep then and did not wake up—
because of this too we must conclude,
this was a divine disposition.

At that time a heavenly being gave to him
a garment suited for the forest life;
His head-dress was carried off when tossed
to the sky—
because of this too we must conclude,
this was a divine disposition.*

Therefore, with respect to his departure, my queen,
please do not think that the two of us are at fault;
I did not act of my free will, nor did this steed,
for he went forth in the company of the gods."

And when the women heard this description 8.50
of the departure of that noble man,
wondrous and attended by many gods,
they were amazed, their grief, as if, destroyed,
but their hearts burned because he had gone forth.

Then Gáutami, her eyes trembling with despair,
grieving like an osprey that had lost its chicks,
lost self-control, wailed aloud, and fainted;
and, her face covered with tears, she then spoke:

«mah”|ôrmimanto mṛdavo ’sitāḥ śubhāḥ
pṛthak pṛthaṅ mūla|ruhāḥ samudgatāḥ
praveritās te bhuvi tasya mūrdha|jā
nar’|êndra|maulī|pariveṣṭana|kṣamāḥ.

pralamba|bāhur mṛga|rāja|vikramo
maha”|rṣabh’|âkṣaḥ kanak’|ôjjvala|dyutiḥ
viśāla|vakṣā ghana|dundubhi|svanas
tathā|vidho ’py āśrama|vāsam arhati.

a|bhāginī nūnam iyaṃ vasuṃ|dharā
tam ārya|karmāṇam an|uttamaṃ patim
gatas tato ’sau guṇavān hi tā|dṛśo
nṛ|paḥ prajā|bhāgya|guṇaiḥ prasūyate.

8.55 sujāta|jāl’|âvatat’|âṅgulī mṛdū
nigūḍha|gulphau bisa|puṣpa|komalau
van’|ânta|bhūmiṃ kaṭhināṃ kathaṃ nu tau
sa|cakra|madhyau caraṇau gamiṣyataḥ.

vimāna|pṛṣṭhe śayan’|āsan’|ôcitaṃ
mah”|ârha|vastr’|âguru|candan’|ârcitam
kathaṃ nu śīt’|ôṣṇa|jal’|āgameṣu
tac|charīram ojasvi vane bhaviṣyati?

"Those hairs on his head, soft and black,
lovely, each growing from its root,
Full of great locks, curling upwards,
fit to be wrapped with a royal head-dress—
have those hairs been thrown on the ground?

With long arms, with the valor of the king of beasts,
with a broad chest, with the eyes of a mighty bull,
A voice like thunder,
glowing with the gleam of gold—
does such a man deserve
to live a hermit's life?

Shall this earth, then, not win him as her lord,
a man who's peerless and of noble deeds,
now that he has gone from here?
For it is through the virtues and the good fortune
of the subjects that such a virtuous king is born.

Those soft feet of his, with lovely webbed toes, 8.55
tender like a flower or lotus fiber,
With concealed ankles, with wheels on the soles—
how will they tread on the rough forest ground?

Used to sitting and lying on the palace roof-top,
bedecked in priceless clothes, aloe,
and sandal paste—
How will his mighty body fare in the forest
in the cold, the heat, and the rain?

kulena sattvena balena varcasā
  śrutena lakṣmyā vayasā ca garvitaḥ
pradātum ev' âbhyucito na yācituṃ
  kathaṃ sa bhikṣāṃ parataś cariṣyati?

śucau sayitvā śayane hiraṇ|maye
  prabodhyamāno niśi tūrya|nisvanaiḥ
kathaṃ bata svapsyati so 'dya me vratī
  paṭ'|âikadeś'|ântarite mahī|tale?»

imaṃ pralāpaṃ karuṇaṃ niśamya tā
  bhujaiḥ pariṣvajya paras|paraṃ striyaḥ
vilocanebhyaḥ salilāni tatyajur
  madhūni puṣpebhya iv' êritā latāḥ.

8.60 tato dharāyām apatad Yaśodharā
  vi|cakravāk" êva rath'|âṅga|sāhvayā
śanaiś ca tat tad vilalāpa viklavā
  muhur muhur gadgada|ruddhayā girā:

«sa mām a|nāthāṃ saha|dharma|cāriṇīm
  apāsya dharmaṃ yadi kartum icchati,
kuto 'sya dharmaḥ saha|dharma|cāriṇīṃ
  vinā tapo yaḥ paribhoktum icchati?

śṛṇoti nūnaṃ sa na pūrva|pārthivān
  Mahāsudarśa|prabhṛtīn pitā|mahān
vanāni patnī|sahitān upeyuṣas,
  tathā hi dharmaṃ mad|ṛte cikīrṣati.

Distinguished by learning, splendor, and strength,
lineage, character, majesty, and youth
Accustomed to giving, not to begging—
how will he from others beg for almsfood?

Used to sleeping in a clean bed of gold,
waking at night to the sound of music—
How will this my ascetic sleep today
on bare ground covered with one piece of cloth?"

Clasping each other with their arms,
as they heard this piteous lament,
the women shed tears from their eyes,
as creepers when they're shaken drip
honey from their flower blossoms.

Yasho·dhara fell on the ground, 8.60
then, like a swan without its mate,
distressed, she softly voiced various laments,
in a voice stifled by repeated sobs:

"If it is his wish to practice dharma,
abandoning me without protector,
forsaking me, his partner in dharma;
From where can he obtain dharma
when he desires ascetic toil
without his partner in dharma?

Perhaps he has not heard of former kings,
his forefathers like Maha·sudársha,
who repaired to the forest with their wives;
For that's the reason why he wants
to practice dharma without me.

makheṣu vā veda|vidhāna|saṃskṛtau
  na dampatī paśyati dīkṣitāv ubhau
samaṃ bubhukṣū parato 'pi tat|phalaṃ
  tato 'sya jāto mayi dharma|matsaraḥ.

dhruvaṃ sa jānan mama dharma|vallabho
  manaḥ priy'|ērṣyā|kalahaṃ muhur mithaḥ
sukhaṃ vibhīr mām apahāya roṣaṇāṃ
  Mah"|êndra|loke 'psaraso jighṛkṣati.

8.65 iyaṃ tu cintā mama—kīdṛśaṃ nu tā
  vapur|guṇaṃ bibhrati tatra yoṣitaḥ
vane yad|arthaṃ sa tapāṃsi tapyate
  śriyaṃ ca hitvā mama bhaktim eva ca?

na khalv iyaṃ svarga|sukhāya me spṛhā,
  na taj janasy' ātmavato 'pi dur|labham;
‹sa tu priyo mām iha vā paratra vā
  kathaṃ na jahyād› iti me mano|rathaḥ.

a|bhāginī yady aham āyat'|êkṣaṇaṃ
  śuci|smitaṃ bhartur udīkṣituṃ mukham
na manda|bhāgyo 'rhati Rāhulo 'py ayaṃ
  kadā cid aṅke parivartituṃ pituḥ!

Perhaps he does not see that in sacrifices
both husband and wife are consecrated
and are sanctified by the Vedic rites,
that the two enjoy the fruits of these rites,
equally even in the afterlife;
That's the reason why he acts selfishly
with respect to dharma concerning me.

Surely this lover of dharma must know my mind,
ever secretly given to
bickering, jealousy, and love,
That, although I am enraged, he abandons me
so easily and without fear,
wishing to win *ápsaras*es
in the Great Indra's world.

But this thought does trouble me—what sort of 8.65
bodily splendor do women there have,
That for the sake of them he would forsake
royal splendor as well as my love, and
in the forest practice ascetic toil?

It's not that I envy his heavenly joys;
they are not hard to obtain
even for people like me;
But I have just this wish: how can I make
my beloved not forsake me
in this life here or in the next?

If it's my lot not to see my lord's face,
his sweetly smiling face with those long eyes,
Still this poor Ráhula does not deserve
never to be rocked in his father's lap!

aho, nṛśaṃsaṃ su|kumāra|varcasaḥ
su|dāruṇaṃ tasya manasvino manaḥ
kala|pralāpaṃ dviṣato 'pi harṣaṇaṃ
śiśuṃ sutaṃ yas tyajat' īdṛśaṃ bata!

mam' âpi kāmaṃ hṛdayaṃ su|dāruṇaṃ
śilā|mayaṃ v" âpy a|yaso 'pi vā kṛtam
a|nāthavac chrī|rahite sukh'|ôcite
vanaṃ gate bhartari yan na dīryate.»

8.70 it' îha devī pati|śoka|mūrchitā
ruroda dadhyau vilalāpa c' â|sakṛt;
sva|bhāva|dhīr" âpi hi sā satī śucā
dhṛtiṃ na sasmāra cakāra n' ô hriyam.

tatas tathā śoka|vilāpa|viklavāṃ
Yaśodharāṃ prekṣya vasuṃ|dharā|gatām
mah"|âravindair iva vṛṣṭi|tāḍitair
mukhaiḥ sa|bāṣpair vanitā vicukruśuḥ.

samāpta|jāpyaḥ kṛta|homa|maṅgalo
nṛ|pas tu dev'|āyatanād viniryayau
janasya ten' ārta|raveṇa c' āhataś
cacāla vajra|dhvanin" êva vāraṇaḥ.

niśāmya ca Chandaka|Kanthakāv ubhau
sutasya saṃśrutya ca niścayaṃ sthiram
papāta śok'|âbhihato mahī|patiḥ
Śacī|pater vṛtta iv' ôtsave dhvajaḥ.

O how cruel and extremely hard is this man's heart,
though his body is gentle and his mind is sharp,
That he would indeed abandon his infant son,
sweetly babbling, charming even an enemy!

My heart too must be very hard,
made perhaps of iron or stone,
That, bereft of its lord, it does not break,
when its lord, used to comforts,
has repaired to the forest
bereft of royal splendor."

Thus did the queen here, swooning with grief 8.70
for her lord,
weep, brood, and wail over and over again;
though by nature steadfast, that good and pure woman
paid no heed to fortitude and she felt no shame.

Then, seeing Yasho·dhara lying there on the ground,
and overcome by the lamentation and grief,
women wailed aloud, their faces dripping with tears,
looking like large lotuses battered by the rain.

But, having said his mantras and performed
the oblation and the auspicious rites,
as the king was going out of the temple,
he reeled, struck by the wail of the people,
like an elephant by a thunderclap.

Seeing both Chándaka and Kánthaka,
and hearing the firm resolve of his son,
the king fell on the ground, struck down by grief,
like Indra's flag at the end of the feast.

tato muhūrtaṃ suta|śoka|mohito
  janena tuly'|âbhijanena dhāritaḥ
nirīkṣya dṛṣṭyā jala|pūrṇayā hayaṃ
  mahī|tala|stho vilalāpa pārthivaḥ:

8.75 «bahūni kṛtvā samare priyāṇi me
  mahat tvayā Kanthaka vipriyaṃ kṛtam;
guṇa|priyo yena vane sa me priyaḥ
  priyo 'pi sann a|priyavat praveritaḥ.

tad adya māṃ vā naya tatra yatra sa,
  vraja drutaṃ vā punar enam ānaya;
ṛte hi tasmān mama n' âsti jīvitaṃ
  vigāḍha|rogasya sad|auṣadhād iva.

Suvarṇaniṣṭhīvini mṛtyunā hṛte
  su|duṣ|karaṃ yan na mamāra Saṃjayaḥ
ahaṃ punar dharma|ratau sute gate
  mumukṣur ātmānam an|ātmavān iva.

vibhor daśa|kṣatra|kṛtaḥ prajāpateḥ
  par'|âpara|jñasya Vivasvad|ātmanaḥ
priyeṇa putreṇa satā vinā|kṛtaṃ
  kathaṃ na muhyed dhi mano Manor api.

Then, fainting briefly with grief for his son,
he was held up by men of equal rank;
and looking at the horse with tearful eyes,
the king cried out still lying upon the ground:

"After doing many favors for me in battle, 8.75
you have done me, Kánthaka, a great disfavor;
In that, acting like a foe, though you are a friend,
you have cast off in the forest
my love, the lover of virtue.

Therefore, either take me today to where he is,
or rush there speedily and bring him back again;
For without him there is no life for me,
as for a gravely ill man
without the right medicine.

Sáñjaya did the impossible when he did not die,
as Suvárna·nishthívin was carried away by death;*
But I, now that my son devoted to dharma has gone,
wish to release my self, like a man
with no self-control.

Manu, the great creator, founder of ten royal lines,
the son of Vivásvat, perceiving the near
and the far—
How could not the mind of even Manu
be bewildered,
if separated from his beloved and virtuous son?

Ajasya rājñas tanayāya dhīmate
nar'|âdhipāy' Êndra|sakhāya me spṛhā,
gate vanaṃ yas tanaye divaṃ gato
na mogha|bāṣpaḥ kṛpaṇaṃ jijīva ha.

8.80 pracakṣva me, bhadra, tad āśram'|âjiraṃ
hṛtas tvayā yatra sa me jal'|âñjaliḥ.
ime parīpsanti hi taṃ pipāsavo
mam' āsavaḥ preta|gatiṃ yiyāsavaḥ.»

iti tanaya|viyoga|jāta|duḥkhaḥ
kṣiti|sadṛśaṃ saha|jaṃ vihāya dhairyam
Daśaratha iva Rāma|śoka|vaśyo
bahu vilalāpa nṛ|po vi|saṃjña|kalpaḥ.

śruta|vinaya|guṇ'|ânvitas tatas taṃ
mati|sacivaḥ pravayāḥ puro|hitaś ca
sama|dhṛtam idam ūcatur yathāvan
na ca paritapta|mukhau na c' âpy a|śokau:

«tyaja, nara|vara, śokam. ehi dhairyaṃ.
ku|dhṛtir iv' ârhasi dhīra n' âśru moktum;
srajam iva mṛditām apāsya lakṣmīṃ
bhuvi bahavo nṛ|pā vanāny atīyuḥ.

I envy the king who was Indra's friend,
the wise son of King Aja;
When his son went to the forest, he went to heaven,
without living a miserable life
and shedding futile tears.*

Point out to me, my dear, where is that hermitage 8.80
to which you have carried off my water-giver?*
For these lifebreaths of mine thirstily long for him,
wishing to travel along the path of the dead."

Thus did the king, grieving at being separated
from his son,
give up his innate steadfastness comparable
to the earth's,
and utter countless lamentations as if
he were deranged,
like Dasha·ratha over Rama, as he succumbed to grief.*

Then, his counselor, endowed with learning
discipline, and virtue, and his chaplain
advanced in years, said to him truthfully
in measured words without forlorn faces,
and yet not unaffected by sorrow:

"Give up sorrow, O best of men, and be steadfast;
do not cry, steadfast man,
like someone who's feeble;
Casting aside sovereignty like a spoilt garland,
many kings on earth have repaired to the forest.

api ca niyata eṣa tasya bhāvaḥ
smara vacanaṃ tad ṛṣeḥ pur" Âsitasya
na hi sa divi na cakra|varti|rājye
kṣaṇam api vāsayituṃ sukhena śakyaḥ.

8.85 yadi tu, nṛ|vara, kārya eva yatnas
tvaritam udāhara yāvad atra yāvaḥ,
bahu|vidham iha yuddham astu tāvat
tava tanayasya vidheś ca tasya tasya.»

nara|patir atha tau śaśāsa: «tasmād
drutam ita eva yuvām abhiprayātam!
na hi mama hṛdayaṃ prayāti śāntiṃ
vana|śakuner iva putra|lālasasya.»

«paramam» iti nar'|êndra|śāsanāt tau
yayatur amātya|purohitau vanaṃ tat;
«kṛtam» iti sa|vadhū|janaḥ sa|dāro
nṛ|patir api pracakāra śeṣa|kāryam.

iti Buddhacarite mahā|kāvye 'ntaḥ|pura|vilāpo nām' âṣṭamaḥ sargaḥ.

This resolve of his, moreover, is inevitable;
remember what the seer Ásita foretold long ago;
For one can't make him live happily even a moment
in heaven or in the kingdom of
a World Conqueror.

But, best of men, if we must do this task, 8.85
quickly command and we will go to him;
Let a battle then be waged here on many fronts
between your son and the diverse rules
of scripture."

Then, the king commanded the two of them:

"So set out quickly from this place, you two!
For my heart cannot find peace,
Like a forest bird yearning for its son."

The two said "Yes" and, carrying out the king's decree,
set out to the forest, chaplain and counselor;
And thinking, "The task is done,"
the king, for his part, carried out the remainder
of the rites,
along with his daughters-in-law and wife.

Thus ends the eighth canto named "Lamenting in the Seraglio"
of the great poem "Life of the Buddha."

CANTO 9
SEARCH FOR THE PRINCE

9.1 TATAS TADĀ mantri|purohitau tau
bāṣpa|pratod'|âbhihatau nṛpeṇa
viddhau sad|aśvāv iva sarva|yatnāt
sauhārda|śīghraṃ yayatur vanaṃ tat.

tam āśramaṃ jāta|pariśramau tāv
upetya kāle sadṛś'|ânuyātrau
rāja'|rddhim utsṛjya vinīta|ceṣṭāv
upeyatur Bhārgava|dhiṣṇyam eva.

tau nyāyatas taṃ pratipūjya vipraṃ
ten' ârcitau tāv api c' ânurūpam
kṛt'|āsanau Bhārgavam āsana|sthaṃ
chittvā kathām ūcatur ātma|kṛtyam:

«śuddh'|âujasaḥ śuddha|viśāla|kīrter
Ikṣvāku|vaṃśa|prabhavasya rājñaḥ
imaṃ janaṃ vettu bhavān adhītaṃ
śruta|grahe mantra|parigrahe ca.

9.5 tasy' Êndra|kalpasya Jayanta|kalpaḥ
putro jarā|mṛtyu|bhayaṃ titīrṣuḥ
ih' âbhyupetaḥ kila tasya hetor;
āvām upetau bhagavān avaitu.»

THE TWO THEN went to the forest, 9.1
chaplain and counselor,
spurred on at that time by the king
with the goad of tears,
striving hard, like fine steeds prodded with spurs,
with great dispatch due to their strong friendship.

The two in time with a fitting escort
reached the hermitage, completely worn out;
discarding royal pomp, their mien subdued,
they approached the abode of Bhárgava.*

The two worshipped the brahmin according to rule,
and he in turn honored them in a fitting way;
when both they and Bhárgava had taken their seats,
they cut out the small talk and told him their business:

"The two of us, please know, are appointed
by the king born in the Ikshváku race,
whose might is pure, as also his wide fame;
The one to sustain the sacred scriptures,
the other to maintain royal counsel.

That king, who's comparable to Indra, 9.5
has a son similar to Jayánta;
He came here, we've heard, wishing to transcend
the dangers coming from old age and death;
know, lord, that we have come because of him."

tau so 'bravīd: «asti sa dīrgha|bāhuḥ
 prāptaḥ kumāro na tu n' âvabuddhaḥ
‹dharmo 'yam āvartaka› ity avetya
 yātas tv Arāḍ'|âbhimukho mumukṣuḥ.»

tasmāt tatas tāv upalabhya tattvaṃ
 taṃ vipram āmantrya tad" âiva sadyaḥ
khinn'|âvakhinnāv iva rāja|bhaktyā
 prasasratus tena yataḥ sa yātaḥ.

yāntau tatas tau mṛjayā vihīnam
 apaśyatāṃ taṃ vapuṣ" ôjjvalantam
upopaviṣṭaṃ pathi vṛkṣa|mūle
 sūryaṃ ghan'|ābhogam iva praviṣṭam.

yānaṃ vihāy' ôpayayau tatas taṃ
 purohito mantra|dhareṇa s'|ârdham,
yathā vana|sthaṃ saha|Vāmadevo
 Rāmaṃ didṛkṣur munir Aurvaśeyaḥ.

9.10 tāv arcayām āsatur arhatas taṃ
 div' îva Śukr'|Âṅgirasau Mah"|êndram
pratyarcayām āsa sa c' ârhatas tau
 div' îva Śukr'|Âṅgirasau Mah"|êndraḥ.

kṛt'|âbhyanujñāv abhitas tatas tau
 niṣedatuḥ Śākya|kula|dhvajasya;
virejatus tasya ca saṃnikarṣe
 Punar|Vasū yoga|gatāv iv' Êndoḥ.

To those two he said:

"Yes, the long-armed prince did indeed come here,
young in age but not in intelligence;
But knowing that this dharma leads to rebirth,
he went to see Aráda seeking release."

The two, then, when they learned what had happened from him,
bade farewell to the brahmin and, although wearied,
yet as if unwearied out of love for their king,
set off immediately to where the prince had gone.

The two, then, as they went along, saw him,
unwashed, yet radiant with innate beauty,
seated by the road underneath a tree,
like the sun within a halo of clouds.

Then, the chaplain together with the counselor,
left the carriage and came up to him, as the sage
Aurvashéya along with Vama·deva did,
wishing to see Rama living in the forest.*

The two paid due homage to him, as in heaven 9.10
Shukra and Ángirasa did to Great Indra;
he too paid due homage to them, as in heaven
Great Indra did to Shukra and Ángirasa.*

The two sat down then, having obtained his consent,
on both sides of that banner of the Shakya race;
and in his presence they shone, like Punar
and Vasu in conjunction with the Moon.*

tam vṛkṣa|mūla|stham abhijvalantaṃ
  puro|hito rāja|sutaṃ babhāṣe,
yath"|ôpaviṣṭaṃ divi Pārijāte
  Bṛhaspatiḥ Śakra|sutaṃ Jayantam.

«tvac|choka|śalye hṛday'|âvagāḍhe
  mohaṃ gato bhūmi|tale muhūrtam,
kumāra, rājā nayan'|âmbu|varṣo
  yat tvām avocat tad idaṃ nibodha:

‹jānāmi dharmaṃ prati niścayaṃ te,
  paraimi te bhāvinam etam artham;
ahaṃ tv a|kāle vana|saṃśrayāt te
  śok'|âgnin" âgni|pratimena dahye.

9.15 tad ehi, dharma|priya, mat|priy'|ârthaṃ
  dharm'|ârtham eva tyaja buddhim etām,
ayaṃ hi mā śoka|rayaḥ pravṛddho
  nadī|rayaḥ kūlam iv' âbhihanti.

megh'|âmbu|kakṣ'|âdriṣu yā hi vṛttiḥ
  samīraṇ'|ârk'|âgni|mah"|âśanīnām
tāṃ vṛttim asmāsu karoti śoko
  vikarṣaṇ'|ôcchoṣaṇa|dāha|bhedaiḥ.

tad bhuṅkṣva tāvad vasudh"|ādhipatyaṃ,
  kāle vanaṃ yāsyasi śāstra|dṛṣṭe;
an|iṣṭa|bandhau kuru mayy apekṣāṃ
  sarveṣu bhūteṣu dayā hi dharmaḥ.

The chaplain spoke to the son of the king,
as he sat effulgent under the tree;
as in heaven Brihas·pati spoke to Shakra's son,
Jayánta, seated under the Paradise tree.*

"The king fell on the ground for a moment,
his heart struck by the dart of grief for you;
Listen, prince, to what the king said to you,
as streams of tears kept flowing from his eyes:

'I know that you have resolved to follow dharma,
and, I realize, this will be your future goal;
but I am burnt up by this fire, the fire of grief,
for you have gone to the forest at the wrong time.

So, for love of me, come back, lover of dharma, 9.15
for the sake of dharma itself, give up this plan,
for this swollen current of my grief assaults me,
like the swollen current of a river its bank.

For what the wind, sun, fire, and thunderbolt,
do to clouds, water, hay, and to mountains,
the same my grief does to me, by tearing,
by parching, by burning, by shattering.*

So enjoy now lordship of earth, and at the time
the scriptures prescribe you will go to the forest;
show kindness to this unlucky father of yours,
for dharma is compassion toward all creatures.

na c' âiṣa dharmo vana eva siddhaḥ;
pure 'pi siddhir niyatā yatīnām;
buddhiś ca yatnaś ca nimittam atra,
vanaṃ ca liṅgaṃ ca hi bhīru|cihnam.

maulī|dharair aṃsa|viṣakta|hāraiḥ
keyūra|viṣṭabdha|bhujair nar'|êndraiḥ
lakṣmy|aṅka|madhye parivartamānaiḥ
prāpto gṛha|sthair api mokṣa|dharmaḥ.

9.20 Dhruv'|ânujau yau Bali|Vajrabāhū
Vaibhrājam Āṣāḍham ath' Ântidevam
Videha|rājaṃ Janakaṃ tath" âiva
[Śālva]|Drumaṃ Sena|jitaś ca rājñaḥ—

etān gṛha|sthān nṛ|patīn avehi
naiḥśreyase dharma|vidhau vinītān
ubhau 'pi* tasmād yugapad bhajasva
citt'|ādhipatyaṃ* ca nṛpa|śriyaṃ ca.

icchāmi hi tvām upaguhya gāḍhaṃ
kṛt'|âbhiṣekaṃ salil'|ārdram eva
dhṛt'|ātapatraṃ samudīkṣamāṇas
ten' âiva harṣeṇa vanaṃ praveṣṭum.›

And this dharma is achieved not just in forests;
ascetics do achieve it even in cities;
in this regard the means are effort and intent;
forest and emblems are the marks of a coward.*

Kings, even while remaining householders
cradled in the lap of royal fortune
  crowns upon their heads,
  pearl strings on shoulders,
  arms bound with bracelets,
have won the dharma of release—

  Bali and Vajra·bahu, 9.20
    the younger brothers of Dhruva,
  Vaibhrája, Ashádha, and Anti·deva,
  Jánaka, likewise, the king of Vidéha,
  Druma of Shalva and the Sénajit kings—

Know that these householder kings
    were well trained
in dharma rules leading to highest bliss;
therefore, you should enjoy both together,
lordship over mind and royal fortune.*

For my desire is to hug you closely,
still wet after your royal anointing,
to see you with the royal parasol
held over your head, and with that same joy
to depart to the forest.'

ity abravīd bhūmi|patir bhavantaṃ
vākyena bāṣpa|grathit'|âkṣareṇa;
śrutvā bhavān arhati tat|priy'|ârthaṃ
snehena tat|sneham anuprayātum.

śok'|âmbhasi tvat|prabhave hy agādhe
duḥkh'|ârṇave majjati Śākya|rājaḥ;
tasmāt tam uttāraya nātha|hīnaṃ,
nir|āśrayaṃ magnam iv' ârṇave nauḥ.

9.25 Bhīṣmeṇa Gaṅg"|ôdara|saṃbhavena
Rāmeṇa Rāmeṇa ca Bhārgaveṇa
śrutvā kṛtaṃ karma pituḥ priy'|ârthaṃ
pitus tvam apy arhasi kartum iṣṭam.

saṃvardhayitrīṃ samavehi devīm
Agastya|juṣṭāṃ diśam a|prayātām
pranaṣṭa|vatsām iva vatsalāṃ gām
ajasram ārtāṃ karuṇaṃ rudantīm.

haṃsena haṃsīm iva viprayuktāṃ,
tyaktāṃ gajen' êva vane kareṇum,
ārtāṃ sa|nāthām api nātha|hīnāṃ
trātuṃ vadhūm arhasi darśanena.

ekaṃ sutaṃ bālam an|arha|duḥkhaṃ
saṃtāpam antar|gatam udvahantam
taṃ Rāhulaṃ mokṣaya bandhu|śokād
Rāh'|ûpasargād iva pūrṇa|candram.

So did the king address you with these words,
pronounced haltingly while choking with tears;
Hearing that, you should do him this favor:
return his love for you with your own love.

The Shakya king is sinking in a sea of grief,
a fathomless sea of sorrow rising from you;
So, raise him up, who is without a protector,
as a boat does a man sinking
in the ocean without a float.

Bhishma, who sprang from the womb of Ganga, 9.25
Rama, and Rama the son of Bhrigu—
Hearing what they did to please their fathers,
you too must do what your father desires.*

Know that the queen who brought you up,
although to Agástya's region she has not gone,*
The queen is anguished,
crying piteously all the time,
like a loving cow that has lost its calf.

Like a pen separated from the cob,
like an elephant forsaken
within a forest by her mate,
Your anguished wife, who is widowed
although her husband is alive,
you must rescue her with your sight.

Your only son, so young, not deserving such grief,
who bears the torment in his heart,
Rescue Ráhula from the grief for his father,
like the Full Moon from Rahu's grasp.*

śok'|âgninā tvad|virah'|êndhanena
  niḥśvāsa|dhūmena tamaḥ|śikhena
tvad|darśan'|âmbv icchati dahyamānam
  antaḥ|puraṃ c' âiva puraṃ ca kṛtsnam.»

9.30 sa bodhi|sattvaḥ paripūrṇa|sattvaḥ
  śrutvā vacas tasya purohitasya
dhyātvā muhūrtaṃ guṇavad guṇa|jñaḥ
  pratyuttaraṃ praśritam ity uvāca:

«avaimi bhāvaṃ tanaye pitṝṇāṃ,
  viśeṣato yo mayi bhūmi|pasya;
jānann api vyādhi|jarā|vipadbhyo
  bhītas tv a|gatyā sva|janaṃ tyajāmi.

draṣṭuṃ priyaṃ kaḥ sva|janaṃ hi n' êcchen,
  n' ânte yadi syāt priya|viprayogaḥ;
yadā tu bhūtv" âpi ciraṃ viyogas
  tato guruṃ snigdham api tyajāmi.

madd|hetukaṃ yat tu nar'|âdhipasya
  śokaṃ bhavān āha, na tat priyaṃ me,
yat svapna|bhūteṣu samāgameṣu
  saṃtapyate bhāvini viprayoge.

evaṃ ca te niścayam etu buddhir
  dṛṣṭvā vicitraṃ jagataḥ pracāram:
saṃtāpa|hetur na suto, na bandhur;
  a|jñāna|naimittika eṣa tāpaḥ.

The seraglio and the entire city, being burnt up
by the fire of grief fueled
by separation from you,
A fire whose smoke is their sighs,
and anguish the flames,
crave for the water of your sight."

The bodhisattva, his spirit completely full,* 9.30
listened to the remarks of the chaplain;
knowing what is excellent, he thought for a while,
and gave this excellent and meek reply:

"I recognize the love fathers have for their sons,
above all the love the king bears for me;
Although I know it, I'm forced to forsake my kin,
by the fear of sickness, old age, and death.

If in the end one were not severed from dear ones,
then who would not wish to see his dear kin;
But when there's severance even after a long time,
even my loving father I forsake.

You spoke about the king's grief on account of me;
I am not pleased that he is so distressed,
Amidst associations as fleeting as dreams,
when separation is bound to take place.

And when you see the jumbled process of this world,
your mind ought to arrive at this verdict:
The cause of anguish is neither father nor son;
ignorance is the cause of this anguish.

9.35 yath"|âdhvagānām iha saṃgatānāṃ
kāle viyogo niyataḥ prajānām,
prājño janaḥ ko nu bhajeta śokaṃ
bandhu|pratijñāta|janair vihīnaḥ?

ih' âiti hitvā sva|janaṃ paratra
pralabhya c' êh' âpi punaḥ prayāti;
gatv" âpi tatr' âpy aparatra gacchaty
evaṃ jane tyāgini ko 'nurodhaḥ?

yadā ca garbhāt prabhṛti pravṛttaḥ
sarvāsv avasthāsu vadhāya mṛtyuḥ,
kasmād a|kāle vana|saṃśrayaṃ me
putra|priyas tatra|bhavān avocat?

bhavaty a|kālo viṣay'|âbhipattau,
kālas tath" âiv' ârtha|vidhau pradiṣṭaḥ;
kālo jagat karṣati sarva|kālān
nirvāhake śreyasi n' âsti kālaḥ.

rājyaṃ mumukṣur mayi yac ca rājā,
tad apy udāraṃ sadṛśaṃ pituś ca;
pratigrahītuṃ mama na kṣamaṃ tu
lobhād apathy'|ânnam iv' āturasya.

9.40 kathaṃ nu moh'|āyatanaṃ nṛ|patvaṃ
kṣamaṃ prapattuṃ viduṣā nareṇa,
s'|ôdvegatā yatra madaḥ śramaś ca
par'|âpacāreṇa ca dharma|pīḍā?

Parting in due course is as certain for creatures, 9.35
as for travelers here who come together;*
What wise man would succumb to grief,
when parted from those called kinsfolk?

A man comes here forsaking his kin there,
having tricked them here, he departs again;*
Even after going there, he goes elsewhere;
how can you be attached to those,
who constantly abandon you?

From the time a man comes out of the womb
death is set to slay him at every stage;
So how could His Lordship, in his love for his son,
say that I went to the forest at the wrong time?

There is a wrong time to enjoy pleasures,
a time is ordained also for obtaining wealth;
Time tears up this world all the time;
but there's no appointed time
for what procures final bliss.

That the king wants to surrender the realm to me,
that too is noble and befitting my father;
Yet it is not proper for me to accept it,
like a sick man out of greed
consuming unhealthy food.

How can it be right for a wise man to accept 9.40
kingship that is delusion's dwelling place,
Where anxiety, pride, and fatigue lurk, and damage
to dharma by mistreating other men?

jāmbūnadaṃ harmyam iva pradīptaṃ
 viṣeṇa saṃyuktam iv' ôttam'|ânnam
grāh'|ākulaṃ c' âmbv iva s'|âravindaṃ
 rājyaṃ hi ramyaṃ vyasan'|āśrayaṃ ca.

itthaṃ ca rājyaṃ na sukhaṃ na dharmaḥ
 pūrve yathā jāta|ghṛṇā nar'|êndrāḥ
vayaḥ|prakarṣe '|parihārya|duḥkhe
 rājyāni muktvā vanam eva jagmuḥ.

varaṃ hi bhuktāni tṛṇāny araṇye
 toṣaṃ paraṃ ratnam iv' ôpaguhya,
sah'|ôṣitaṃ śrī|sulabhair na c' âiva
 doṣair a|dṛśyair iva kṛṣṇa|sarpaiḥ.

ślāghyaṃ hi rājyāni vihāya rājñāṃ
 dharm'|âbhilāṣeṇa vanaṃ praveṣṭum;
bhagna|pratijñasya na t' ûpapannaṃ
 vanaṃ parityajya gṛhaṃ praveṣṭum.

9.45 jātaḥ kule ko hi naraḥ sa|sattvo
 dharm'|âbhilāṣeṇa vanaṃ praviṣṭaḥ
kāṣāyam utsṛjya vimukta|lajjaḥ
 Puraṃdarasy' âpi puraṃ śrayeta?

lobhādd hi mohād atha vā bhayena
 yo vāntam annaṃ punar ādadīta,
lobhāt sa mohād atha vā bhayena
 saṃtyajya kāmān punar ādadīta.

For a kingdom is charming yet full of dangers,
like a golden castle that is on fire,
like exquisite food that's mixed with poison,
like a lotus pond filled with crocodiles.

A kingdom thus provides neither dharma nor joy;
so when kings of old reached old age
With its inescapable pains and felt disgust,
they abandoned their kingdoms,
and repaired to the forest.

For it is better to eat grass in the forest,
hiding one's supreme contentment,
as one would a priceless jewel,
Than to abide with the latent dangers
rampant in royal power,
as with concealed black snakes.

For it's praiseworthy for kings to forsake kingdoms
and enter the forest aspiring to dharma;
But it's not fitting for someone to return home,
abandoning the forest and breaking his vow.

For what man of spirit from a good family, 9.45
who has repaired to the forest seeking dharma,
Would without any shame discard the ochre robe
even to take refuge in Indra's citadel?

For, if a man, out of greed, delusion, or fear,
would take back the food he has vomited,
That man, indeed, out of greed, delusion, or fear,
would take back the pleasures he has renounced.

yaś ca pradīptāc charaṇāt kathaṃ cin
niṣkramya bhūyaḥ praviśet tad eva,
gārhasthyam utsṛjya sa dṛṣṭa|doṣo
mohena bhūyo 'bhilaṣed grahītum.

yā ca śrutir ‹mokṣam avāptavanto
nṛ|pā gṛha|sthā iti› n' âitad asti!
śama|pradhānaḥ kva ca mokṣa|dharmo,
daṇḍa|pradhānaḥ kva ca rāja|dharmaḥ?

śame ratiś cec, chithilaṃ ca rājyaṃ;
rājye matiś cec, chama|viplavaś ca;
śamaś ca taikṣṇyaṃ ca hi n' ôpapannaṃ
śīt'|ôṣṇayor aikyam iv' ôdak'|âgnyoḥ.

9.50 tan niścayād vā vasudh"|âdhipās te
rājyāni muktvā śamam āptavantaḥ,
rājy'|âṅgitā vā nibhṛt'|êndriyatvād
a|naiṣṭhike mokṣa|kṛt'|âbhimānāḥ.

teṣāṃ ca rājye 'stu śamo yathāvat,
prāpto vanaṃ n' âham a|niścayena;
chittvā hi pāśaṃ gṛha|bandhu|saṃjñaṃ
muktaḥ punar na pravivikṣur asmi.»

Only a man who, after somehow getting out
of a burning house, would enter it once again,
Will out of delusion wish to take back again
the household life that he has given up,
after he had seen its dangers.

As for the scripture that householder kings
have attained release,
that cannot be!
The dharma of release, where calm prevails,
And the dharma of kings, where force prevails—
how far apart are they!

If a king delights in calm, his realm falls apart,
if his mind is on his realm, his calm is destroyed;
For calmness and fierceness are incompatible,
like the union of fire and water, heat and cold.

So, certainly, either those kings 9.50
gave up their realms and obtained calm,
Or remaining within the realm, they projected
release on a non-final state,
because their senses were controlled.

Let's say they duly attained calm within the realm;
I've not reached the forest with mind undecided;
For I am free, I've cut the snare called
home and kin;
I have no desire to enter that snare again."

ity ātma|vijñāna|guṇ'|ânurūpaṃ
mukta|spṛhaṃ hetumad ūrjitaṃ ca
śrutvā narendr'|âtmajam uktavantaṃ
pratyuttaraṃ mantra|dharo 'py uvāca:

«yo niścayo dharma|vidhau tav' âyaṃ
n' âyaṃ na yukto na tu kāla|yuktaḥ;
śokāya dattvā pitaraṃ vayaḥ|sthaṃ
syād dharma|kāmasya hi te na dharmaḥ.

nūnaṃ ca buddhis tava n' âti|sūkṣmā
dharm'|ârtha|kāmeṣv a|vicakṣaṇā vā
hetor a|dṛṣṭasya phalasya yas tvaṃ
pratyakṣam arthaṃ paribhūya yāsi.

9.55 ‹punar|bhavo 'st' îti› ca ke cid āhur
‹n' âst' îti› ke cin niyata|pratijñāḥ;
evaṃ yadā saṃśayito 'yam arthas
tasmāt kṣamaṃ bhoktum upasthitā śrīḥ.

bhūyaḥ pravṛttir yadi kā cid asti,
raṃsyāmahe tatra yath'|ôpapattau;
atha pravṛttiḥ parato na kā cit
siddho '|prayatnāj jagato 'sya mokṣaḥ.

‹ast' îti› ke cit para|lokam āhur,
mokṣasya yogaṃ na tu varṇayanti;
agner yathā hy auṣṇyam apāṃ dravatvaṃ
tadvat pravṛttau Prakṛtiṃ vadanti.

The prince made this speech, freed from all longings,
spoken with spirit and finely argued,
befitting his self, knowledge, and virtue;
having heard it the counselor replied:

"It is not that this decision of yours
to practice dharma is not right,
just that this is not the right time;
For to condemn your old father to grief
is surely not your dharma,
you who delight in dharma.

Perhaps your mind is not too sharp,
or not conversant with
dharma, wealth, and pleasure;
That you leave to win an unseen result,
disdaining the object before your eyes.

Now, some assert that rebirth does take place, 9.55
others deny it with great confidence;
When this matter is thus in doubt, it's right
that you enjoy the sovereignty at hand.

If there is continued existence beyond this,
we will rejoice there in accordance with our birth;
But if there's no existence in the hereafter,
this world will be released without any effort.

Some say that the world beyond does exist,
but they do not teach the path to release;
For Nature's relation to existence,
they say, is like that of heat to fire,
or liquidity to water.

ke cit ‹sva|bhāvād› iti varṇayanti
śubh'|âśubhaṃ c' âiva bhav'|âbhavau ca;
svābhāvikaṃ sarvam idaṃ ca yasmād,
ato 'pi mogho bhavati prayatnaḥ.

yad indriyāṇāṃ niyataḥ pracāraḥ
priy'|âpriyatvaṃ viṣayeṣu c' âiva
saṃyujyate yaj jaray" ārtibhiś ca—
kas tatra yatno? nanu sa sva|bhāvaḥ.

9.60 adbhir hut'|âśaḥ śamam abhyupaiti,
tejāṃsi c' āpo gamayanti śoṣam;
bhinnāni bhūtāni śarīra|saṃsthāny
aikyaṃ ca gatvā jagad udvahanti.

yat pāṇi|pād'|ôdara|pṛṣṭha|mūrdhnāṃ
nirvartate garbha|gatasya bhāvaḥ
yad ātmanas tasya ca tena yogaḥ,
svābhāvikaṃ tat kathayanti taj|jñāḥ.

kaḥ kaṇṭakasya prakaroti taikṣṇyaṃ,
vicitra|bhāvaṃ mṛga|pakṣiṇāṃ vā?
sva|bhāvataḥ sarvam idaṃ pravṛttaṃ;
na kāma|kāro 'sti, kutaḥ prayatnaḥ?

Some explain that good and evil,
existence and non-existence
are caused by inherent nature;
Because this whole world operates
by means of inherent nature,
for that reason too effort is useless.

That senses operate in specific confines,
that sensual objects are either pleasing or not,
that people are subject to sickness and old age—
From inherent nature, surely, all that proceeds;
what is the use of effort in all this?

A fire becomes extinguished by water, 9.60
whereas water becomes dried up by fire;
Disparate elements based within the body,
when they become united, give rise to the world.

That, entering the womb, it develops
hands, feet, abdomen, back, and head;
That his soul then is united with it—
all this, experts in these matters explain,
is just the work of inherent nature.

Who produces the sharpness of a thorn?
Or the diversity of beasts and birds?
All this happens through inherent nature;
there is no role here for willful action,
how much less for any human effort?

sargaṃ vadant' Îśvaratas tath" ânye;
  tatra prayatne puruṣasya ko 'rthaḥ?
ya eva hetur jagataḥ pravṛttau,
  hetur nivṛttau niyataḥ sa eva.

ke cid vadanty ātma|nimittam eva
  prādur|bhavaṃ c' âiva bhava|kṣayaṃ ca;
prādur|bhavaṃ tu pravadanty a|yatnād
  yatnena mokṣ'|âdhigamaṃ bruvanti.

9.65 naraḥ pitṝṇām an|ṛṇaḥ prajābhir
  vedair ṛṣīṇāṃ kratubhiḥ surāṇām;
utpadyate s'|ârdham ṛṇais tribhis tair;
  yasy' âsti mokṣaḥ, kila tasya mokṣaḥ.

ity evam etena vidhi|krameṇa
  mokṣaṃ sa|yatnasya vadanti taj|jñāḥ;
prayatnavanto 'pi hi vikrameṇa
  mumukṣavaḥ khedam avāpnuvanti.

tat, saumya, mokṣe yadi bhaktir asti,
  nyāyena sevasva vidhiṃ yath'|ôktam;
evaṃ bhaviṣyaty upapattir asya
  saṃtāpa|nāśaś ca nar'|âdhipasya.

Others, likewise, proclaim that creation
proceeds from Íshvara; what then*
is the use of human effort?
The very cause of the world's existence
is doubtless the cause of its cessation.

Some say that the self alone is the cause
of beings emerging and ceasing to be;
But, their emergence is without effort,
they say, while release is gained through effort.

A man is released from his debts 9.65
to his ancestors through offspring,
to seers through studying the Vedas,
and to the gods through sacrifice;
A man is born with these three debts,
whoever has become released from these,
for him alone, they say, there is release.*

Release is open to one, experts say,
who strives following this sequence of rules;
Those who desire release violating that sequence,*
only get fatigued though they expend
much effort.

So, my dear, if you are devoted to release,
properly follow the rule I have pointed out;
Thus your release will be achieved,
and the king's grief will be removed.

yā ca pravṛttā tava doṣa|buddhis
tapo|vanebhyo bhavanaṃ praveṣṭum,
tatr' âpi cintā tava, tāta, mā bhūt:
pūrve 'pi jagmuḥ sva|gṛhān vanebhyaḥ—

tapo|vana|stho 'pi vṛtaḥ prajābhir
jagāma rājā puram Ambarīṣaḥ;
tathā mahīṃ viprakṛtām an|āryais
tapo|vanād etya rarakṣa Rāmaḥ;

9.70 tath" âiva Śālv'|âdhipatir Drum'|ākhyo
vanāt sa|sūnur nagaraṃ viveśa;
brahma'|rṣi|bhūtaś ca muner Vasiṣṭhād
dadhre śriyaṃ Sāṃkṛtir Antidevaḥ.

evaṃ|vidhā dharma|yaśaḥ|pradīptā
vanāni hitvā bhavanāny atīyuḥ;
tasmān na doṣo 'sti gṛhaṃ prayātuṃ
tapo|vanād dharma|nimittam eva.»

As to your view that it is wrong
to return home from the ascetic grove,
On that too do not be concerned;
people even in ancient times
did return home from the forest—

although he resided in an ascetic grove,
King Ambarísha did return to his city
when he was petitioned by his subjects;*

Rama returned from the ascetic grove,
likewise, and protected the earth,
when it was beset by barbarians;*

the king of Shalvas named Druma, 9.70
likewise, returned to the city
from the forest along with his sons;*

Anti·deva also, the Sánkriti,
who was a brahmin seer,
accepted royal power
from the sage Vasíshtha.*

People like these, who blazed with the fame
of dharma,
left the forest and returned to their homes;
When it's for dharma's sake, therefore,
it is not wrong to return home
from the ascetic grove."

tato vacas tasya niśamya mantriṇaḥ
priyaṃ hitaṃ c' âiva nṛ|pasya cakṣuṣaḥ
a|nūnam a|vyastam a|saktam a|drutaṃ
dhṛtau sthito rāja|suto 'bravīd vacaḥ:

«ih' ‹âsti n' âst' îti› ya eṣa saṃśayaḥ
parasya vākyair na mam' âtra niścayaḥ;
avetya tattvaṃ tapasā śamena ca
svayaṃ grahīṣyāmi yad atra niścitam.

na me kṣamaṃ saṃśaya|jaṃ hi darśanaṃ
grahītum a|vyakta|paras|par'|āhatam;
budhaḥ para|pratyayato hi ko vrajej
jano 'ndhakāre 'ndha iv' ândha|deśikaḥ?

9.75 a|dṛṣṭa|tattvasya sato 'pi kiṃ tu me
śubh'|âśubhe saṃśayite śubhe matiḥ;
vṛth" âpi khedo hi varaṃ śubh'|ātmanaḥ
sukhaṃ na tattve 'pi vigarhit'|ātmanaḥ.

imaṃ tu dṛṣṭv" āgamam a|vyavasthitaṃ
yad uktam āptais tad avehi sādhv iti;
prahīṇa|doṣatvam avehi c' āptatāṃ,
prahīṇa|doṣo hy an|ṛtaṃ na vakṣyati.

The prince listened to these words,
wholesome and kind,
of the counselor, who is the king's eye;
then, firm in his resolve, he gave this reply,
without deficiency or prolixity,
without hesitation or rapidity:

"As to the doubt whether rebirth exists or not,
my judgment will not be based
on another's words;
Perceiving the truth by calm and ascetic toil,
I shall myself render the judgment on this point.

For it is not right that I accept a doctrine,
obscure and contradictory, produced by doubt;
For what wise man would follow another's belief,
like a blind man in the dark, a guide who is blind?

Although I have not seen the truth, 9.75
yet when there is a doubt between
what's good and bad I choose the good;
For better the toil of one seeking the good,
though it be in vain,
Than the comfort of one given to evil,
though it is the truth.

But seeing that these scriptures are unfounded,
know that what adepts state is what is good;
And know that adepts are men without faults,
for men without faults do not tell untruths.

gṛha|praveśaṃ prati yac ca me bhavān
  uvāca Rāma|prabhṛtīn nidarśanam,
na te pramāṇaṃ; na hi dharma|niścayeṣv
  alaṃ pramāṇāya parikṣata|vratāḥ.

tad evam apy eva ravir mahīṃ pated
  api sthiratvaṃ Himavān giris tyajet
a|dṛṣṭa|tattvo viṣay'|ônmukh'|êndriyaḥ
  śrayeya na tv eva gṛhān pṛthag|janaḥ.

ahaṃ viśeyaṃ jvalitaṃ hut'|âśanaṃ
  na c' â|kṛt'|ârthaḥ praviśeyam ālayam.»
iti pratijñāṃ sa cakāra garvito
  yath"|êṣṭam utthāya ca nir|mamo yayau.

9.80 tataḥ sa|bāṣpau saciva|dvijāv ubhau
  niśamya tasya sthiram eva niścayam
viṣaṇṇa|vaktrāv anugamya duḥkhitau
  śanair a|gatyā puram eva jagmatuḥ.

tat|snehād atha nṛ|pateś ca bhaktitas tau
  s'|âpekṣaṃ pratiyayatuś ca tasthatuś ca;
dur|dharṣaṃ ravim iva dīptam ātma|bhāsā
  taṃ draṣṭuṃ na hi pathi śekatur, na moktum.

You give the example of Rama and others
on the question of one's returning home,
but they have no binding authority;
For in decisions regarding dharma,
apostates from vows lack authority.

Therefore, although the sun may fall to earth,
or Himálaya lose its fixity,
I'll not return home like a common man,
whose senses yearn for sensual things,
and who has not perceived the truth.

I would rather enter a blazing fire,
than return home without reaching my aim."

Thus did he proudly proclaim his resolve;
and, according to his wish, he got up
and went away, free of all selfish thoughts.

Then, hearing that firm decision of his, 9.80
both minister and brahmin followed him,
tearful and sad, with their faces downcast;
but not finding any other recourse,
the two returned slowly to the city.

The two, because of their love for the prince,
and due to their devotion to the king,
now went back anxiously and now stood still;
for, being unapproachable like the sun,
and blazing forth with the light of his self,
they could not on the road gaze upon him,
and yet they just could not let go of him.

tau jñātuṃ parama|gater gatiṃ tu tasya
pracchannāṃś cara|puruṣāñ chucīn vidhāya
«rājānaṃ priya|suta|lālasaṃ nu gatvā
drakṣyāvaḥ katham» iti jagmatuḥ kathaṃ cit.

iti Buddhacarite mahā|kāvye Kumār'|ânveṣaṇo nāma navamaḥ sargaḥ.

The two, then, appointed trustworthy spies
in disguise to find out the path he took,
he who had taken to the highest path;
and thinking,

> "How can we go and see the king
> pining for his beloved son?"

the two somehow went on their way.

Thus ends the ninth canto named "Search for the Prince"
of the great poem "Life of the Buddha."

CANTO 10

ENCOUNTER WITH KING SHRENYA

10.1 Sa rāja|vatsaḥ pṛthu|pīna|vakṣās
tau havya|mantr'|âdhikṛtau vihāya
uttīrya Gaṅgāṃ pracalat|taraṅgāṃ
śrīmad|gṛhaṃ Rājagṛhaṃ jagāma.

śailaiḥ su|guptaṃ ca vibhūṣitaṃ ca
dhṛtaṃ ca pūtaṃ ca śivais tap'|ôdaiḥ
pañc'|âcal'|âṅkaṃ nagaraṃ prapede
śāntaḥ Svayaṃbhūr iva nāka|pṛṣṭham.

gāmbhīryam ojaś ca niśāmya tasya
vapuś ca dīptaṃ puruṣān atītya
visismaye tatra janas tadānīṃ
sthāṇu|vratasy' êva Vṛṣa|dhvajasya.

taṃ prekṣya yo 'nyena yayau, sa tasthau;
yas tatra tasthau, pathi so 'nvagacchat;
drutaṃ yayau yaḥ, sa jagāma dhīraṃ;
yaḥ kaś cid āste sma, sa c' ôtpapāta.

10.5 kaś cit tam ānarca janaḥ karābhyāṃ,
sat|kṛtya kaś cic chirasā vavande,
snigdhena kaś cid vacas" âbhyananda,
n' âinaṃ jagām' â|pratipūjya kaś cit.

THE PRINCE, whose chest was broad and stout, 10.1
left the two who were charged
with rituals and counsel,
crossed the Ganges with its swift waves,
and went to Raja·griha with splendid mansions.

He reached the city marked by the five hills,
well-protected and adorned by the hills,
upheld and cleansed by auspicious hot springs,
calmly, like Svayam·bhu the heavenly crest.*

At that time, seeing his profundity and vigor,
his effulgent body surpassing the human,
like that of the bull-bannered one
who had taken the pillar vow,*
people living there were amazed.

Whoever was going by another way stood still,
whoever was standing on that road followed him,
whoever was going fast began to walk slowly,
whoever was seated sprang up,
upon seeing him.

Some venerated him with folded hands, 10.5
some in honoring him bent down their heads,
some greeted him with affectionate words,
no one went by without worshipping him.

tam̩ jihriyuḥ prekṣya vicitra|veṣāḥ
prakīrṇa|vācaḥ pathi maunam īyuḥ.
dharmasya sākṣād iva sam̩nikarṣe
na kaś cid a|nyāya|matir babhūva.

anya|kriyāṇām api rāja|mārge
strīṇām̩ nṛṇām̩ ca bahu|māna|pūrvam
tam̩ deva|kalpam̩ nara|deva|sūnum̩
nirīkṣamāṇā na tatarpa dṛṣṭiḥ.

bhruvau lalāṭam̩ mukham īkṣaṇe vā
vapuḥ karau vā caraṇau gatim̩ vā—
yad eva yas tasya dadarśa tatra
tad eva tasy' âtha babandha cakṣuḥ.

dṛṣṭvā ca s'|ōrṇa|bhruvam āyat'|âkṣam̩
jvalac|charīram̩ śubha|jāla|hastam
tam̩ bhikṣu|veṣam̩ kṣiti|pālan'|ârham̩
sam̩cukṣubhe Rājagṛhasya Lakṣmīḥ.

10.10 Śreṇyo 'tha bhartā Magadh'|âjirasya
bāhyād vimānād vipulam̩ jan'|âugham
dadarśa, papraccha ca tasya hetum̩;
tatas tam asmai puruṣaḥ śaśam̩sa:

Those who were pompously dressed felt ashamed,
those chattering on the road fell silent
  upon seeing him.

No one had an improper thought,
as if they were in the presence
of dharma in visible form.

Men and women on the royal highway,
although they were busy with other tasks,
as they looked with great reverence at that
godlike son of that god of men,
their gaze was still not satisfied.

Brows, forehead, mouth, or eyes,
body, hands, feet, or gait—
whatever part of his a man looked at,
his eyes then became riveted on that.

The Royal fortune of Raja·griha
became alarmed when she caught sight of him,
  a curl of hair between his brows,
  a radiant body and long eyes,
  hands that were beautiful and webbed,
wearing the garb of mendicant,
but worthy of ruling the world.

Then Shrenya, lord of the Mágadha realm, 10.10
saw throngs of men from his outer palace,
and inquired about the reason for it;
then, an official of his informed him:

«jñānaṃ paraṃ vā pṛthivī|śriyaṃ vā
viprair ya ukto 'dhigamiṣyat' îti
sa eṣa Śāky'|âdhipates tanū|jo
nirīkṣyate pravrajito janena.»

Tataḥ śrut'|ârtho manas" āgat'|āstho
rājā babhāṣe puruṣaṃ tam eva:
«vijñāyatāṃ kva pratigacchat' îti»
«tath" êty» ath' âinaṃ puruṣo 'nvagacchat.

a|lola|cakṣur yuga|mātra|darśī
nivṛtta|vāg yantrita|manda|gāmī
cacāra bhikṣāṃ sa tu bhikṣu|varyo
nidhāya gātrāṇi calaṃ ca cetaḥ.

ādāya bhaikṣaṃ ca yath"|ôpapannaṃ
yayau gireḥ prasravaṇaṃ viviktam
nyāyena tatr' âbhyavahṛtya c' âinan
mahī|dharaṃ Pāṇḍavam āruroha.

10.15 tasminn avau lodhra|van'|ôpagūḍhe
mayūra|nāda|pratipūrṇa|kuñje
kāṣāya|vāsāḥ sa babhau nṛ|sūryo
yath" ôdayasy' ôpari bāla|sūryaḥ.

tatr' âinam ālokya sa rāja|bhṛtyaḥ
Śreṇyāya rājñe kathayāṃ cakāra;
saṃśrutya rājā sa ca bāhumānyāt
tatra pratasthe nibhṛt'|ânuyātraḥ.

"This here is the son of the Shakya king,
about whom brahmins predicted
that he'd attain knowledge supreme
or sovereignty over the earth;
He has become an itinerant monk,
and people are looking at him."

When he heard the reason, then, confidence returned to the mind of the king, and he told the same man:

"Find out where he is going."

The man said, "I will," and followed the prince.

But, that best of mendicants went begging
with steady eyes fixed just a yard in front,
in silence, walking slowly with restraint,
controlling his limbs and his lively mind.

Taking whatever almsfood he obtained,
he went to a lonely stream in the hills;
and, after eating that food as prescribed,
he climbed up the Pándava hill.

On that hill overspread with *lodhra* groves, 10.15
its thickets alive with cries of peacocks,
dressed in ochre robe that human sun blazed,
like the young sun over the eastern hills.

Spying him there, the officer of the king
disclosed the matter to Shrenya, the king;
hearing that, the king set off to that spot
with a small guard out of respect for him.

sa Pāṇḍavaṃ Pāṇḍava|tulya|vīryaḥ
śail'|ôttamaṃ śaila|samāna|varṣmā
maulī|dharaḥ siṃha|gatir nṛ|siṃhaś
calat|saṭaḥ siṃha iv' āruroha.

tataḥ sma tasy' ôpari śṛṅga|bhūtaṃ
śānt'|êndriyaṃ paśyati Bodhi|sattvam
paryaṅkam āsthāya virocamānaṃ
śaś'|âṅkam udyantam iv' âbhra|kuñjāt.

taṃ rūpa|lakṣmyā ca śamena c' âiva
dharmasya nirmāṇam iv' ôpaviṣṭam
sa|vismayaḥ praśrayavān nar'|êndraḥ
Svayaṃbhuvaṃ Śakra iv' ôpatasthe.

10.20 taṃ nyāyato nyāya|vidāṃ variṣṭhaṃ
sametya papraccha ca dhātu|sāmyam;
sa c' âpy avocat sadṛśena sāmnā
nṛ|paṃ manaḥ|svāsthyam an|āmayaṃ ca.

tataḥ śucau vāraṇa|karṇa|nīle
śilā|tale saṃniṣasāda rājā;
upopaviśy' ânumataś ca tasya
bhāvaṃ vijijñāsur idaṃ babhāṣe:

«prītiḥ parā me bhavataḥ kulena
kram'|āgatā c' âiva parīkṣitā ca;
jātā vivakṣā; sva|vayo yato me,
tasmād idaṃ sneha|vaco nibodha.

Equal in valor to the Pándavas,
with a stature similar to a hill,
with a lion's gait, with a royal head-dress,
that man-lion climbed the Pándava, the best
of hills, like a lion with a bouncing mane.*

Then, atop that hill, like another peak,
the bodhisattva with his organs stilled,
he saw sitting cross-legged and shining bright,
like the moon rising from a clump of clouds.

He sat with calm and resplendent beauty,
like the image of dharma; with reverence
and in amazement the king approached him,
the way Shakra once approached Svayam·bhu.*

According to rule the king approached him, 10.20
who was the best of those who know the rules,
and inquired about his well-being;
he too with equal deference asked the king
about his health and peace of mind.*

Then, the king sat down upon a clean rock,
that was as dark as an elephant's ear;
seated close to him with his permission,
and wishing to know his mind, the king said:

"I have the strongest friendship with your family,
an ancestral friendship that has been well tested;*
Because you are my age, I want to talk to you;
listen, therefore, to these my affectionate words.

Āditya|pūrvaṃ vipulaṃ kulaṃ te
navaṃ vayo dīptam idaṃ vapuś ca;
kasmād iyaṃ te matir a|kramena
bhaikṣāka ev' âbhiratā, na rājye?

gātraṃ hi te lohita|candan'|ârhaṃ,
kāṣāya|saṃśleṣam an|arham etat;
hastaḥ prajā|pālana|yogya eṣa,
bhoktuṃ na c' ârhaḥ para|dattam annam.

10.25 tat, saumya, rājyaṃ yadi paitṛkaṃ tvaṃ
snehāt pitur n' êcchasi vikrameṇa,
na ca kramaṃ marṣayituṃ matis te,
bhuṅkṣv' ârdham asmad|viṣayasya śīghram.

evaṃ hi na syāt sva|jan'|âvamardaḥ
kāla|krameṇ' âpi śama|śrayā śrīḥ,
tasmāt kuruṣva praṇayaṃ mayi tvaṃ;
sadbhiḥ sahīyā hi satāṃ samṛddhiḥ.

atha tv idānīṃ kula|garvitatvād
asmāsu viśrambha|guṇo na te 'sti,
vyūḍhāny anīkāni vigāhya bāṇair
mayā sahāyena parān jigīṣa.

Your family is mighty, rising from the sun,
you are young in age, and your body is radiant;
Why then did you resolve,
quite against the sequence,
to follow the mendicant life and not kingship?*

For your body is worthy of red sandal paste,
not contact with an ochre robe;
This hand of yours is fit to govern the people,
and deserves not to take food given by others.

If, therefore, my dear, because you love your father, 10.25
you do not desire to take your father's kingdom
in violation of the proper sequence,
And cannot bear to wait for the proper sequence,
then quickly take a half of my kingdom.

In this way you will not hurt your kinsfolk,
and sovereignty also will come to you
peacefully and in the proper sequence;
Please do this kind favor for me, therefore,
for association with the virtuous
makes the virtuous prosper.

Or if out of family pride
you will not place your trust in me,
Charge into the battle lines with arrows,
and, with me as ally, vanquish your foes.

tad buddhim atr' ânyatarām vṛṇīṣva;
dharm'|ârtha|kāmān vidhivad bhajasva;
vyatyasya rāgād iha hi tri|vargaṃ
prety' êha ca bhraṃśam avāpnuvanti.

yo hy artha|dharmau paripīḍya kāmaḥ
syād, dharma|kāmau paribhūya c' ârthaḥ,
kām'|ârthayoś c' ôparameṇa dharmas
tyājyaḥ sa kṛtsno, yadi kāṅkṣito 'rthaḥ.

10.30 tasmāt tri|vargasya niṣevaṇena
tvaṃ rūpam etat sa|phalaṃ kuruṣva;
dharm'|ârtha|kām'|âdhigamaṃ hy an|ūnaṃ
nṛṇām an|ūnaṃ puruṣ'|ârtham āhuḥ.

tan niṣ|phalau n' ârhasi kartum etau
pīnau bhujau cāpa|vikarṣaṇ'|ârhau
Māndhātṛvaj jetum imau hi yogyau
lokān api trīn iha, kiṃ punar gām!

snehena khalv etad ahaṃ bravīmi
n' āiśvarya|rāgeṇa na vismayena;
imaṃ hi dṛṣṭvā tava bhikṣu|veṣaṃ
jāt'|ânukampo 'smy api c' āgat'|âśruḥ.

Choose, therefore, any one of these options;
devote yourself as prescribed
to dharma, wealth, and pleasure;
For by inverting here the triple set
through passion one goes to ruin
here and in the hereafter.

For when pleasure impairs wealth and dharma,
when wealth suppresses dharma and pleasure,
Or when dharma wipes out pleasure and wealth,
one should abandon the odd one out,
if one wishes
to attain the goal in its entirety.

By pursuing, therefore, the triple set, 10.30
make this lovely body of yours bear fruit;
For when a man gains in their entirety
dharma, wealth, and pleasure, they say
he has achieved the purpose of
human life in its entirety.

So, it's not right that you should let
these two stout arms
fit for drawing a bow remain unproductive;
For, like Mandhátri, they have the capacity
to conquer all the three worlds,
how much more this earth?

It's out of love that I say this to you,
not out of pride or through lust for lordship;
For seeing this mendicant garb of yours,
I am moved to compassion,
and tears well up in my eyes.

yāvat sva|vaṃśa|pratirūpa|rūpaṃ
  na te jar" âbhyety abhibhūya bhūyaḥ,
tad bhuṅkṣva, bhikṣ"|āśrama|kāma, kāmān;
  kāle 'si kartā, priya|dharma, dharmam.

śaknoti jīrṇaḥ khalu dharmam āptuṃ,
  kām'|ôpabhogeṣv a|gatir jarāyāḥ;
ataś ca yūnaḥ kathayanti kāmān,
  madhyasya vittaṃ, sthavirasya dharmam.

10.35 dharmasya c' ârthasya ca jīva|loke
  prathyarthi|bhūtāni hi yauvanāni;
saṃrakṣyamāṇāny api dur|grahāṇi
  kāmā yatas tena pathā haranti.

vayāṃsi jīrṇāni vimarśavanti
  dhīrāṇy avasthāna|parāyaṇāni;
alpena yatnena śam'|ātmakāni
  bhavanty a|gaty" âiva ca lajjayā ca.

ataś ca lolaṃ viṣaya|pradhānaṃ
  pramattam a|kṣāntam a|dīrgha|darśi
bahu|cchalaṃ yauvanam abhyatītya
  nistīrya kāntāram iv' āśvasanti.

tasmād a|dhīraṃ capala|pramādi
  navaṃ vayas tāvad idaṃ vyapaitu;
kāmasya pūrvaṃ hi vayaḥ śaravyaṃ
  na śakyate rakṣitum indriyebhyaḥ.

Before old age, therefore, overtakes you,
ruining the beauty that befits your line,
Enjoy pleasures, you who take pleasure in
the mendicant order of life;
In time you will practice dharma,
you who find delight in dharma.

Surely, when you are old you can practice dharma,
old age lacks capacity to enjoy pleasures;
And, therefore, they assign pleasure for youth,
wealth for the middle-aged,
and dharma for the old.

For the time of youth in this human world 10.35
is the enemy of dharma and wealth;
Though well guarded, youth is hard to secure,
as by that path pleasures carry it off.

Old age is resolute, given to reflection,
and intent on stability;
It attains tranquility with little effort,
because of shame and impotence.

When people have crossed beyond youth,
restless, rash, impatient, and short-sighted,
given to deceit, to pleasures of sense,
They breathe a deep sigh of relief,
as when they have crossed a desert.

So, let this fickle time of youth pass by,
it is indecisive and negligent;
For the early years are Kama's target,
they cannot be guarded from the senses.

ath' ô cikīrṣā tava dharma eva,
yajasva yajñaṃ kula|dharma eṣaḥ;
yajñair adhiṣṭhāya hi nāka|pṛṣṭhaṃ
yayau Marutvān api nāka|pṛṣṭham.

10.40 suvarṇa|keyūra|vidaṣṭa|bāhavo
maṇi|pradīp'|ôjjvala|citra|maulayaḥ
nṛpa'|rṣayas tāṃ hi gatiṃ gatā makhaiḥ
śrameṇa yām eva maha"|rṣayo yayuḥ.»

ity evaṃ Magadha|patir vaco babhāṣe
yaḥ samyag Valabhid iva bruvan babhāse;
tac chrutvā na sa vicacāla rāja|sūnuḥ
Kailāso girir iva n'|âika|citra|sānuḥ.

iti Buddhacarite mahā|kāvye 'śva|ghoṣa|kṛte
Śreṇy'|âbhigamano nāma daśamaḥ sargaḥ.

But if what you want to practice is just dharma,
make sacrificial offerings,
which is your family dharma;
For having stepped on heaven's crest
through sacrifice,
even Marútvat attained the crest of heaven.*

For the royal sages have attained the same state, 10.40
their arms bound with golden armlets,
Their head-dresses radiant with the glitter of gems,
that the great sages attained through ascetic toil."

In this manner did the king of Mágadha speak,
shining like Válabhid as he fittingly spoke;
when he heard that, the son of the king did not sway,
like mount Kailása with its many sparkling peaks.

Thus ends the tenth canto named "Encounter with King Shrenya" of the great poem "Life of the Buddha" composed by Ashva·ghosha.

CANTO 11
CONDEMNATION OF PASSION

11.1 Ath' âivam|ukto Magadh'|âdhipena
suhṛn|mukhena pratikūlam artham,
sva|stho '|vikāraḥ kula|śauca|śuddhaḥ
Śauddhodanir vākyam idaṃ jagāda:

«n' āścaryam etad bhavato vidhānaṃ
jātasya Haryaṅka|kule viśāle
yan mitra|pakṣe tava, mitra|kāma,
syād vṛttir eṣā pariśuddha|vṛtteḥ.

a|satsu maitrī sva|kul'|ânuvṛttā
na tiṣṭhati, śrīr iva viklaveṣu;
pūrvaiḥ kṛtāṃ prīti|paraṃparābhis
tām eva santas tu vivardhayanti.

ye c' ârtha|kṛcchreṣu bhavanti loke
samāna|kāryāḥ su|hṛdāṃ manuṣyāḥ,
mitrāṇi tān' îti paraimi buddhyā;
sva|sthasya vṛddhiṣv iha ko hi na syāt?

11.5 evaṃ ca ye dravyam avāpya loke
mitreṣu dharme ca niyojayanti,
avāpta|sārāṇi dhanāni teṣāṃ
bhraṣṭāni n' ânte janayanti tāpam.

Now, when the Mágadha king had said this, 11.1
harmful advice beneath his friendly face,
the son of Shuddhódana said to him,
while he remained tranquil and unperturbed,
made pure by his family purity:

"This your arrangement causes no surprise,
that you should behave thus toward your friend;
Born in the illustrious Haryánka line,*
you are pure in conduct,
devoted to your friends.

Ancestral friendships don't last among evil men,
as sovereign power lasts not among timid men;
But a friendship established by their ancestors,
good men enhance through a series
of friendly acts.

When their friends are in dire straits in this world,
men who continue to share the same tasks,
I deem them in my heart to be true friends;
who will not befriend a man,
prosperous and in good health?

Thus, when people obtain wealth in this world, 11.5
and use it for their friends and for dharma,
They obtain the full value of their wealth,
and if, in the end, it is lost,
it causes no remorse.

su|hṛttayā c' āryatayā ca, rājan,
  khalv eṣa yo māṃ prati niścayas te;
atr' ânuneṣyāmi su|hṛttay" âiva
  brūyām ahaṃ n' ôttaram anyad atra.

ahaṃ jarā|mṛtyu|bhayaṃ viditvā
  mumukṣayā dharmam imaṃ prapannaḥ
bandhūn priyān aśru|mukhān vihāya
  prāg eva kāmān a|śubhasya hetūn.

n' āśīviṣebhyo hi tathā bibhemi,
  n' âiv' âśanibhyo gaganāc cyutebhyaḥ,
na pāvakebhyo 'nila|saṃhitebhyo,
  yathā bhayaṃ me viṣayebhya eva.

kāmā hy a|nityāḥ kuśal'|ârtha|caurā
  riktāś ca māyā|sadṛśāś ca loke;
āśāsyamānā api mohayanti
  cittaṃ nṛṇāṃ, kiṃ punar ātma|saṃsthāḥ?

11.10 kām'|âbhibhūtā hi na yānti śarma
  tri|piṣṭape, kiṃ bata martya|loke;
kāmaiḥ sa|tṛṣṇasya hi n' âsti tṛptir,
  yath" êndhanair vāta|sakhasya vahneḥ.

jagaty an|artho na samo 'sti kāmair,
  mohāc ca teṣv eva janaḥ prasaktaḥ;
tattvaṃ viditv" âivam an|artha|bhīruḥ
  prājñaḥ svayaṃ ko 'bhilaṣed an|artham?

It's from friendship, surely, and your noble nature,
that you made, O king, this decision about me;
It's with friendship that I will gratify you here,
on this I'll not give you a different answer.

When I realized the danger of old age and death,
I took to this dharma seeking release,
Forsaking my beloved kinsmen as they wept,
how much more, then, pleasures that cause evil.

For I have no fear of venomous snakes,
or even of bolts falling from the sky,
Or of fires that are whipped up by the wind,
as much as I fear the objects of sense.

For pleasures are fleeting, robbing wealth and virtue,
they are empty, like phantoms in this world;
Even when wished for,
they delude the minds of men;
how much more when actually possessed?

For men overwhelmed by pleasures find no relief 11.10
in triple heaven, much less in this mortal world;
For pleasures do not sate a man full of desires,
as firewood a fire accompanied by the wind.

There is no evil equal to pleasures
in the world, yet it's to them that people
are attached through delusion;
Knowing that this is the truth,
what wise man who fears evil
will on his own yearn for evil?

samudra|vastrām api gām avāpya
pāraṃ jigīṣanti mah"|ârṇavasya;
lokasya kāmair na vitṛptir asti
patadbhir ambhobhir iv' ârṇavasya.

devena vṛṣṭe 'pi hiraṇya|varṣe
dvīpān samagrāṃś caturo 'pi jitvā
Íakrasya c' ârdh'|āsanam apy avāpya,
Māndhātur āsīd viṣayeṣv a|tṛptiḥ.

bhuktv" âpi rājyaṃ divi devatānāṃ
Śatakratau Vṛtra|bhayāt pranaṣṭe
darpān maha"|rṣīn api vāhayitvā
kāmeṣv a|tṛpto Nahuṣaḥ papāta.

11.15 Aiḍaś ca rājā tri|divaṃ vigāhya
nītv" âpi devīṃ vaśam Urvaśīṃ tām,
lobhād ṛṣibhyaḥ kanakaṃ jihīrṣur
jagāma nāśaṃ viṣayeṣv a|tṛptaḥ.

Though they have won the earth
girded by the ocean,
they wish to conquer
what's beyond the great ocean;
Men are not sated by gaining pleasures,
as the great ocean by rushing waters.

Although the heavens rained down gold for him,
although he conquered all four continents,
and although he won half of Shakra's throne,
Yet Mandhátri's craving for sense objects
remained unappeased.

Although he enjoyed kingship over gods in heaven,
when Indra absconded from his fear of Vritra,
and through pride made even the great seers
carry him,
Yet Náhusha fell, while his craving for pleasures
remained unappeased.*

Although King Aida conquered the triple heaven, 11.15
even brought goddess Úrvashi into his power,
Yet through greed he desired to seize
gold from the seers,
and came to ruin while his craving
for sense objects
remained unappeased.*

Baler Mah"|Êndraṃ Nahuṣaṃ Mah"|Êndrād
  Indraṃ punar ye Nahuṣād upeyuḥ;
svarge kṣitau vā viṣayeṣu teṣu
  ko viśvased bhāgya|kul'|âkuleṣu?

cīr'|âmbarā mūla|phal'|âmbu|bhakṣā
  jaṭā vahanto 'pi bhujaṅga|dīrghāḥ
yair n' ânya|kāryā munayo 'pi bhagnāḥ,
  kaḥ kāma|saṃjñān mṛgayeta śatrūn?

Ugrāyudhaś c' ôgra|dhṛt'|āyudho 'pi
  yeṣāṃ kṛte mṛtyum avāpa Bhīṣmāt;
cint" âpi teṣām a|śivā vadhāya
  sad|vṛttināṃ, kiṃ punar a|vratānām?

āsvādam alpaṃ viṣayeṣu matvā
  saṃyojan'|ôtkarṣam a|tṛptim eva
sadbhyaś ca garhāṃ niyataṃ ca pāpaṃ;
  kaḥ kāma|saṃjñaṃ viṣam ādadīta?

11.20 kṛṣy|ādibhiḥ karmabhir arditānāṃ
  kām'|ātmakānāṃ ca niśamya duḥkham
svāsthyaṃ ca kāmeṣv a|kutūhalānāṃ
  kāmān vihātuṃ kṣamam ātmavadbhiḥ.

In heaven or earth, who would put his trust
in this sensual realm that is subject
to the ups and downs of fate,
A realm that passed from Bali to Great Indra,
from Great Indra to Náhusha,
and from Náhusha back again to Indra?*

Who would seek the enemies called pleasures,
by whom even the sages were vanquished,
Sages who were withdrawn from other tasks,
subsisting on water, fruits, and roots,
wearing bark and even dreadlocks
that were as long as snakes?

For their sake did Ugráyudha,
though armed with a dreadful weapon,
perish at the hands of Bhishma;*
Their very thought is unlucky and leads to death
even the virtuous, how much more
then those who are non-observant?

Who'd drink the poison called pleasures,
knowing that in objects of sense
The taste is trivial, the bondage is great,
and there is no satisfaction?
They invite the disdain of good people;
the resultant sin is certain.

Hearing about the sorrow of passionate men 11.20
harassed by the labor of tillage and the like,
And the content of those indifferent to pleasures,
it behooves self-possessed men
to relinquish pleasures.

jñeyā vipat kāmini kāma|saṃpat,
siddheṣu kāmeṣu madaṃ hy upaiti;
madād a|kāryaṃ kurute, na kāryaṃ,
yena kṣato dur|gatim abhyupaiti.

yatnena labdhāḥ parirakṣitāś ca
ye vipralabhya pratiyānti bhūyaḥ,
teṣv ātmavān yācitak'|ôpameṣu
kāmeṣu vidvān iha ko rameta?

anviṣya c' ādāya ca jāta|tarṣā
yān a|tyajantaḥ pariyānti duḥkham
loke tṛṇ'|ôlkā|sadṛśeṣu teṣu
kāmeṣu kasy' ātmavato ratiḥ syāt?

an|ātmavanto hṛdi yair vidaṣṭā
vināśam archanti na yānti śarma.
kruddh'|ôgra|sarpa|pratimeṣu teṣu
kāmeṣu kasy' ātmavato ratiḥ syāt?

11.25 asthi kṣudh"|ārtā iva sārameyā
bhuktv" âpi yān n' âiva bhavanti tṛptāḥ,
jīrṇ'|âsthi|kaṅkāla|sameṣu teṣu
kāmeṣu kasy' ātmavato ratiḥ syāt?

Being fortunate in pleasures should be viewed
as a misfortune for men of passion,
for attainment of pleasures leads to pride,
Pride makes them do what's wrong
and not what's right,
and when they are struck down by that,
they come to an unhappy end.

What man here, who's self-possessed and wise,
would delight in pleasures,
arduously attained and well protected,
Pleasures that cheat you and leave you again,
much like something received on loan?

What man who's self-possessed
would delight in pleasures,
that are like torches of straw in this world?
When pursued and grasped, they excite craving,
but when left unabandoned lead to grief.

What man who's self-possessed
would delight in pleasures,
that are like snakes, fierce and enraged?
Stung by them on the heart,
men who aren't self-possessed
go to their death and obtain no relief.

What man who's self-possessed 11.25
would delight in pleasures,
that are like a skeleton of dry bones?
Even when enjoyed, men get no satisfaction,
like a famished dog that's eating a bone.

ye rāja|caur'|ôdaka|pāvakebhyaḥ
sādhāraṇatvāj janayanti duḥkham,
teṣu praviddh'|āmiṣa|saṃnibheṣu
kāmeṣu kasy' ātmavato ratiḥ syāt?

yatra sthitānām abhito vipattiḥ
śatroḥ sakāśād api bāndhavebhyaḥ,
hiṃsreṣu teṣv āyatan'|ôpameṣu
kāmeṣu kasy' ātmavato ratiḥ syāt?

girau vane c' âpsu ca sāgare ca
yān bhraṃśam archanti vilaṅghamānāḥ,
teṣu druma|prāgra|phal'|ôpameṣu
kāmeṣu kasy' ātmavato ratiḥ syāt?

tīvraiḥ prayatnair vividhair avāptāḥ
kṣaṇena ye nāśam iha prayānti,
svapn'|ôpabhoga|pratimeṣu teṣu
kāmeṣu kasy' ātmavato ratiḥ syāt?

11.30 yān arjayitv" âpi na yānti śarma
vivardhayitvā paripālayitvā,
aṅgāra|karṣū|pratimeṣu teṣu
kāmeṣu kasy' ātmavato ratiḥ syāt?

What man who's self-possessed
would delight in pleasures,
that are like a raw-flesh bait being thrown down?
Because they're like a king, a thief, water, and fire,
pleasures only give rise to suffering.

What man who's self-possessed
would delight in pleasures,
that are like dangerous habitations?
Those dwelling in them face misfortunes
from all sides,
at the hands of enemies and kinsfolk.

What man who's self-possessed
would delight in pleasures,
that are like fruits at the top of a tree?
People leap up at them and come to utter ruin,
in mountains, forests, rivers, and oceans.

What man who's self-possessed
would delight in pleasures,
that are like delights enjoyed in a dream?
Although acquired with painful and diverse efforts,
pleasures are destroyed here in an instant.

What man who's self-possessed 11.30
would delight in pleasures,
that are like trenches filled with burning coals?
Although they are secured, enhanced, and protected,
people do not find relief in pleasures.

vināśam īyuḥ Kuravo yad|arthaṃ
  Vṛṣṇy|Andhakā Mekhala|Daṇḍakāś ca.
sūn"|âsi|kāṣṭha|pratimeṣu teṣu
  kāmeṣu kasy' ātmavato ratiḥ syāt?

Sund'|Ôpasundāv asurau yad|artham
  anyo|'nya|vaira|prasṛtau vinaṣṭau,
sauhārda|viśleṣa|kareṣu teṣu
  kāmeṣu kasy' ātmavato ratiḥ syāt?

yeṣāṃ kṛte vāriṇi pāvake ca
  kravy'|âtsu c' ātmānam ih' ôtsṛjanti,
sapatna|bhūteṣv a|śiveṣu teṣu
  kāmeṣu kasy' ātmavato ratiḥ syāt?

kām'|ârtham a|jñaḥ kṛpaṇaṃ karoti,
  prāpnoti duḥkhaṃ vadha|bandhanādi;
kām'|ârtham āśā|kṛpaṇas tapasvī
  mṛtyuṃ śramaṃ c' ârchati jīva|lokaḥ.

11.35 gītair hriyante hi mṛgā vadhāya;
  rūp'|ârtham agnau śalabhāḥ patanti;
matsyo giraty āyasam āmiṣ'|ârthī;
  tasmād an|arthaṃ viṣayāḥ phalanti.

What man who's self-possessed
would delight in pleasures,
that are like the wood and knives
of a slaughter house?
For their sake the Kurus went to their destruction,
as also Vrishni-Ándhakas
and the Mékhala-Dándakas.*

What man who's self-possessed
would delight in pleasures,
that tend only to split apart friendships?
For their sake demons Sunda and Upasúnda
hated each other and were thus destroyed.*

What man who's self-possessed
would delight in pleasures,
that are, in fact, sinister enemies?
For their sake people here deliver their bodies
to water, fire, and predatory beasts.

For pleasure's sake ignorant men do wretched things,
incur sufferings such as jail and death;
For pleasure's sake mankind endures
both toil and death,
tormented and made wretched by yearning.

For deer are lured by songs to their death; 11.35
moths fall into the fire lured by its charm;
Fish swallow the hook, greedy for the bait;
objects of sense, therefore, bring misfortune.

‹kāmās tu bhogā› iti yan|matiḥ syād
bhogā na ke cit pariganyamānāḥ;
vastr'|ādayo dravya|guṇā hi loke
duḥkha|pratīkāra iti pradhāryāḥ.

iṣṭaṃ hi tarṣa|praśamāya toyaṃ,
kṣun|nāśa|hetor aśanaṃ tath" âiva,
vāt'|ātap'|âmbv|āvaraṇāya veśma,
kaupīna|śīt'|āvaraṇāya vāsaḥ,

nidrā|vighātāya tath" âiva śayyā,
yānaṃ tath" âdhva|śrama|nāśanāya,
tath" āsanaṃ sthāna|vinodanāya,
snānaṃ mṛj"|ārogya|bal'|āśrayāya.

duḥkha|pratīkāra|nimitta|bhūtās
tasmāt prajānāṃ viṣayā, na bhogāḥ.
‹aśnāmi bhogān› iti ko 'bhyupeyāt
prājñaḥ pratīkāra|vidhau pravṛttaḥ?

11.40 yaḥ pitta|dāhena vidahyamānaḥ
‹śīta|kriyāṃ bhoga› iti vyavasyet,
duḥkha|pratīkāra|vidhau pravṛttaḥ
kāmeṣu kuryāt sa hi bhoga|saṃjñām.

kāmeṣv an|aikāntikatā ca yasmād
ato 'pi me teṣu na bhoga|saṃjñā;
ya eva bhāvā hi sukhaṃ diśanti
ta eva duḥkhaṃ punar āvahanti.

'But pleasures are enjoyments,' some may think,
yet none should be reckoned as enjoyments;
For clothes and other objects in the world
should be reckoned as remedies for pain.

For one desires water to slake one's thirst,
food, likewise, to assuage one's hunger,
House for shelter against wind, heat, and rain,
clothes for the cold and to cover the loins.

A bed, likewise, to expel drowsiness,
a carriage to avert travel's fatigue,
A seat too as a respite from standing,
and bathing to ensure
strength, health, and cleanliness.

The objects of sense, therefore, are not enjoyments,
but means of curing people's suffering.
What wise man, while employing remedies,
would think 'I am relishing enjoyments?'

A man who, as he's burning with bilious fever, 11.40
decides 'cold remedies are enjoyments,'
He, indeed, while using remedies for suffering,
would give the name 'enjoyment' to pleasures.

Given that there's nothing absolute in pleasures,
for that reason too I don't call them 'enjoyments;'
For the same things that provide joy,
do, in their turn, bring pain as well.

gurūṇi vāsāṃsy agurūṇi c' âiva
sukhāya śīte hy, a|sukhāya gharme;
candr'|âṃśavaś candanam eva c' ôṣṇe
sukhāya, duḥkhāya bhavanti śīte.

dvandvāni sarvasya yataḥ prasaktāny
alābha|lābha|prabhṛtīni loke,
ato 'pi n' âikānta|sukho 'sti kaś cin
n' âikānta|duḥkhaḥ puruṣaḥ pṛthivyām.

dṛṣṭvā vimiśrāṃ sukha|duḥkhatāṃ me,
rājyaṃ ca dāsyaṃ ca mataṃ samānam;
nityaṃ hasaty eva hi n' âiva rājā,
na c' âpi saṃtapyata eva dāsaḥ.

11.45 ‹ājñā nṛ|patye 'bhyadhik" êti› yat syān
mahānti duḥkhāny ata eva rājñaḥ;
āsaṅga|kāṣṭha|pratimo hi rājā,
lokasya hetoḥ parikhedam eti.

rājye nṛ|pas tyāgini bahv|a|mitre
viśvāsam āgacchati ced vipannaḥ;
ath' âpi viśrambham upaiti n' êha,
kiṃ nāma saukhyaṃ cakitasya rājñaḥ?

yadā ca jitv" âpi mahīṃ samagrāṃ
vāsāya dṛṣṭaṃ puram ekam eva;
tatr' âpi c' âikaṃ bhavanaṃ niṣevyaṃ,
śramaḥ par'|ârthe nanu rāja|bhāvaḥ.

For aloewood and heavy clothes provide
joy when it's cold but pain when it is hot;
Moonbeams and sandal paste, likewise, provide
joy when it's hot but pain when it is cold.

Because opposites such as gain and loss
are the lot of everyone in this world;
For that reason too no man on this earth
tastes absolute joy or absolute pain.

Seeing that joy and pain are always mixed,
I reckon king and slave to be the same;
For, surely, a king does not always laugh,
and a slave is not always in distress.

A king has great authority, one may argue; 11.45
but that is the very cause of a king's distress;
For a king, much like a carrying-pole,
for the people's sake endures great travail.

If a king places faith in his kingdom,
fickle and full of enemies, he's doomed;
But if he fails to place his trust in it,
then what happiness does a king enjoy,
when he is trembling with fright?

When even after conquering the entire earth,
we see that he gets just one city to dwell in;
When even there he lives in just one residence;
does not sovereignty consist in
toiling for other people's sake?

rājño 'pi vāso|yugam ekam eva,
kṣut|saṃnirodhāya tath" ânna|mātrā;
śayyā tath" âik'|āsanam ekam eva;
śeṣā viśeṣā nṛ|pater madāya.

tuṣṭy|artham etac ca phalaṃ yad' îṣṭam
ṛte 'pi rājyān mama tuṣṭir asti.
tuṣṭau ca satyāṃ puruṣasya loke
sarve viśeṣā nanu nir|viśeṣāḥ.

11.50 tan n' âsmi kāmān prati saṃpratāryaḥ
kṣemaṃ śivaṃ mārgam anuprapannaḥ;
smṛtvā su|hṛttvaṃ tu punaḥ punar māṃ
brūhi ‹pratijñāṃ khalu pālay' êti.›

na hy asmy amarṣeṇa vanaṃ praviṣṭo,
na śatru|bāṇair avadhūta|mauliḥ,
kṛta|spṛho n' âpi phal'|âdhikebhyo,
gṛhṇāmi n' âitad vacanaṃ yatas te.

yo danda|śūkaṃ kupitaṃ bhujaṅ|gaṃ
muktvā vyavasyedd hi punar grahītum
dāh'|ātmikāṃ vā jvalitāṃ tṛṇ'|ôlkāṃ,
saṃtyajya kāmān sa punar bhajeta.

Even a king wears only one pair of garments,
and eats as much food as would allay his hunger;
He sleeps in one bed and sits on a single seat;
other opulence only puffs up a king's pride.

If one desires this fruit to obtain contentment,
I'm content even without a kingdom.
When a man has obtained contentment
in this world,
don't all luxuries seem quite ordinary?

I cannot be impelled, therefore, toward pleasures, 11.50
for I've set out on the auspicious path to peace;
But recalling our friendship, say to me
again and again:
'Hold fast to your pledge!'

For I entered the forest not out of anger,
enemy arrows did not take away my crown,
I do not crave ever higher rewards;
therefore I decline this offer of yours.

Having cast off an angry snake itching to bite,
or a fiery hay torch, whose nature is to burn,
Should a man decide to hold them again,
he would embrace once again
pleasures he had once renounced.

andhāya yaś ca spṛhayed an|andho,
baddhāya mukto vidhanāya c' āḍhyaḥ,
unmatta|cittāya ca kalya|cittaḥ:
spṛhāṃ sa kuryād viṣay'|ātmakāya.

bhaikṣ'|ôpabhog" îti ca n' ânukampyaḥ
kṛtī jarā|mṛtyu|bhayaṃ titīrṣuḥ
ih' ôttamaṃ śānti|sukhaṃ ca yasya
paratra duḥkhāni ca saṃvṛtāni.

11.55 lakṣmyāṃ mahatyām api vartamānas
tṛṣṇ"|âbhibhūtas tv anukampitavyaḥ
prāpnoti yaḥ śānti|sukhaṃ na c' êha
paratra duḥkhaiḥ pratigṛhyate ca.

evaṃ tu vaktuṃ bhavato 'nurūpaṃ
sattvasya vṛttasya kulasya c' âiva;
mam' âpi voḍhuṃ sadṛśaṃ pratijñāṃ
sattvasya vṛttasya kulasya c' âiva.

ahaṃ hi saṃsāra|śareṇa viddho
viniḥsṛtaḥ śāntim avāptu|kāmaḥ;
n' êccheyam āptuṃ tri|dive 'pi rājyaṃ
nir|āmayaṃ, kiṃ bata mānuṣeṣu!

The sighted man who envies a blind man,
a free man who envies a prisoner,
a wealthy man who envies a pauper,
a sane man who envies one who's insane:
That man would envy a person
who's a slave to objects of sense.

One should not pity a man for eating almsfood,
a skillful man who wishes to cross beyond
the dangers of old age and death,
A man who enjoys the highest joy of peace here,
and escapes suffering in the hereafter.

One should pity a man overwhelmed by longing, 11.55
although he enjoys the greatest sovereign power,
A man who does not obtain the joy of peace here,
and is gripped by suffering in the hereafter.

But to speak like this is in keeping with
your character, conduct, and family;
To keep my pledge too is in keeping with
my character, conduct, and family.

For, pierced by the arrow of this samsaric life,
I have departed desiring to obtain peace;
I do not desire unhindered kingship
even in the triple heaven;
how much less then among humans!

‹tri|varga|sevām,› nṛ|pa, yat tu ‹kṛtsnataḥ
paro manuṣy'|ârtha› iti tvam āttha mām,
‹an|artha› ity eva mam' âtra darśanaṃ
kṣayī tri|vargo hi na c' âpi tarpakaḥ.

pade tu yasmin na jarā na bhīr na ruṅ
na janma n' âiv' ôparamo na c' ādhayaḥ,
tam eva manye puruṣ'|ârtham uttamaṃ
na vidyate yatra punaḥ punaḥ kriyā.

11.60 yad apy avocaḥ ‹paripālyatāṃ jarā
navaṃ vayo gacchati vikriyām› iti,
a|niścayo 'yaṃ, capalaṃ hi dṛśyate;
jar" âpy a|dhīrā dhṛtimac ca yauvanam.

sva|karma|dakṣaś ca yad" ântiko jagad
vayaḥsu sarveṣv a|vaśaṃ vikarṣati,
vināśa|kāle katham a|vyavasthite
jarā pratīkṣyā viduṣā śam'|êpsunā?

jar"|āyudho vyādhi|vikīrṇa|sāyako
yad" ântiko vyādha iv' â|śivaḥ sthitaḥ
prajā|mṛgān bhāgya|van'|āśritāṃs tudan,
vayaḥ|prakarṣaṃ prati ko mano|rathaḥ?

As to what you said to me, that the triple set
when followed in its entirety
is for humans the highest good;
My view on this is that it's truly an evil,
for the triple set is fleeting
and fails to satisfy.

The state in which there is no old age and no fear,
no sickness and no birth, no death and no distress,
That alone I take as the highest good for men,
in which there is no repeated activity.

As to what you said: 'Wait until old age, 11.60
youth is liable to vacillation;'
That is not fixed, there is uncertainty;
old age too can be fickle,
while youth is often steadfast.

When Death, who is so skilled at his work,
drags the world
helplessly in all periods of life,
How can a wise man seeking peace await old age,
when the time of death is so uncertain?

When Death stands like an ominous hunter,
using old age as his weapon,
spraying the arrows of sickness,
Striking down people as if they were deer
entering the forest of doom,
How can one dream about a ripe old age?

ato yuvā vā stha|viro 'tha vā śiśus
  tathā tvarāvān iha kartum arhati,
yathā bhaved dharmavataḥ kṛt'|ātmanaḥ
  pravṛttir iṣṭā vinivṛttir eva vā.

yad āttha c' âp' ‹iṣṭa|phalāṃ kul'|ôcitāṃ
  kuruṣva dharmāya makha|kriyām› iti,
namo makhebhyo—na hi kāmaye sukhaṃ
  parasya duḥkha|kriyayā yad iṣyate.

11.65 paraṃ hi hantuṃ vi|vaśaṃ phal'|êpsayā
  na yukta|rūpaṃ karuṇ"|ātmanaḥ sataḥ;
kratoḥ phalaṃ yady api śāśvataṃ bhavet,
  tath" âpi kṛtvā, kim u yat kṣay'|ātmakam?

bhavec ca dharmo yadi n' âparo vidhir
  vratena śīlena manaḥ|śamena vā,
tath" âpi n' âiv' ârhati sevituṃ kratuṃ
  viśasya yasmin param ucyate phalam.

ih' âpi tāvat puruṣasya tiṣṭhataḥ
  pravartate yat para|hiṃsayā sukham,
tad apy an|iṣṭaṃ sa|ghṛṇasya dhīmato;
  bhav'|ântare kiṃ bata yan na dṛśyate?

So, whether one is young, old, or even a child,
one should quickly act in such a way here
That, endowed with dharma, with a perfected self,
one will win the continued life one seeks,
or the total cessation of such life.

As to what you said:
'For dharma's sake perform the sacrificial rites,
as is your family custom,
rites that yield the desired results;'
My respects to sacrificial rites—
but I do not covet joy that is sought
by inflicting pain on another being.

For to kill some hapless being to obtain results 11.65
does not befit a good and compassionate man,
Even if that rite yields everlasting results;
how much less when the results are ephemeral?

Even if dharma were not a different process,
through vows, moral restraints,
tranquility of mind,
Yet it is not right to perform rites whose result
is said to derive from killing another being.

Now, even the pleasure that a man living here
derives from his harming another being,
Is unwelcome to a wise compassionate man;
how much more in the hereafter,
regarding an unseen pleasure?

na ca pratāryo 'smi phala|pravṛttaye
bhaveṣu, rājan, ramate na me manaḥ;
latā iv' âmbho|dhara|vṛṣṭi|tāḍitāḥ
pravṛttayaḥ sarva|gatā hi cañcalāḥ.

ih' āgataś c' âham ito didṛkṣayā
muner Arāḍasya vimokṣa|vādinaḥ
prayāmi c' âdy' âiva. nṛ|p' âstu te śivam,
vacaḥ kṣamethā mama tattva|niṣṭhuram.

11.70 av' Êndravad divy, ava śaśvad arkavad,
guṇair ava, śreya ih' âva, gām ava,
av' āyur, āryair ava, sat|sutān ava,
śriyaś ca, rājann, ava dharmam ātmanaḥ.

him'|âri|ket'|ûdbhava|saṃbhav'|ântare
yathā dvi|jo yāti vimokṣayaṃs tanum,
him'|âri|śatru|kṣaya|śatru|ghātane
tath" ântare yāhi vimokṣayan manaḥ.»

You can't lure me to act for the sake of results;
my mind, king, delights not in existential states;
For, like creepers battered by showers
from rain clouds,
actions are unsteady and darting everywhere.

I have come here and I will leave today
desiring to see the sage Aráda,
who teaches release.
Good fortune to you, king,
and bear with my words
speaking a harsh truth.

Be glad like Indra in heaven, ever shine like the sun, 11.70
flourish with virtues and obtain here
the highest bliss,
Protect the earth, obtain long life,
flourish with Aryas,
protect the sons of the virtuous,
possess sovereign power,
And, O King, follow the dharma proper to you.*

As fire, the twice-born, when it encounters
rain pouring from a cloud that springs
from smoke,
sign of the enemy of cold,
proceeds releasing its form,
So proceed, releasing your mind by killing
the foes of the destruction of darkness,
the foe of the sun, the enemy of cold."*

nṛ|po 'bravīt s'|âñjalir āgata|spṛho:
«yath"|êṣṭam āpnotu bhavān a|vighnataḥ.
avāpya kāle kṛta|kṛtyatām imāṃ
mam' âpi kāryo bhavatā tv anugrahaḥ.»

sthiraṃ pratijñāya «tath" êti» pārthive
tataḥ sa Vaiśvaṃtaṛam āśramaṃ yayau;
parivrajantaṃ tam udīkṣya vismito
nṛ|po 'pi vavrāja puriṃ Girivrajam.

iti Buddhacarite mahā|kāvye Kāma|vigarhaṇo nām'
âikā|daśaḥ sargaḥ.

With joined hands the king said, full of longing:

"May you obtain what you desire,
free from hindrance.
Having in time achieved success in your task,
Deign to show me also your favor."

Saying "Yes," he made a firm promise to the king,
and set out to the Vaishvántara hermitage;
seeing him wandering thus, the king was amazed,
and went back to the city of Giri·vraja.

Thus ends the eleventh canto named "Condemnation of Passion"
of the great poem "Life of the Buddha."

CANTO 12
THE MEETING WITH ARÁDA

12.1 Tataḥ śama|vihārasya
muner Ikṣvāku|candramāḥ
Arāḍasy' āśramaṃ bheje
vapuṣā pūrayann iva.

sa Kālāma|sa|gotreṇa
ten' āloky' âiva dūrataḥ
uccaiḥ «sv|āgatam» ity uktaḥ
samīpam upajagmivān.

tāv ubhau nyāyataḥ pṛṣṭvā
dhātu|sāmyaṃ paras|param,
dāravyor medhyayor vṛṣyoḥ
śucau deśe niṣedatuḥ.

tam āsīnaṃ nṛpa|sutaṃ
so 'bravīn muni|sattamaḥ
bahumāna|viśālābhyāṃ
darśanābhyāṃ pibann iva:

12.5 «viditaṃ me yathā, saumya,
niṣkrānto bhavanād asi
chittvā sneha|mayaṃ pāśaṃ
pāśaṃ dṛpta iva dvi|paḥ.

sarvathā dhṛtimac c' âiva
prājñaṃ c' âiva manas tava
yas tvaṃ prāptaḥ śriyaṃ tyaktvā
latāṃ viṣa|phalām iva.

THEN, THAT moon of the Ikshvákus 12.1
reached the cloister of Aráda,
a sage who abided in peace,
filling it, as if, with his grace.

The sage of the Kaláma line,
just as he saw him from afar,
declared in a loud voice: "Welcome!"
and the prince then drew close to him.

They both asked according to rule
about each other's health;
then they sat down in a clean spot
on pure stools made of wood.

After the king's son was seated,
that best of sages said to him,
drinking him in, as if, with eyes
extended wide in deep respect:

"I already know, my dear, 12.5
how you set out from your home,
Having cut the fetters of affection,
like an enraged elephant its fetters.

Your mind is clearly wise:
steadfast in every way,
For you have come forsaking sovereign power,
like a creeper bearing poisonous fruit.

n' âścaryaṃ jīrṇa|vayaso
  yaj jagmuḥ pārthivā vanam
apatyebhyaḥ śriyaṃ dattvā
  bhukt'|ôcchiṣṭām iva srajam.

idaṃ me matam āścaryaṃ,
  nave vayasi yad bhavān
a|bhuktv" âiva śriyaṃ prāptaḥ
  sthito viṣaya|gocare.

tad vijñātum imaṃ dharmaṃ
  paramaṃ bhājanaṃ bhavān;
jñāna|plavam adhiṣṭhāya
  śīghraṃ duḥkh'|ârṇavaṃ tara.

12.10 śiṣye yady api vijñāte
  śāstraṃ kālena varṇyate,
gāmbhīryād vyavasāyāc ca
  na parīkṣyo bhavān mama.»

iti vākyam Arāḍasya
  vijñāya sa nara'|rṣabhaḥ
babhūva parama|prītaḥ
  provāc' ôttaram eva ca:

«viraktasy' âpi yad idaṃ
  saumukhyaṃ bhavataḥ param
a|kṛt'|ârtho 'py anen' âsmi
  kṛt'|ârtha iva saṃprati.

It is no great wonder that aged kings
should go away to the forest,
Bestowing sovereign power on their children,
like a used and cast-off garland.

Now, I consider this a great wonder,
that you, while still a young man
Living in the thick of sensual pleasures,
should come here even before
you have enjoyed sovereign power.

You are, therefore, the paramount vessel
to comprehend this, the supreme dharma;
Get into this boat of knowledge,
quickly cross the ocean of grief.

Though this science is taught after a time, 12.10
when a student has undergone the test,
Because you're so profound and resolute,
there's no need for me to test you at all."

Hearing these words of Aráda,
that bull among men,
was filled with great joy,
and made this reply:

"By this your great kindness to me,
although you are freed from passion,
I feel I've now attained my goal,
although I've not attained it yet.

didṛkṣur iva hi jyotir,
  yiyāsur iva daiśikam,
tvad|darśanam ahaṃ manye
  titīrṣur iva ca plavam.

tasmād arhasi tad vaktuṃ
  vaktavyaṃ yadi manyase
jarā|maraṇa|rogebhyo
  yath" âyaṃ parimucyate.»

12.15 ity Arāḍaḥ kumārasya
  māhātmyād eva coditaḥ
saṃkṣiptaṃ kathayāṃ cakre
  svasya śāstrasya niścayam:

«śrūyatām ayam asmākaṃ
  siddhāntaḥ, śṛṇvatāṃ vara:
yathā bhavati saṃsāro
  yathā c' âiva nivartate.

Prakṛtiś ca Vikāraś ca
  janma mṛtyur jar" âiva ca—
tat tāvat Sattvam ity uktaṃ,
  sthira|sattva, parehi tat.

tatra tu Prakṛtiṃ nāma
  viddhi, prakṛti|kovida:
pañca bhūtāny, ahaṃ|kāraṃ,
  buddhim, a|vyaktam eva ca.

As a light for a man longing to see,
  as a guide for a man longing to trek,
As a boat for a man longing to cross,
  so do I regard your philosophy.

So deign to explain it to me,
  if you think it's right to explain,
So that I shall become free,
  from old age, death, and disease."

This eulogy by the prince 12.15
spurred Aráda to explain
succinctly the conclusions
of his system of thought:

"Listen, O best of listeners,
  to this settled doctrine of ours:
How samsara comes into being,
  likewise, how it ceases to be.

Primal nature and Transformation,
  birth, death, and old age—
All that is called Being, please understand,
  you whose being is firm.*

Among these, know that the Primal nature,
  you who know primary constituents,
Consists of the five elements, ego,
  the intellect, and the unmanifest.*

Vikāra iti budhyasva
viṣayān indriyāṇi ca,
pāṇi|pādaṃ ca vādaṃ ca
pāy'|ûpasthaṃ tathā manaḥ.

12.20 asya kṣetrasya vijñānāt
Kṣetra|jña iti saṃjñi ca;
‹Kṣetra|jña› iti c' ātmānaṃ
kathayanty ātma|cintakāḥ.

sa|śiṣyaḥ Kapilaś c' êha
pratibuddhir iti smṛtiḥ.
sa|putro '|pratibuddhas tu
Prajāpatir ih' ôcyate.

jāyate jīryate c' âiva
bādhyate mriyate ca yat,
tad vyaktam iti vijñeyam;
a|vyaktaṃ tu viparyayāt.

a|jñānaṃ karma tṛṣṇā ca
jñeyāḥ saṃsāra|hetavaḥ;
sthito 'smiṃs tritaye jantus
tat sattvaṃ n' âtivartate—

vi|pratyayād, ahaṃ|kārāt,
saṃdehād, abhisaṃplavāt,
a|viśeṣ'|ân|upāyābhyāṃ,
saṅgād, abhyavapātataḥ.

Recognize that Transformation
is the senses and sense objects,
Hands and feet, as also the mouth,
anus, genitals, and the mind.*

Because it cognizes this field, 12.20
what is conscious is called
the Knower of the field;
But those who contemplate the self,
call the self 'Knower of the field.'*

Kápila with his pupils, tradition says,
is the Conscious in this system;
Praja·pati with his sons is said to be
the Unconscious in this system.*

What is born, what grows old,
what is bound, and what dies:
All that, you should know, is the Manifest;
the Unmanifest is known
by the opposite of these.

Ignorance, action, desire, you should know,
are the causes of samsara;
When a creature is mired in these three,
it will never transcend that Being—

by reason of wrong knowledge and ego,
confusion and wrong association,
non-discrimination and wrongful means,
attachment and falling away.

12.25 tatra vi|pratyayo nāma
viparītaṃ pravartate,
anyathā kurute kāryaṃ
mantavyaṃ manyate 'nyathā.

‹bravīmy aham, ahaṃ vedmi,
gacchāmy aham, ahaṃ sthitaḥ› —
it' îh' âivam ahaṃ|kāras tv,
an|ahaṃ|kāra, vartate.

yas tu bhāvān a|saṃdigdhān
ekī|bhāvena paśyati
mṛt|piṇḍavad, a|saṃdeha,
saṃdehaḥ sa ih' ôcyate.

‹ya ev' âhaṃ, sa ev' êdaṃ,
mano, buddhiś ca, karma ca;
yaś c' âiv' âiṣa gaṇaḥ, so 'ham:›
iti yaḥ, so 'bhisaṃplavaḥ.

a|viśeṣaṃ, viśeṣa|jña,
pratibuddh'|â|prabuddhayoḥ
prakṛtīnāṃ ca yo veda,
so '|viśeṣa iti smṛtaḥ.

12.30 namas|kāra|vaṣaṭ|kārau
prokṣaṇ'|âbhyukṣaṇ'|ādayaḥ—
an|upāya iti prājñair,
upāya|jña, praveditaḥ.

Among these, wrong knowledge 12.25
  proceeds aberrantly,
Doing wrongly what has to be done,
  thinking wrongly what must be thought.

'I speak, I know,
  I go, I stand'—
The ego proceeds thus in this system,
  O you who are free of ego.

When one sees as unified
  things that are not commingled,
Like a ball of earth, O unconfused one,
  it is called confusion in this system.

'I am the very same as mind,
  intellect, and activity;
I'm truly the same as this group:'
  that is wrong association.

When one fails to discriminate,
  you who know to discriminate,
Between the Conscious and the Unconscious,
  and among Primal nature's constituents,
  tradition calls it non-discrimination.

The ritual sounds *namah* and *vashat*,* 12.30
  ritual sprinklings and annointings—
The wise declare these to be wrongful means,
  O you who know the rightful means.

sajjate yena dur|medhā
  mano|vāg|buddhi|karmabhiḥ
viṣayeṣv, an|abhiṣvaṅga,
  so 'bhiṣvaṅga iti smṛtaḥ.

‹mam' êdam› ‹aham asy' êti›
  yad duḥkham abhimanyate,
vijñeyo 'bhyavapātaḥ sa
  saṃsāre yena pātyate.

ity a|vidyāṃ hi vidvān sa
  pañca|parvāṃ samīhate
tamo mohaṃ mahā|mohaṃ
  tāmisra|dvayam eva ca.

tatr' ālasyaṃ tamo viddhi,
  mohaṃ mṛtyuṃ ca janma ca;
mahā|mohas tv, a|saṃmoha,
  kāma ity eva gamyatām.

12.35 yasmād atra ca bhūtāni
  pramuhyanti mahānty api,
tasmād eṣa, mahā|bāho,
  mahā|moha iti smṛtaḥ.

tāmisram iti c' â|krodha,
  krodham ev' âdhikurvate;
viṣādaṃ c' ândha|tāmisram,
  a|viṣāda, pracakṣate.

By which a fool is attached to the objects of sense,
through mind, speech, intellect, and acts,
That, traditions tells us, is attachment,
O you who are unattached.

When one imagines suffering with the thought,
'This is linked to me' and 'I'm linked to this,'
That should be recognized as falling away,
by which one is made to fall into samsara.

In this way, that wise one maintains,
that ignorance has five sections:
Gloom, delusion, great delusion,
likewise, the two kinds of darkness.*

Among these, know that gloom is laziness,
and delusion consists of death and birth;
O you without delusion, understand
that great delusion is simply passion.

Because even great beings are 12.35
deluded in this regard;
Therefore, O you who possess great arms,
tradition calls it great delusion.

By darkness, O angerless one,
they refer simply to anger,
Blind darkness, they say, is dejection,
O you who are free of dejection.

anay" â|vidyayā bālaḥ
samyuktaḥ pañca|parvayā
saṃsāre duḥkha|bhūyiṣṭhe
janmasv abhiniṣicyate.

draṣṭā, śrotā ca, mantā ca,
kārya|karaṇam eva ca
‹aham› ity evam āgamya
saṃsāre parivartate.

ih' âibhir hetubhir, dhīman,
janma|srotaḥ pravartate;
hetv|a|bhāvāt phal'|â|bhāva
iti vijñātum arhati!

12.40 tatra samyaṅ|matir vidyān,
mokṣa|kāma, catuṣṭayam:
pratibuddh'|â|prabuddhau ca
vyaktam a|vyaktam eva ca.

yathāvad etad vijñāya
Kṣetra|jño hi catuṣṭayam,
ājavaṃjavatāṃ hitvā
prāpnoti padam a|kṣaram.

ity|arthaṃ brāhmaṇā loke
parama|brahma|vādinaḥ
brahma|caryaṃ carant' îha
brāhmaṇān vāsayanti ca.»

Permeated by this ignorance
  with five sections, a foolish man
Is forced into birth after birth,
  in samsara where pain prevails.

When a person thinks that he is
  the seer, the hearer, the thinker,
And the agent of the result,
  he goes around in samsara.

In this system, wise one, these
  are the causes by means of which
  the stream of births keeps rolling on;
You should understand:
  when there is no cause,
  there'll be no effect!

Of these, you who desire release, 12.40
  a right thinking man
  ought to know these four:
The Conscious and the Unconscious,
  the Manifest and the Unmanifest.

For the Knower of the field, when he
  has properly fathomed these four,
Gives up the stream of births and deaths
  and reaches the undecaying state.

To this end brahmins in the world,
  expounding the highest brahman,
Walk the brahma-course in our system,
  and likewise instruct other brahmins."

iti vākyam idaṃ śrutvā
munes tasya nṛp'|ātmajaḥ
abhyupāyaṃ ca papraccha
padam eva ca naiṣṭhikam:

«brahma|caryam idaṃ caryaṃ
yathā yāvac ca yatra ca,
dharmasy' âsya ca paryantaṃ
bhavān vyākhyātum arhati.»

12.45 ity Arāḍo yathā|śāstraṃ
vispaṣṭ'|ârthaṃ samāsataḥ
tam ev' ânyena kalpena
dharmam asmai vyabhāṣata:

«ayam ādau gṛhān muktvā
bhaikṣākaṃ liṅgam āśritaḥ
samudācāra|vistīrṇaṃ
śīlam ādāya vartate.

saṃtoṣaṃ param āsthāya
yena tena yatas tataḥ
viviktaṃ sevate vāsaṃ
nir|dvandvaḥ śāstra|vit kṛtī.

tato rāgād bhayaṃ dṛṣṭvā,
vairāgyāc ca paraṃ śivam,
nigṛhṇann indriya|grāmaṃ
yatate manasaḥ śame.

After he listened to this speech
of that sage, the son of the king,
inquired further about the means,
also about the final state:

"How does one walk this brahma-course?
For how long a time? And where?
What's the limit of this dharma?
Please, Sir, explain that to me."

Aráda explained to him in this way, 12.45
the same dharma in a different way,
in concise form and clear language,
in accordance with sacred texts:

"At the outset, he leaves his home,
puts on a mendicant's emblem;
And lives adhering to a rule of life
embracing all standards of good conduct.

Becoming supremely content
with whatever he gets
from anyone at all,
He lives in a secluded place,
free from the pairs of opposites,
skillful, learned in sacred texts.

Then, seeing that from passion comes danger,
from detachment, likewise, the highest bliss,
He restrains all his sense organs
and strives to quieten his mind.

ath' ô viviktaṃ kāmebhyo
vyāpād'|ādibhya eva ca
viveka|jam avāpnoti
pūrva|dhyānaṃ vitarkavat.

12.50 tac ca dhyāna|sukhaṃ prāpya
tat tad eva vitarkayan,
a|pūrva|sukha|lābhena
hriyate bāliśo janaḥ.

śamen' âivaṃ|vidhen' âyaṃ
kāma|dveṣa|vigarhiṇā
Brahma|lokam avāpnoti
paritoṣeṇa vañcitaḥ.

jñātvā vidvān vitarkāṃs tu
manaḥ|saṃkṣobha|kārakān
tad|viyuktam avāpnoti
dhyānaṃ prīti|sukh'|ânvitam.

hriyamāṇas tayā prītyā
yo viśeṣaṃ na paśyati,
sthānaṃ bhāsvaram āpnoti
deveṣv ābhāsvareṣu saḥ.

yas tu prīti|sukhāt tasmād
vivecayati mānasam,
tṛtīyaṃ labhate dhyānaṃ
sukhaṃ prīti|vivarjitam.

Thereupon, he attains the first level of trance
rising from discrimination
and containing discursive thought,
Insulated from all passions,
from malevolence and the like.

When he has experienced that joy of trance, 12.50
pondered it over and over again,
The fool is carried away by gaining
a hitherto unexperienced joy.

Through tranquility of this sort,
that holds love and hate in disdain,
That man attains the brahma-world,
deceived by overwhelming joy.

But when the wise man realizes that
discursive thought perturbs the mind,
He attains the trance that's divorced from that,
and containing delight and joy.

When one's carried away by that delight
and does not perceive a superior state,
One obtains the state of luminescence
among the gods who are luminescent.

But one who dissociates his mind
from that delight and from that joy,
Obtains the third level of trance,
containing joy without delight.

12.55 yas tu tasmin sukhe magno
na viśeṣāya yatnavān,
śubha|kṛtsnaiḥ sa sāmānyaṃ
sukhaṃ prāpnoti daivataiḥ.

tādṛśaṃ sukham āsādya
yo na rajyaty upekṣakaḥ,
caturthaṃ dhyānam āpnoti
sukha|duḥkha|vivarjitam.

tatra ke cid vyavasyanti
mokṣa ity abhimāninaḥ
sukha|duḥkha|parityāgād
a|vyāpārāc ca cetasaḥ.

asya dhyānasya tu phalaṃ
samaṃ devair bṛhat|phalaiḥ
kathayanti bṛhat|kālaṃ
bṛhat|prajñā|parīkṣakāḥ.

samādher vyutthitas tasmād
dṛṣṭvā doṣāṃś charīriṇām
jñānam ārohati prājñaḥ
śarīra|vinivṛttaye.

12.60 tatas tad dhyānam utsṛjya
viśeṣe kṛta|niścayaḥ
kāmebhya iva sa prājño
rūpād api virajyate.

But he who gets himself mired in that joy 12.55
and does not strive for a superior state,
Obtains a joy equal to that
of the Shubha·kritsna gods.

When after obtaining that kind of joy,
a man becomes indifferent
and is not enamored with it,
He gains the fourth level of trance
that's devoid of sorrow and joy.

In that state, through their imagination,
some conclude that it is release,
Because joy and sorrow are forsaken,
and the mind ceases to function.

Those who explore the knowledge of the Great,*
however, describe the fruit of this trance
As lasting over a great span of time
together with the Brihat·phala gods.

Seeing the faults of embodied beings,
a wise man comes out of that trance
And sets his mind on that knowledge
that would rid him of his body.

Then, having cast aside that trance, 12.60
he sets his sight on a higher state;
As he once withdrew from pleasures,
so now the wise man withdraws
also from visible form.

śarīre khāni yāny asmin
　tāny ādau parikalpayan
ghaneṣv api tato dravyeṣv
　ākāśam adhimucyate.

ākāśa|gatam ātmānaṃ
　saṃkṣipya tv aparo budhaḥ,
tad ev' ân|antataḥ paśyan
　viśeṣam adhigacchati.

adhyātma|kuśalas tv anyo
　nivarty' ātmānam ātmanā,
kiṃ cin n' âst' îti saṃpaśyann
　ākiṃcanya iti smṛtaḥ.

tato muñjād iṣīk" êva
　śakuniḥ pañjarād iva
Kṣetra|jño niḥsṛto dehān
　‹mukta› ity abhidhīyate.

12.65 etat tat paramaṃ brahma
　nir|liṅgaṃ dhruvam a|kṣaram
yan ‹mokṣa› iti tattva|jñāḥ
　kathayanti manīṣiṇaḥ.

ity upāyaś ca mokṣaś ca
　mayā saṃdarśitas tava;
yadi jñātaṃ, yadi rucir,
　yathāvat pratipadyatām.

First he forms a mental picture
of the empty holes within his body;
Then he focuses his mind on
the empty space in solid objects too.

But another wise man draws together
the self spread over empty space,
And, deeming that alone as eternal,
arrives at a superior state.

But another versed in the inner self,
effacing his self with the self,
Perceives that there exists nothing at all;
tradition calls him one for whom
nothing exists at all.

Then, like a reed from its grass sheath,
or like a bird from a bird-cage,
Knower of the field, from body freed,
is designated 'released being.'

This here is the supreme brahman, 12.65
without a distinguishing mark,
constant and imperishable,
Which wise men who perceive the truth
describe as 'release.'

I've thus explained clearly to you
the means, as also the release;
If you understand it, if you like it,
then undertake it in the proper way.

Jaigīṣavyo 'tha Janako
  vṛddhaś c' âiva Parāśaraḥ
imaṃ panthānam āsādya
  muktā hy anye ca mokṣiṇaḥ.»

iti tasya sa tad vākyaṃ
  gṛhītvā tu vicārya ca,
pūrva|hetu|bala|prāptaḥ
  pratyuttaram uvāca ha:

«śrutaṃ jñānam idaṃ sūkṣmaṃ
  parataḥ parataḥ śivam;
Kṣetra|jñasy' â|parityāgād
  avaimy etad a|naiṣṭhikam.

12.70 Vikāra|Prakṛtibhyo hi
  Kṣetra|jñaṃ muktam apy aham
manye prasava|dharmāṇaṃ
  bīja|dharmāṇam eva ca.

viśuddho yady api hy ātmā
  nirmukta iti kalpyate;
bhūyaḥ pratyaya|sad|bhāvād
  a|muktaḥ sa bhaviṣyati.

ṛtu|bhūmy|ambu|virahād
  yathā bījaṃ na rohati,
rohati pratyayais tais tais
  tadvat so 'pi mato mama.

For Jaigishávya and Jánaka,
as also the Elder Paráshara,
Attained release by taking to this path,
as also others who have sought release."*

The prince, however, took note
of his speech and gave it thought;
and endowed with the power of
impulses from previous births,
he gave this reply:

"I have listened to this subtle knowledge
that grows progressively more and more pure;
But since the Field-knower is not forsaken,
I think it is short of the absolute.

For, although the Knower of the field is freed 12.70
from Primal nature and Transformations,
Yet I think it still has the quality
of giving birth and serving as a seed.*

For, though the soul, being wholly pure,
you consider to be released;
Yet, because the causal roots are present,
it will once again become unreleased.

A seed will not sprout in the wrong season,
or when water and good soil are absent;
It sprouts when those causal roots are present;
that holds true, I think, also for the soul.

yat karm'|â|jñāna|tṛṣṇānāṃ
  tyāgān mokṣaś ca kalpyate,
atyantas tat|parityāgaḥ
  saty ātmani na vidyate.

hitvā hitvā trayam idaṃ
  viśeṣas t' ûpalabhyate;
ātmanas tu sthitir yatra
  tatra sūkṣmam idaṃ trayam.

12.75 sūkṣmatvāc c' âiva doṣāṇām,
  a|vyāpārāc ca cetasaḥ,
dīrghatvād āyuṣaś c' âiva—
  mokṣas tu parikalpyate.

ahaṃkāra|parityāgo
  yaś c' âiṣa parikalpyate—
saty ātmani parityāgo
  n' âhaṃ|kārasya vidyate.

saṃkhy"|ādibhir a|muktaś ca
  nir|guṇo na bhavaty ayam;
tasmād a|sati nairguṇye
  n' âsya mokṣo 'bhidhīyate.

guṇino hi guṇānāṃ ca
  vyatireko na vidyate;
rūp'|ôṣṇābhyāṃ virahito
  na hy agnir upalabhyate.

And if you contend that release is effected
by giving up action, ignorance, and desire;
Their complete abandonment is impossible,
so long as one upholds the existence of the soul.

The ongoing abandonment of these three,
indeed, brings about a superior state;
Yet, where the soul continues to endure,
these three will remain in a subtle form.

The faults are subtle, the mind is dormant, 12.75
and the span of life is, likewise, prolonged—
On that basis one imagines
that it is the state of release.

This abandonment of ego
that you imagine to take place—
When there's a soul, the abandonment
of the ego cannot take place.

This soul is not attributeless
when it is not released
from number and the like;*
And it is not viewed as released,
when it's not free of attributes.

For there exists no disjuncture between
attributes and the one possessing them;
For it's not possible to perceive fire
that's devoid of heat and visible form.

prāg dehān na bhaved dehī,
prāg guṇebhyas tathā guṇī;
tasmād ādau vimuktaḥ san
śarīrī badhyate punaḥ.

12.80 Kṣetra|jño vi|śarīraś ca
jño vā syād a|jña eva vā,
yadi jño jñeyam asy' âsti
jñeye sati na mucyate.

ath' â|jña iti siddho vaḥ,
kalpitena kim ātmanā?
vin" âpi hy ātman" â|jñānaṃ
prasiddhaṃ kāṣṭha|kuḍyavat.

parataḥ paratas tyāgo
yasmāt tu guṇavān smṛtaḥ,
tasmāt sarva|parityāgān
manye kṛtsnāṃ kṛt'|ârthatām.»

iti dharmam Arāḍasya
viditvā, na tutoṣa saḥ;
«a|kṛtsnam» iti vijñāya
tata pratijagāma ha.

Prior to the body there does not exist
 a possessor of the body;
 and prior to attributes there is
 no possessor of attributes;
Therefore, although released at first,
 a possessor of the body
 is bound over again.

And, without the body, the Knower of the field 12.80
 should be either a knower or not a knower;
If he's a knower, there's something for him to know;
 and if there is something for him to know,
 then he is not released.

If, on the contrary, your settled view
 is that he is not a knower,
 then why do you invent a soul?
For non-knowing is truly established
 even without a soul,
 as in a log or wall.

Progressively greater abandonment,
 tradition says, is more perfect;
Therefore, I think that abandoning all
 leads to the full attainment of the goal."

Learning Aráda's dharma as described
did not bring him any satisfaction;
when he realized that it was incomplete,
he went away from there.

viśeṣam atha śuśrūṣur
Udrakasy' āśramaṃ yayau;
ātma|grāhāc ca tasy' âpi
jagṛhe na sa darśanam.

12.85 saṃjñ"|â|saṃjñitvayor doṣaṃ
jñātvā hi munir Udrakaḥ,
ākiṃcanyāt paraṃ lebhe
saṃjñ"|â|saṃjñ"|ātmikāṃ gatim.

yasmāc c' ālambane sūkṣme
saṃjñ"|â|saṃjñe tataḥ param
n' â|saṃjñī n' âiva saṃjñ" êti
tasmāt tatra gata|spṛhaḥ.

yataś ca buddhis tatr' âiva
sthit" ânyatr' â|pracāriṇī,
sūkṣm" â|paṭvī tatas tatra
n' â|saṃjñitvaṃ na saṃjñitā.

yasmāc ca tad api prāpya
punar āvartate jagat,
Bodhi|sattvaḥ paraṃ prepsus
tasmād Udrakam atyajat.

tato hitv" āśramaṃ tasya
śreyo|'rthī kṛta|niścayaḥ
bheje Gayasya rāja'|rṣer
Nagarī|saṃjñam āśramam.

He then went to Údraka's hermitage,
seeking to learn about a higher state;
but he didn't accept Údraka's doctrine,
because he also believed in a soul.

For the sage Údraka perceived the fault 12.85
of cognition and of non-cognition,
and attained the state beyond nothingness,
that's characterized by neither
cognition nor non-cognition.*

Because cognition and non-cognition
are both states that contain subtle substrates,
so he thought that the state beyond them was
neither cognition nor non-cognition,
and, therefore, he longed for that.

Because the intellect, subtle and static, remains
in that state alone, without proceeding elsewhere,
therefore, in that state there's neither
cognition nor non-cognition.

But, because even after attaining that state
a man returns once again to the world,
the bodhisattva then left Údraka behind,
aiming to attain a state beyond that.

Then, after he had left his hermitage,
seeking after bliss, firmly resolute,
he repaired to the royal seer Gaya's
hermitage, having the name Nágari.

12.90 atha Nairañjanā|tīre
śucau śuci|parākramaḥ
cakāra vāsam ekānta|
vihār'|âbhiratir muniḥ.

[tatas] tat|pūrvam [āśritān]
pañc'|êndriya|vaś'|ôddhatān
tapaḥ|[saṃśraya]|vratino
bhikṣūn pañca niraikṣata.

te c' ôpatasthur dṛṣṭv" âtra
bhikṣavas taṃ mumukṣavaḥ
puṇy'|ârjita|dhan'|ārogyam
indriy'|ârthā iv' ēśvaram.

saṃpūjyamānas taiḥ prahvair
vinayād anuvartibhiḥ
tad|vaśa|sthāyibhiḥ śiṣyair
lolair mana iv' êndriyaiḥ—

«mṛtyu|janm'|ânta|karaṇe
syād upāyo 'yam?» ity atha
duṣ|karāṇi samārebhe
tapāṃsy an|aśanena saḥ.

12.95 upavāsa|vidhīn n' âikān
kurvan nara|durācarān
varṣāṇi ṣaṭ śama|prepsur
akarot kārśyam ātmanaḥ.

Then, that sage, whose valor was pure, 12.90
finding delight in solitude,
made his abode on the pure bank
of the river Nairáñjana.

There he saw five mendicants who
had come there before, given to
vows and austerities, puffed up
by control of the five senses.

Seeing him there and desiring release,
the mendicants came to him, as objects
of sense come to a person of high rank,
whose meritorious deeds
had won him wealth and health.

As they waited upon him with reverence,
living as pupils under his control
and obedient because of their training,
like fickle senses waiting on the mind—

he then undertook fierce austerities
by fasting, thinking that
that was the means whereby
death and birth are destroyed.

Observing many kinds of fast, 12.95
difficult for men to perform,
he shriveled up his body for
six years in his pursuit of calm.

anna|kāleṣu c' âik'|âikaiḥ
sa kola|tila|taṇḍulaiḥ
a|pāra|pāra|saṃsāra|
pāraṃ prepsur apārayat.

dehād apacayas tena
tapasā tasya yaḥ kṛtaḥ,
sa ev' ôpacayo bhūyas
tejas" âsya kṛto 'bhavat.

kṛśo 'py a|kṛśa|kīrti|śrīr
hlādaṃ cakre 'nya|cakṣuṣām
kumudānām iva śarac|
chukla|pakṣ'|ādi|candramāḥ.

tvag|asthi|śeṣo niḥ|śeṣair
medaḥ|piśita|śoṇitaiḥ
kṣīṇo 'py a|kṣīṇa|gāmbhīryaḥ
samudra iva sa vyabhāt.

12.100 atha kaṣṭa|tapaḥ|spaṣṭa|
vyartha|kliṣṭa|tanur muniḥ
bhava|bhīrur imāṃ cakre
buddhiṃ buddhatva|kāṅkṣayā.

The farther shore of samsara,
the shore that has no farther shore,
yearning to reach, he subsisted
by consuming during mealtimes
one jujube, one sesame seed,
and a single grain of rice.

Whatever diminution of body
was created by his austerities,
it was augmented to the same extent
by the power of his inner energy.

Although he was decayed in his body,
but his splendor and glory undecayed,
he brought delight to the eyes of others,
like the autumn moon to night lotuses
at the beginning of the bright fortnight.

Although shrunk in body,
reduced to skin and bones,
drained of fat, flesh, and blood,
yet, with his profundity unimpaired,
he sparkled like the sea.

Then, the sage, his body clearly tortured 12.100
for no purpose by vile austerities,
and afraid of continued existence,
made this resolve, longing for Buddhahood:

«n' âyaṃ dharmo virāgāya,
na bodhāya, na muktaye;
jambu|mūle mayā prāpto
yas tadā, sa vidhir dhruvaḥ.

na c' âsau dur|balen' āptuṃ
śakyam» ity āgat'|ādaraḥ
śarīra|bala|vṛddhy|artham
idaṃ bhūyo 'nvacintayat:

«kṣut|pipāsā|śrama|klāntaḥ
śramād a|svastha|mānasaḥ
prāpnuyān manas" âvāpyaṃ
phalaṃ katham a|nirvṛtaḥ?

nirvṛtiḥ prāpyate samyak
satat'|êndriya|tarpaṇāt
saṃtarpit'|êndriyatayā
manaḥ|svāsthyam avāpyate.

12.105 svastha|prasanna|manasaḥ
samādhir upapadyate,
samādhi|yukta|cittasya
dhyāna|yogaḥ pravartate.

dhyāna|pravartanād dharmāḥ
prāpyante yair avāpyate
dur|labhaṃ śāntam a|jaraṃ
paraṃ tad a|mṛtaṃ padam.»

"This dharma will not lead to detachment,
to Awakening or release;
The path I attained at that time
under the rose apple tree
was indeed the certain path.*

But that path cannot be traversed
by a man who is weak."

Thus, with a sense of urgency
he reflected on this again
to increase his bodily strength:

"When a man is worn out
by hunger, thirst, and fatigue,
his mind unwell with fatigue,
How will he, who is not tranquil, attain
the fruit that the mind alone can attain?

Tranquility is properly attained
by always making the senses content;
When the senses are well content,
wellness of the mind is attained.

Mental concentration springs up 12.105
when one's mind is well and serene,
And practice of trance advances
when concentration grips one's mind.

And by the advancement of trance,
one attains the dharmas by which
Is attained that supreme state hard to obtain,
a state that is unaging, immortal, and calm."

tasmād āhāra|mūlo 'yam
  upāya iti niścayaḥ
āhāra|karaṇe dhīraḥ
  kṛtv" â|mita|matir matim.

snāto Nairañjanā|tīrād
  uttatāra śanaiḥ kṛśaḥ
bhakty" âvanata|śākh"|âgrair
  datta|hastas taṭa|drumaiḥ.

atha gop'|âdhipa|sutā
  daivatair abhicoditā
udbhūta|hṛday'|ānandā
  tatra Nandabal" āgamat—

12.110 sita|śaṅkh'|ôjjvala|bhujā
  nīla|kambala|vāsinī
sa|phena|mālā|nīl'|âmbur
  Yamun" êva sarid varā.

sā śraddhā|vardhita|prītir
  vikasal|locan'|ôtpalā
śirasā praṇipaty' âinaṃ
  grāhayām āsa pāyasam.

kṛtvā tad|upabhogena
  prāpta|janma|phalāṃ sa tām
bodhi|prāptau samartho 'bhūt
  saṃtarpita|ṣaḍ|indriyaḥ.

Having concluded, therefore, that
this process was rooted in food,
steadfast, and with boundless wisdom,
he resolved to partake of food.

When he had taken his bath, he climbed slowly up
the bank of the Nairáñjana in his feeble state,
and the trees on the bank gave him a helping hand,
by devoutly lowering the tips of their boughs.

Then, the daughter of a cowherd chief,
Nanda·bala, impelled by the gods,
the joy of her heart spilling over,
arrived at that spot—

wearing a dark-blue garment, 12.110
her arms sparkling with white shells,
she looked like Yámuna, best of rivers,
with its dark-blue water enwreathed with foam.

Her joy enhanced by her faith,
her lotus-eyes opened wide,
she bowed her head before him
and made him take the milk rice.

By eating that he caused her to
obtain the reward of her birth;
he became, with his six senses content,
able to attain the Awakening.

paryāpt'|āpyāna|mūrtiś ca
  s'|ârdhaṃ sva|yaśasā muniḥ
kānti|dhairye babhār' âikaḥ
  śaś'|âṅk'|ârṇavayor dvayoḥ.

«āvṛtta» iti vijñāya
  taṃ jahuḥ pañca bhikṣavaḥ
manīṣiṇam iv' ātmānaṃ
  nirmuktaṃ pañca dhātavaḥ.

12.115 vyavasāya|dvitīyo 'tha
  śādval'|āstīrṇa|bhūtalam
so 'śvattha|mūlaṃ prayayau
  bodhāya kṛta|niścayaḥ.

tatas tadānīṃ gaja|rāja|vikramaḥ
  pada|svanen' ân|upamena bodhitaḥ
mahā|muner āgata|bodhi|niścayo
  jagāda Kālo bhujag'|ôttamaḥ stutim:

«yathā, mune, tvac|caraṇ'|âvapīḍitā
  muhur muhur niṣṭanat' îva medinī
yathā ca te rājati sūryavat prabhā
  dhruvaṃ tvam iṣṭaṃ phalam adya bhokṣyase.

His body along with his fame
having reached complete amplitude,
the sage in his single person
bore the stability and charm
of the ocean and the moon.

The five mendicants left him,
thinking he had relapsed,
as the five elements leave
the wise and released soul.

Then, with resolve as his companion, 12.115
resolving to attain Awakening,
he repaired to the foot of a bo-tree,
under which the ground was covered with grass.

At that time, then, Kala, the best of snakes,
with the valor of the elephant king,
awakened by the unrivaled sound of his feet,
knowing the sage's resolve to be awakened,
uttered this eulogy:

"As, O sage, the earth thunders again and again
at the pounding of your feet;
As your radiance, likewise, shines forth like the sun,
so surely you will enjoy
the result you wish today.

yathā bhramantyo divi cāṣa|paṅktayaḥ
pradakṣiṇaṃ tvāṃ, kamal'|âkṣa, kurvate,
yathā ca saumyā divi vānti vāyavas
tvam adya Buddho niyataṃ bhaviṣyasi.»

tato bhujaṅga|pravareṇa saṃstutas
tṛṇāny upādāya śucīni lāvakāt
kṛta|pratijño niṣasāda bodhaye
mahā|taror mūlam upāśritaḥ śuceḥ.

12.120 tataḥ sa paryaṅkam a|kampyam uttamaṃ
babandha supt'|ôraga|bhoga|piṇḍitam
«bhinadmi tāvad bhuvi n' âitad āsanaṃ
na yāmi yāvat kṛta|kṛtyatām» iti.

tato yayur mudam a|tulāṃ div'|âukaso
vavāśire na mṛga|gaṇāḥ na pakṣiṇaḥ
na sasvanur vana|taravo 'nil'|āhatāḥ
kṛt'|āsane bhagavati niścit'|ātmani.

iti Buddhacarite mahā|kāvye 'rāḍa|darśano nāma
dvādaśaḥ sargaḥ.

As the row of blue jays fluttering in the sky
  are flying around you, O lotus-eyed one,
  keeping you to their right,
As the gentle breezes are blowing in the sky,
  so surely you will become
  an Awakened One, today."

Praised in this manner by that best of snakes,
from a reaper he then obtained some grass,
repaired to the foot of that great pure tree,
and sat down with the vow
to become awakened.

Then, he took up the posture with folded legs, 12.120
supreme, unshakable, drawn together
like the coils of a sleeping snake, thinking:

"I'll not break this posture on earth
  until I have fulfilled my task."

Then, heavenly beings felt unparalleled joy,
the birds and the throngs of beasts made no noise,
the forest trees did not rustle
though shaken by the wind,
  when the Lord took up his posture
  firm in his resolve.

Thus ends the twelfth canto named "The Meeting with Aráda"
of the great poem "Life of the Buddha."

CANTO 13
VICTORY OVER MARA

13.1 TASMIN VIMOKṢĀYA kṛta|pratijñe
rāja'|ṛṣi|vaṃśa|prabhave maha"|ṛṣau
tatr' ôpaviṣṭe prajaharṣa lokas
tatrāsa sad|dharma|ripus tu Māraḥ.

yaṃ Kāma|devaṃ pravandanti loke
citr'|āyudhaṃ puṣpa|śaraṃ tath" âiva,
kāma|pracār'|âdhipatiṃ tam eva
mokṣa|dviṣaṃ Māram udāharanti.

Tasy' ātma|jā Vibhrama|Harṣa|Darpās
tisro 'rati|Prīti|Tṛṣaś ca kanyāḥ
papracchur enaṃ manaso vikāraṃ
sa tāṃś ca tāś c' âiva vaco 'bhyuvāca:

«asau munir niścaya|varma bibhrat
sattv'|āyudhaṃ buddhi|śaraṃ vikṛṣya
jigīṣur āste viṣayān madīyān,
tasmād ayaṃ me manaso viṣādaḥ.

13.5 yadi hy asau mām abhibhūya yāti
lokāya c' ākhyāty apavarga|mārgam,
śūnyas tato 'yaṃ viṣayo mam' âdya
vṛttāc cyutasy' êva Videha|bhartuḥ.

tad yāvad ev' âiṣa na labdha|cakṣur
mad|gocare tiṣṭhati yāvad eva,
yāsyāmi tāvad vratam asya bhettuṃ
setuṃ nadī|vega iv' âti|vṛddhaḥ.»

WHEN THAT GREAT seer, who was born in a line of royal seers, sat down there with the pledge 13.1
to win release, the world rejoiced, and yet
Mara, foe of true dharma, shook with fright.

The one that people in the world call god Kama,
the one with flower arrows and colorful bow,
the one who oversees the working of passions,
that same one they call Mara, the foe of release.

His three sons—Fluster, Thrill, and Pride,
and his three girls—Discontent, Delight, and Thirst,
asked why his mind was so troubled;
he said this to his boys and girls:

"That sage wearing the armor of resolve,
drawing the bow of courage
with the arrow of insight,
Sits there desiring to conquer my realms;
that's why my mind is despondent.

For, if he succeeds in vanquishing me, 13.5
proclaims to the world the path to release,
Then today this my realm will be empty,
like that of the Vidéha king
when he strayed from the correct path.*

So, while he has not yet obtained insight,
while he still remains within my domain,
I will proceed there to break up his vow,
as a river's swollen current a dike."

tato dhanuḥ puṣpa|mayaṃ gṛhītvā
  śarān jagan|moha|karāṃś ca pañca
so 'śvattha|mūlaṃ sa|suto 'bhyagacchad
  a|svāsthya|kārī manasaḥ prajānām.

atha praśāntaṃ munim āsana|sthaṃ
  pāraṃ titīrṣuṃ bhava|sāgarasya
viṣajya savyaṃ karam āyudh'|âgre
  krīḍan śareṇ' êdam uvāca Māraḥ:

«uttiṣṭha, bhoḥ kṣatriya, mṛtyu|bhīta!
  cara sva|dharmaṃ, tyaja mokṣa|dharmam;
bāṇaiś ca yajñaiś ca vinīya lokaṃ
  lokāt padaṃ prāpnuhi Vāsavasya.

13.10 panthā hi niryātum ayaṃ yaśasyo
  yo vāhitaḥ pūrvatamair nar'|êndraiḥ;
jātasya rāja'|rṣi|kule viśāle
  bhaikṣākam a|ślāghyam idaṃ prapattum.

ath' âdya n' ôttiṣṭhasi, niścit'|ātman,
  bhava sthiro, mā vimucaḥ pratijñām!
may" ôdyato hy eṣa śaraḥ sa eva
  yaḥ Śūrpake mīna|ripau vimuktaḥ.

spṛṣṭaḥ sa c' ânena kathaṃ cid Aiḍaḥ
  Somasya napt" âpy abhavad vicittaḥ,
sa c' âbhavac Chantanur a|svatantraḥ;
  kṣīṇe yuge kiṃ bata dur|balo 'nyaḥ?

Then, taking up his bow made of flowers
and the five arrows that delude the world,
the one who troubles the minds of people
went to the foot of the bo-tree
accompanied by his children.

Then, placing his left hand on the bow tip
and fondling an arrow, Mara said
to the sage seated calm and motionless,
seeking to cross the ocean of existence:

"Rise up, O Warrior, afraid of death!
Follow the dharma that's your own,
abandon the dharma of release;
By subduing the world with arrows and rites,
from this world you will attain Indra's realm.

For to travel along this path brings fame, 13.10
a path traversed by the most ancient kings;
Begging brings ignominy to one born
in a great lineage of royal seers.

Or if you, resolute man, won't rise up today,
remain steadfast, do not recant your pledge!
For I have raised this, the same arrow that I hurled
at Shúrpaka, the enemy of fish!*

Scarcely grazed by it,
Aida went out of his mind,
although he was Moon's grandson;
and Shántanu lost his self-will;*
How much more some feeble man,
in this most decadent age?

tat kṣipram uttiṣṭha, labhasva saṃjñāṃ!
  bāṇo hy ayaṃ tiṣṭhati lelihānaḥ.
priyā|vidheyeṣu rati|priyeṣu
  yaṃ cakravākeṣv iva n' ôtsṛjāmi.»

ity evam|ukto 'pi yadā nir|āstho
  n' âiv' āsanaṃ Śākya|munir bibheda,
śaraṃ tato 'smai visasarja Māraḥ
  kanyāś ca kṛtvā purataḥ sutāṃś ca.

13.15 tasmiṃs tu bāṇe 'pi sa vipramukte
  cakāra n' āsthāṃ na dhṛteś cacāla;
dṛṣṭvā tath" âinaṃ viṣasāda Māraś
  cintā|parītaś ca śanair jagāda:

«Śail'|êndra|putrīṃ prati yena viddho
  devo 'pi Śambhuś calito babhūva,
na cintayaty eṣa tam eva bāṇaṃ!
  kiṃ syād a|citto? na śaraḥ sa eṣaḥ?

tasmād ayaṃ n' ârhati puṣpa|bāṇaṃ
  na harṣaṇaṃ n' âpi rater niyogam,
arhaty ayaṃ bhūta|gaṇair a|saumyaiḥ
  saṃtrāsan'|ātarjana|tāḍanāni.»

So, rise up quick and come to your senses,
for this arrow is set, licking its chops!
I won't shoot men servile to their lovers
and delighting in sexual pleasures,
as I won't shoot at *chakra·vaka* ducks."

When the sage of the Shakyas paid no heed
and did not even give up his posture,
even after he was so admonished,
Mara then discharged the arrow at him,
placing his sons and girls in front of him.

But even after he shot the arrow at him, 13.15
he paid no heed and did not veer from his resolve;
seeing him thus, Mara was despondent,
and, filled with anxiety, he spoke softly:

"Shambhu, although a god, was stirred with love
for the daughter of the mountain
when struck with this arrow;*
Yet this one takes no notice of that same arrow!
Has he no heart?
Or is this not the same arrow?

He's not a suitable object, therefore,
for the flower-arrow, for arousal,
or even to rouse erotic passion;
He's only fit to be frightened, threatened,
and beaten up by the fierce throngs of fiends."

sasmāra Māraś ca tataḥ sva|sainyaṃ
vighnaṃ śame Śākya|muneś cikīrṣan,
nān"|āśrayāś c' ânucarāḥ parīyuḥ
śala|druma|prāsa|gād'|âsi|hastāḥ—

varāha|mīn'|âśva|khar'|ôṣṭra|vaktrā,
vyāghra'|rkṣa|siṃha|dvirad'|ânanāś ca,
ek'|êkṣaṇā n'|âika|mukhās tri|śīrṣā,
lamb'|ôdarāś c' âiva pṛṣ'|ôdarāś ca;

13.20 a|jānu|sakthā, ghaṭa|jānavaś ca,
daṃṣṭr'|āyudhāś c' âiva, nakh'|âyudhāś ca,
karaṅka|vaktrā, bahu|mūrtayaś ca,
bhagn'|ârdha|vaktrāś ca, mahā|mukhāś ca;

bhasm'|âruṇā, lohita|bindu|citrāḥ,
khaṭvāṅga|hastā, hari|dhūmra|keśāḥ,
lamba|srajo, vāraṇa|lamba|karṇāś,
carm'|âmbarāś c' âiva, nir|ambarāś ca;

No sooner, then, had Mara thought of his army,
wishing to hinder the calm of the Shakya sage,
than his cohorts in diverse forms gathered round him,
carrying in their hands spears, trees, javelins, clubs,
and swords—

some with faces of boars, fish, horses, donkeys,
and camels,
some with the guise of tigers, bears, lions,
and elephants,
some with one eye, some with many mouths,
some with three heads,
some with enormous stomachs,
some with spotted bellies;

some without knees, some without thighs, 13.20
some with knees the size of pots,
some armed with tusks, some armed with talons,
some with skulls as faces, some with many bodies,
some with half their faces torn off,
some with colossal mouths;

some having the color of ash,
some with blood-red spots,
some carrying ascetic staves with skulls at the top,
some with hair smoke-colored like a monkey's,
some with hanging garlands,
some with ears as big as an elephant's,
some wearing animal skins, some completely naked;

śvet'|ârdha|vaktrā, harit'|ârdha|kāyās,
tāmrāś ca, dhūmrā, harayo, 'sitāś ca,
vyāl'|ôttar'|āsaṅga|bhujās tath" âiva,
praghuṣṭa|ghaṇṭ"|ākula|mekhalāś ca;

tāla|pramāṇāś ca gṛhīta|śūlā,
daṃṣṭrā|karālāś ca śiśu|pramāṇāḥ,
urabhra|vaktrāś ca vihaṃgam'|âkṣā,
mārjāra|vaktrāś ca manuṣya|kāyāḥ;

prakīrṇa|keśāḥ, śikhino, 'rdha|muṇḍā,
rakt'|âmbarā, vyākula|veṣṭanāś ca,
prahṛṣṭa|vaktrā, bhṛkuṭī|mukhāś ca,
tejo|harāś c' âiva, mano|harāś ca.

13.25 ke cid vrajanto bhṛśam āvavalgur,
anyo|'nyam āpupluvire tath" ânye,
cikrīḍur ākāśa|gatāś ca ke cit,
ke cic ca cerus taru|mastakeṣu;

nanarta kaś cid bhramayaṃs tri|śūlaṃ,
kaś cid vipusphūrja gadāṃ vikarṣan,
harṣeṇa kaś cid vṛṣavan nanarda,
kaś cit prajajvāla tanū|ruhebhyaḥ.

evaṃ|vidhā bhūta|gaṇāḥ samantāt
tad bodhi|mūlaṃ parivārya tasthuḥ
jighṛkṣavaś c' âiva jighāṃsavaś ca
bhartur niyogaṃ paripālayantaḥ.

some with half their faces white,
some with half their bodies green,
some copper-colored, some smoke-colored,
some tawny, some black,
some wearing snakes as their upper garments,
some with clanging bells hanging from their girdles;

some as tall as palmyra trees and carrying spears,
some the size of children with protruding fangs,
some with faces of sheep and the eyes of birds,
some with faces of cats and the bodies of men;

some with disheveled hair, some wearing topknots,
some with half-shaven heads,
some wearing red clothes,
some with their turbans in disarray,
some with excited faces, some with frowning faces,
some draining the energy, some drawing the mind;

some leapt wildly as they dashed around, 13.25
some jumped upon one another,
some frolicked rising up into the sky,
some hopped across the tree tops;

one danced, brandishing a trident,
one roared, dragging a club,
one bellowed with joy, like a bull,
one blazed fire from every hair.

Throngs of fiends of these kinds stood encircling
the foot of that bo-tree on every side,
eager to seize and eager to kill,
awaiting their master's orders.

tam preksya Mārasya ca pūrva|rātre
Śākya'|rṣabhasy' âiva ca yuddha|kālam—
na dyauś cakāśe, pṛthivī cakampe,
prajajvaluś c' âiva diśaḥ sa|śabdāḥ;
viṣvag vavau vāyur udīrṇa|vegas,
tārā na rejur, na babhau śaś'|âṅkaḥ,
tamaś ca bhūyo vitatāna rātriḥ,
sarve ca saṃcukṣubhire samudrāḥ.

13.30 mahībhṛto dharma|parāś ca nāgā
mahā|muner vighnam a|mṛṣyamāṇāḥ
Māraṃ prati krodha|vivṛtta|netrā
niḥśaśvasuś c' âiva, jajṛmbhire ca.

śuddh'|âdhivāsā vibudha'|rṣayas tu
sad|dharma|siddhy|artham abhipravṛttāḥ
Māre 'nukampāṃ manasā pracakrur
virāga|bhāvāt tu na roṣam īyuḥ.

tad bodhi|mūlaṃ samavekṣya kīrṇaṃ
hiṃs"|ātmanā Māra|balena tena
dharm'|ātmabhir loka|vimokṣa|kāmair
babhūva hāhā|kṛtam antarīkṣe.

upaplavaṃ dharma|vidhes tu tasya
dṛṣṭvā sthitaṃ Māra|balaṃ maha"|rṣiḥ
na cukṣubhe n' âpi yayau vikāraṃ
madhye gavāṃ siṃha iv' ôpaviṣṭaḥ.

Seeing in the early night the time of battle
raging between Mara and the bull of Shakyas—

the sky lost its glimmer and the earth shook,
the directions blazed forth with a loud sound,
the wind raged wildly in all directions,
stars did not sparkle, the moon did not shine,
the night unfolded a denser darkness,
and all the oceans began to shudder.

The serpents given to dharma who bore the earth, 13.30
unable to bear that hindrance to the great sage,
hissed aloud, and at Mara they unfurled their hoods,
their eyes rolling with anger.

But the divine seers residing in the pure realm,
engaged in gaining success in the true dharma,
displayed compassion toward Mara in their minds,
and, because they were devoid of passion,
did not give way to anger.

Seeing the foot of the bo-tree besieged
by those murderous forces of Mara,
those beings who were devoted to dharma,
and who longed for the release of the world,
cried out "Ha! Ha!" in the sky.

But when the great seer saw Mara's forces
ready to upset the course of dharma,
he neither trembled nor was he perturbed,
like a lion seated among cows.

Māras tato bhūta|camūm udīrṇām
 ājñāpayām āsa bhayāya tasya;
svaiḥ svaiḥ prabhāvair atha s" âsya senā
 tad|dhairya|bhedāya matiṃ cakāra.

13.35 ke cic calan|n'|âika|vilambi|jihvās,
 tīkṣṇ'|âgra|daṃṣṭrā hari|maṇḍal'|âkṣāḥ,
vidārit'|āsyāḥ sthira|śaṅku|karṇāḥ—
 saṃtrāsayantaḥ kila nāma tasthuḥ.

tebhyaḥ sthitebhyaḥ sa tathā|vidhebhyaḥ
 rūpeṇa bhāvena ca dāruṇebhyaḥ
na vivyathe n' ôdvivije maha"|rṣiḥ
 krīḍat|su|bālebhya iv' ôddhatebhyaḥ—

kaś cit tato roṣa|vivṛtta|dṛṣṭis
 tasmai gadām udyamayāṃ cakāra
tastambha bāhuḥ sa|gadas tato 'sya
 Puraṃdarasy' êva purā sa|vajraḥ.

ke cit samudyamya śilās tarūṃś ca
 viṣehire n' âiva munau vimoktum;
petuḥ sa|vṛkṣāḥ sa|śilās tath" âiva
 vajr'|âvabhagnā iva Vindhya|pādāḥ.

Then to his frenzied army of fiends,
Mara gave orders to frighten him;
his troops, then, each with its special power,
set their minds to breaking his resolve.

They stood there trying to frighten him— 13.35

some with multiple tongues
dangling and quivering,
some with sharp and pointed fangs,
some with eyes like the sun's orb,
some with gaping mouths,
some with ears upright like spikes.

As they stood in such guise,
dreadful in form and mien,
the great seer was no more alarmed
or frightened of them
than of little children ebullient as they play—

then, one, his eyes rolling with rage,
lifted up his club at the sage,
but the hand holding the club froze,
like Puran·dara's hand of old
that was holding the bolt.

Some lifted rocks and trees at him,
but could not hurl them at the sage;
they fell down with the trees and rocks,
like the outcrops of the Vindhya
when they're struck by the bolt.*

kaiś cit samutpatya nabho vimuktāḥ
śilāś ca vṛkṣāś ca paraśvadhāś ca
tasthur nabhasy eva na c' âvapetuḥ
saṃdhy"|âbhra|pādā iva n'|âika|varṇāḥ.

13.40 cikṣepa tasy' ôpari dīptam anyaḥ
kaḍaṅgaraṃ parvata|śṛṅga|mātram,
yan|mukta|mātraṃ gagana|stham eva
tasy' ânubhāvāc chata|dhā paphāla.

kaś cij jvalann arka iv' ôditaḥ khād
aṅgāra|varṣaṃ mahad utsasarja
cūrṇāni cāmīkara|kandarāṇāṃ
kalp'|âtyaye Merur iva pradīptaḥ.

tad bodhi|mūle pravikīryamāṇam
aṅgāra|varṣaṃ tu sa|visphuliṅgam
maitrī|vihārād ṛṣi|sattamasya
babhūva rakt'|ôtpala|pattra|varṣaḥ.

śarīra|citta|vyasan'|ātapais tair
evaṃ|vidhais taiś ca nipātyamanaiḥ
n' âiv' āsanāc Chākya|muniś cacāla
sva|niścayaṃ bandhum iv' ôpaguhya.

ath' âpare nirjigilur mukhebhyaḥ
sarpān vijīrṇebhya iva drumebhyaḥ;
te mantra|baddhā iva tat|samīpe
na śaśvasur n' ôtsasṛpur na celuḥ.

Some, leaping up into the sky,
hurled at him rocks, axes, and trees;
but they hung in the sky and did not fall,
like the multi-hued rays of twilight clouds.

Another flung a blazing stack of straw, 13.40
as large as a mountain peak;
but as it was thrown and still in the sky,
it shattered into a hundred pieces
by his miraculous power.

One, blazing like the rising sun, released
a great shower of burning coals from the sky,
like mount Meru ablaze at eon's end
showering lava fragments from golden rifts.

But that shower of burning coals with flying sparks,
sprinkling around the foot of the bo-tree,
became a shower of red lotus petals
by the universal benevolence
practiced by that foremost of seers.

While he was assaulted with these tribulations
and torture of body and mind of various kinds,
the Shakya sage did not waver from his posture,
guarding his resolve as if it were a kinsman.

Still others, then, disgorged snakes
from their mouths
as if from rotten tree trunks;
but in his presence those snakes did not hiss,
they did not raise their heads or move about,
as if tied down by a spell.

13.45 bhūtv" âpare vāri|dharā bṛhantaḥ
sa|vidyutaḥ s'|âśani|caṇḍa|ghoṣāḥ
tasmin drume tatyajur aśma|varṣaṃ
tat puṣpa|varṣaṃ ruciraṃ babhūva.

cāpe 'tha bāṇo nihito 'pareṇa
jajvāla tatr' âiva na niṣpapāta,
an|īśvarasy' ātmani dhūyamāno
dur|marṣaṇasy' êva narasya manyuḥ.

pañc'|êṣavo 'nyena tu vipramuktās
tasthur nabhasy eva munau na petuḥ,
saṃsāra|bhīror viṣaya|pravṛttau
pañc'|êndriyāṇ' îva parīkṣakasya.

jighāṃsay" ânyaḥ prasasāra ruṣṭo
gadāṃ gṛhītv" âbhimukho maha"|rṣeḥ;
so '|prāpta|kāmo vi|vaśaḥ papāta
doṣeṣv iv' ân|artha|kareṣu lokaḥ.

strī megha|kālī tu kapāla|hastā
kartuṃ maha"|rṣeḥ kila citta|moham
babhrāma tatr' â|niyataṃ na tasthau
cal'|ātmano buddhir iv' āgameṣu.

13.50 kaś cit pradīptaṃ praṇidhāya cakṣur
netr'|âgnin" āśī|viṣavad didhakṣuḥ;
tatr' âiva n' āsīnam ṛṣiṃ dadarśa
kām'|ātmakaḥ śreya iv' ôpadiṣṭam.

Yet others, transmuted into vast clouds, 13.45
with lightning and fierce sound of thunderbolts,
let loose a shower of stones on that tree;
but it became transformed into
a lovely shower of flowers.

Another fixed an arrow to his bow,
but it flared up there and did not fly off,
like the anger of a poor ill-humored man
igniting within himself.

And five arrows shot by another one
stood still in the sky and did not fall on the sage,
like the five senses before the objects of sense
in a wise man scared of samsaric life.

Another, enraged, rushed at the great sage,
grabbing a club and intending to kill;
but he fell helpless, his aim unattained,
in much the same way as the world descends
into vices that thwart its goals.

A woman, black as a cloud and carrying a skull,
in order to seduce the mind of that great seer,
flitted about there unrestrained and did not halt,
like a fickle man's mind amidst scriptural texts.

One, wishing to burn him with the fire of his eye, 13.50
like a noxious snake, fixed on him his blazing gaze;
but he did not perceive the seer seated right there,
like a man full of passion the ultimate good
that had been clearly pointed out to him.

gurvīṃ śilām udyamayaṃs tath" ânyaḥ
śaśrāma moghaṃ vihata|prayatnaḥ
niḥ|śreyasaṃ jñāna|samādhi|gamyaṃ
kāya|klamair dharmam iv' āptu|kāmaḥ.

tarakṣu|siṃh'|ākṛtayas tath" ânye
praṇedur uccair mahataḥ praṇādān,
sattvāni yaiḥ saṃcukucuḥ samantād
vajr'|āhatā dyauḥ phalat' îti matvā.

mṛgā gajāś c' ārta|ravān sṛjanto
vidudruvuś c' âiva nililyire ca
rātrau ca tasyām ahan' îva digbhyaḥ
khagā ruvantaḥ paripetur ārtāḥ.

teṣāṃ praṇādais tu tathā|vidhais taiḥ
sarveṣu bhūteṣv api kampiteṣu
munir na tatrāsa na saṃcukoca,
ravair Garutmān iva vāyasānām.

13.55 bhay'|āvahebhyaḥ pariṣad|gaṇebhyo
yathā yathā n' âiva munir bibhāya,
tathā tathā dharma|bhṛtāṃ sa|patnaḥ
śokāc ca roṣāc ca sasāda Māraḥ.

bhūtaṃ tataḥ kiṃ cid a|dṛśya|rūpaṃ
viśiṣṭa|bhūtaṃ gagana|stham eva
dṛṣṭva" rṣaye drugdham a|vaira|ruṣṭaṃ
Māraṃ babhāṣe mahatā svareṇa:

Another, likewise, tried to lift a heavy rock,
but he toiled in vain with his efforts frustrated,
like one seeking to win through bodily fatigue
dharma, the ultimate good, that can be attained
only through knowledge and trance.

Others also, in the guise of lions and hyenas,
thunderously roared out deafening roars,
at which animals all around recoiled in fear,
thinking that the sky itself was being split apart
by the strike of a thunderbolt.

Deer and elephants ran helter-skelter,
and hid themselves, howling cries of distress;
during that night, birds flew round in the sky
crying out in distress, as if it were day.

Even though all beings shuddered
at such bellowing of theirs,
the sage trembled not, nor did he recoil,
like Gáruda at the clamor of crows.

The less the sage was fearful of that troop of fiends, 13.55
who were attempting to make him afraid,
the more Mara, foe of those who uphold dharma,
became despondent with sorrow and rage.

Then, a certain being standing in the sky,
high in station, invisible in form,
seeing Mara's malice toward the seer
and his unprovoked animosity,
spoke to him in a loud voice:

«moghaṃ śramaṃ n' ârhasi Māra kartuṃ,
  hiṃsr'|ātmatām utsṛja, gaccha śarma;
n' âiṣa tvayā kampayituṃ hi śakyo
  mahā|girir Merur iv' ânilena.

apy uṣṇa|bhāvaṃ jvalanaḥ prajahyād,
  āpo dravatvaṃ, pṛthivī sthiratvam,
an|eka|kalp'|ācita|puṇya|karmā
  na tv eva jahyād vyavasāyam eṣaḥ.

yo niścayo hy asya, parākramaś ca,
  tejaś ca yad, yā ca dayā prajāsu,
a|prāpya n' ôtthāsyati tattvam eṣa
  tamāṃsy a|hatv" êva sahasra|raśmiḥ.

13.60 kāṣṭhaṃ hi mathnan labhate hut'|âśaṃ,
  bhūmiṃ khanan vindati c' âpi toyam,
nirbandhinaḥ kiṃ cana n' âsty a|sādhyaṃ;
  nyāyena yuktaṃ ca kṛtaṃ ca sarvam.

tal lokam ārtaṃ karuṇāyamāno
  rogeṣu rāg'|ādiṣu vartamānam
mahā|bhiṣaṅ n'|ârhati vighnam eṣa
  jñān'|âuṣadh'|ârthaṃ parikhidyamānaḥ.

"Don't toil in vain, Mara, give up
your murderous intent and go home;
For you can no more shake this man,
than a gust of wind
the great Meru mount.

Fire may well give up its fiery nature,
water its fluidity, earth its stability,
But this man will not give up his resolve,
having piled up merit over countless eons.

For his resolve, valor, and energy,
and his compassion for creatures are such
That he'll not rise without grasping the truth,
as the sun without dispelling the dark.

For one obtains fire by rubbing the wood, 13.60
and one finds water by digging the earth;
There is nothing that is impossible
for the man who is persistent;
Everything can be accomplished,
when it is done the proper way.

In his compassion for this anguished world,
mired in diseases such as passion,
As he toils to find the medicine of knowledge,
it's not proper to hinder this great physician.

hṛte ca loke bahubhiḥ ku|mārgaiḥ
  san|mārgam anvicchati yaḥ śrameṇa,
sa daiśikaḥ kṣobhayituṃ na yuktaṃ
  su|deśikaḥ sārtha iva pranaṣṭe.

sattveṣu naṣṭeṣu mah"|ândha|kāre
  jñāna|pradīpaḥ kriyamāṇa eṣaḥ
āryasya nirvāpayituṃ na sādhu,
  prajvālyamānas tamas' îva dīpaḥ.

dṛṣṭvā ca saṃsāra|maye mah"|âughe
  magnaṃ jagat pāram a|vindamānam
yaś c' êdam uttārayituṃ pravṛttaḥ,
  kaś cintayet tasya tu pāpam āryaḥ?

13.65 kṣamā|śipho dhairya|vigaḍha|mūlaś
  cāritra|puṣpaḥ smṛti|buddhi|śākhaḥ
jñāna|drumo dharma|phala|pradātā
  n' ôtpāṭanaṃ hy arhati vardhamānaḥ.

baddhāṃ dṛḍhaiś cetasi moha|pāśair
  yasya prajāṃ mokṣayituṃ manīṣā,
tasmin jighāṃsā tava n' ôpapannā
  śrānte jagad|bandhana|mokṣa|hetoḥ.

When the world is swept along crooked paths,
he toils in search of the right path;
So, it's no more right to harass that guide
than to harass a skilled navigator
while the caravan is lost.

When creatures are lost in the great darkness,
this man is being made a lamp of wisdom;
It's no more right for you, a gentleman,
to extinguish it, than to extinguish
a lamp set up to shine in the darkness.

Seeing the world plunged in the great flood
of samsara
and unable to find the farther shore,
This man is working to ferry that world across;
what gentleman would entertain
wicked thoughts against him?

For it's not proper to cut down 13.65
this flourishing tree of knowledge,
That provides the fruits of dharma,
whose fibers are patience,
whose deep roots are resolve,
whose flowers are good conduct,
And whose boughs are mindfulness and wisdom.

His intent is to free creatures, whose minds
are bound tight by the bonds of delusion;
It behooves you not to seek to kill him
who labors to free the world from its bonds.

bodhāya karmāṇi hi yāny anena
kṛtāni, teṣāṃ niyato 'dya kālaḥ;
sthāne tath" âsminn upaviṣṭa eṣa
yath" âiva pūrve munayas, tath" âiva.

eṣā hi nābhir vasudhā|talasya
kṛtsnena yuktā parameṇa dhāmnā;
bhūmer ato 'nyo 'sti hi na pradeśo
vegaṃ samādher viṣaheta yo 'sya.

tan mā kṛthāḥ śokam, upehi śāntiṃ,
mā bhūn mahimnā tava Māra mānaḥ;
viśrambhituṃ na kṣamam a|dhruvā śrīś,
cale pade vismayam abhyupaiṣi.»

13.70 tataḥ sa saṃśrutya ca tasya tad vaco
mahā|muneḥ prekṣya ca niṣ|prakampatām
jagāma Māro vimano hat'|ôdyamaḥ
śarair jagac cetasi yair vihanyate.

gata|praharṣā viphalī|kṛta|śramā
praviddha|pāṣāṇa|kaḍaṅgara|drumā
diśaḥ pradudrāva tato 'sya sā camūr
hat'|āśray" êva dviṣatā dviṣac|camūḥ.

For today is the time when the deeds he has done
to obtain Awakening will bear fruit;
At this spot he remains in this manner seated,
in the same way as sages of the past.

For this is the navel of th' earth's surface,
filled with the highest force in its fullness;
There is no other place on earth, therefore,
that can bear the intensity of trance.

So, do not be sad, calm yourself, Mara,
do not become proud because of your might;
Sovereign power is fickle, don't trust in it;
you are puffed up as your base is reeling."

After he listened to those words of his, 13.70
and saw that the great sage couldn't be shaken,
then Mara went away broken-hearted,
his efforts struck down by the same arrows
with which the world is smitten in the heart.

Then his troops fled in every direction,
their euphoria gone, their toil made fruitless,
the rocks, logs, and trees all scattered around,
like enemy troops when their enemy
has killed their chief.

dravati sa|paripakṣe nirjite puṣpa|ketau
jayati jita|tamaske nīrajaske maha"|rṣau
yuvatir iva sahāsā dyauś cakāśe sa|candrā
surabhi ca jala|garbham puṣpa|varṣam papāta.

iti Buddhacarite mahā|kāvye 'śva|ghoṣa|kṛte Māra|vijayo nāma trayodaśaḥ sargaḥ.

As the flower-bannered one fled defeated
along with his cohorts,
passion-free, the great seer stood victorious
and dispelling darkness,
the sky sparkled with the moon,
like a girl with a smile,
and a shower of flowers fell
fragrant and water-filled.

Thus ends the thirteenth canto named “Victory over Mara”
of the great poem “Life of the Buddha”
composed by Ashva·ghosha.

CANTO 14
THE AWAKENING

14.1 TATO MĀRA|balaṃ jitvā
dhairyeṇa ca śamena ca
param'|ârthaṃ vijijñāsuḥ
sa dadhyau dhyāna|kovidaḥ.

sarveṣu dhyāna|vidhiṣu
prāpya c' āiśvaryam uttamam
sasmāra prathame yāme
pūrva|janma|paraṃparām.

«amutr' âham ayaṃ nāma,
cyutas tasmād ih' āgataḥ—»
iti janma|sahasrāṇi
sasmār' ânubhavann iva.

smṛtvā janma ca mṛtyuṃ ca
tāsu tās' ûpapattiṣu,
tataḥ sattveṣu kāruṇyaṃ
cakāra karuṇ"|ātmakaḥ:

14.5 «kṛtv" êha sva|jan'|ôtsargaṃ
punar anyatra ca kriyāḥ*
a|trāṇaḥ khalu loko 'yaṃ
paribhramati cakravat.»

ity evaṃ smaratas tasya
babhūva niyat'|ātmanaḥ
kadalī|garbha|niḥsāraḥ
saṃsāra iti niścayaḥ.

THEN, AFTER defeating Mara's army 14.1
by resolve and tranquility,
that expert in trance went into a trance,
seeking to know the highest truth.

After achieving full control
over all the techniques of trance,
he recalled during the first watch
the series of his former births.

"Over there I had this name;
Departing thence I came here—"

in this way he recalled thousands of births,
as if he were living through them again.

After recalling births and deaths
in all the various rebirth states,
that man, full of compassion, then
felt compassion toward all beings:

"Abandoning its kinsmen here, 14.5
going again to another place,*
The world here is without refuge,
and rolls round and round like a wheel."

As that resolute man recalled
thus the past, he became convinced
that samsara had no substance,
like the core of banana trees.

dvitīye tv āgate yāme
so '|dvitīya|parākramaḥ
divyaṃ lebhe paraṃ cakṣuḥ
sarva|cakṣuṣmatāṃ varaḥ.

tatas tena sa divyena
pariśuddhena cakṣuṣā
dadarśa nikhilaṃ lokam
ādarśa iva nir|male.

sattvānāṃ paśyatas tasya
nikṛṣṭ'|ôtkṛṣṭa|karmaṇām
pracyutiṃ c' ôpapattiṃ ca
vavṛdhe karuṇ"|ātmatā—

14.10 «ime duṣkṛta|karmāṇaḥ
prāṇino yānti dur|gatim;
ime 'nye śubha|karmāṇaḥ
pratiṣṭhante tri|piṣṭape.

upapannāḥ pratibhaye
narake bhṛśa|dāruṇe
amī duḥkhair bahu|vidhaiḥ
pīḍyante kṛpaṇaṃ, bata—

pāyyante kvathitaṃ ke cid
agni|varṇam ayo|rasam;
āropyante ruvanto 'nye
niṣṭapta|stambham āyasam;

And when the second watch appeared,
the one whose valor was unmatched,
the best of all who possess sight,
obtained the highest divine sight.

And then with that sight,
spotless and divine,
he saw the entire world,
as if in a stainless looking glass.

As he witnessed the births and deaths
of beings doing base and lofty deeds,
his compassion waxed ever great—

"These living beings who perform evil deeds 14.10
end up in miserable states;
But these others who perform virtuous deeds,
rise up to the triple heaven.

Born in a fearsome hell,
full of dreadful horrors,
The former, alas, are tortured cruelly
with many torments of diverse kinds—

some are made to drink
fiery molten iron;
others are impaled screaming
upon red-hot iron shafts;

pacyante piṣṭavat ke cid
ayas|kumbhīṣv avāṅ|mukhāḥ;
dahyante karuṇaṃ ke cid
dīpteṣv aṅgāra|rāśiṣu;

ke cit tīkṣṇair ayo|daṃṣṭrair
bhakṣyante dāruṇaiḥ śvabhiḥ;
ke cid dhṛṣṭair ayas|tuṇḍair
vāyasair āyasair iva;

14.15 ke cid dāha|pariśrāntāḥ
śīta|cchāy"|âbhikāṅkṣiṇaḥ
asi|pattra|vanaṃ nīlaṃ
baddhā iva viśanty amī;

pāṭyante dāruvat ke cit
kuṭhārair baddha|bāhavaḥ,
duḥkhe 'pi na vipacyante
karmabhir dhārit'|āsavaḥ.

sukhaṃ syād iti yat karma
kṛtaṃ duḥkha|nivṛttaye,
phalaṃ tasy' êdam a|vaśair
duḥkham ev' ôpabhujyate.

sukh'|ârtham a|śubhaṃ kṛtvā
ya ete bhṛśa|duḥkhitāḥ,
āsvādaḥ sa kim eteṣāṃ
karoti sukham aṇv api?

some are cooked, heads hanging down,
like dough in iron cauldrons;
some are cruelly burnt up
in blazing piles of coal;

some are devoured by fierce and horrid dogs
with teeth made of iron;
some are devoured by insolent Iron-beaks,
as if by iron crows;

some, exhausted by the burning, 14.15
yearn for cooling shade;
and like captive men they enter
the dark forest with leaves of swords;*

some, moreover, with their hands bound,
are split up with axes like logs;
even in pain they do not cease,
their lifebreaths sustained by their deeds;

To bring an end to all their pain
they did a deed expecting joy;
Now they experience helplessly
just this pain, which is its result.

Having done evil deeds to obtain joy,
these are now suffering immense torments;
Does that enjoyment bring to them
even a bit of joy today?

hasadbhir yat kṛtaṃ karma
kaluṣaṃ kaluṣ'|ātmabhiḥ,
etat pariṇate kāle
krośadbhir anubhūyate.

14.20 yady evaṃ pāpa|karmāṇaḥ
paśyeyuḥ karmaṇāṃ phalam,
vameyur uṣṇaṃ rudhiraṃ,
marmasv abhihatā iva.

ime 'nye karmabhiś citraiś
citta|vispanda|saṃbhavaiḥ
tiryag|yonau vicitrāyām
upapannās tapasvinaḥ.

māṃsa|tvag|vāla|dant'|ârthaṃ
vairād api madād api
hanyante kṛpaṇaṃ yatra
bandhūnāṃ paśyatām api.

a|śaknuvanto 'py a|vaśāḥ
kṣut|tarṣa|śrama|pīḍitāḥ
go|'śva|bhūtāś ca vāhyante
pratoda|kṣata|mūrtayaḥ.

vāhyante gaja|bhūtāś ca
balīyāṃso 'pi dur|balaiḥ
aṅkuśa|kliṣṭa|mūrdhānas
tāḍitāḥ pāda|pārṣṇibhiḥ.

The vile deeds that vile men
carried out as they laughed,
The same deeds, when the time has come,
those men experience as they weep.

If the evil-doers could only see 14.20
the fruits of their deeds in this way,
They would indeed vomit hot blood,
as if struck in a vital part.

By reason of the diverse deeds they did,
springing from the disturbance of their minds,
These other unfortunate beings are born
in diverse animal wombs.

In those states they are cruelly killed,
even as their kinsmen look on,
For their flesh and skin, fur and tusks,
or from enmity or for thrill.

When they are born as oxen or horses,
they are driven, bodies wounded by goads,
Though they are incapable and helpless,
tormented by hunger, thirst, and fatigue.

And born as elephants they are driven,
although much stronger, by much weaker men,
Heads wounded by ankus hooks,
and beaten by feet and heels.

14.25 satsv apy anyeṣu duḥkheṣu
duḥkhaṃ yatra viśeṣataḥ
paraspara|virodhāc ca
par'|âdhīnatay" âiva ca.

kha|sthāḥ kha|sthair hi bādhyante
jala|sthā jala|cāribhiḥ
sthala|sthāḥ sthala|saṃsthaiś ca
prāpya c' âiv' êtar'|êtaraiḥ.

upapannās tathā c' ême
mātsary'|ākrānta|cetasaḥ
pitṛ|loke nir|āloke
kṛpaṇaṃ bhuñjate phalam.

sūcī|chidr'|ôpama|mukhāḥ
parvat'|ôpama|kukṣayaḥ
kṣut|tarṣa|janitair duḥkhaiḥ
pīḍyante duḥkha|bhāginaḥ.

āśayā samatikrāntā
dhāryamāṇāḥ sva|karmabhiḥ
labhante na hy amī bhoktuṃ
praviddhāny a|śucīny api.

14.30 puruṣo yadi jānīta
mātsaryasy' ēdṛśaṃ phalam
sarvathā Śibi|vad dadyāc
charīr'|âvayavān api.

Though there are other kinds of pain, 14.25
here pain comes in a special way,
From hatred toward each other
and subservience to others.

For those who live in the sky
oppress those living in the sky
Those who live in water too
oppress those living in water
Those who live on land, likewise,
oppress those living on land
As they seize each other.

And when jealousy overwhelms their minds
these are born in the world of the fathers
Deprived of light, and there they experience
their reward in misery.

With mouths as minute as a needle's eye,
with bellies as enormous as mountains,
These unhappy beings are oppressed
with the pains of hunger and thirst.

For, though overcome by hunger,
yet maintained by their former deeds,
They are unable to swallow
even the filth that's thrown away.

If a man perceived that this 14.30
was the fruit of jealousy,
Like Shibi, he would always give away
even the parts of his very body.

ime 'nye naraka|prakhye
  garbha|saṃjñe '|śuci|hrade
upapannā manuṣyeṣu
  duḥkham archanti jantavaḥ.

[- - - »]

These other creatures take their birth
  in the filthy pool called a womb,
A splitting image of hell,
  and endure pain among men.

[. . ."]

SUMMARY OF CANTOS 14–28

IN THE SANSKRIT text of the *Buddhacarita* the last chapters from the the second half of Canto 14 are missing. They are preserved in Chinese and Tibetan translations. I give below a summary of these Cantos based on the English translation of JOHNSTON.

Canto 14: The Awakening (from verse 32)

During the second watch of that night, Siddhártha sees the births and deaths of creatures. He sees before his eyes their births in hell and gives vivid descriptions of the torments endured by people fallen into hell. He sees also their birth in heaven, as also their fall from heaven after the exhaustion of their merits. He describes the sorrow these creatures feel as they are forced to abandon the pleasures of heaven. Having examined all of life, Siddhártha finds nothing that is of substance; everything is as insubstantial and without a core as the heart of a banana tree.

During the third watch, he meditates on the true nature of the world. This leads gradually to the discovery of the causal chain known as Dependent Origination (*pratītya/samutpāda*) that leads to old age, sickness, and death. He sees that finally it is ignorance that is the driving force behind this causal chain, and that the absence of ignorance leads to the cessation of the causes that give rise to suffering. In this meditative trance, he also grasps that there is no permanent center, no self, anywhere in the world.

During the fourth watch of the night, as dawn was breaking, Siddhártha becomes Awakened; he becomes a Buddha.

There follows a description of the marvelous happenings that accompanied this event. The Buddha sits under the tree for seven days and reflects on the fact that there is no human being capable of receiving his message. He decides to remain immobile, but remembering his promise he thinks of those who may be capable of accepting his message. He is encouraged in this by the gods, who want him to preach his new doctrine.

The gods of the four quarters offer him four begging bowls, which the Buddha combines to create a single bowl. A group of merchants passing nearby offer him almsfood. Then he thinks of preaching to his two former teachers, Aráda Kaláma and Údraka Rama·putra; but he realizes that both are dead. He then thinks of his five companions and starts out to Varánasi.

Canto 15: Turning the Wheel of Dharma

The Buddha sets out to Varánasi, and on the way he meets another mendicant. He sees the Buddha so calm and shining and asks the Buddha who his teacher is. The Buddha replies: "I have no teacher. I have obtained Nirvana; I am not the same as others. Know that I am the Self-existent (*svayaṃ|bhū*) with respect to dharma" (tr. JOHNSTON). The Buddha says that he has discovered the dharma and is going to Varánasi to beat the drum of the deathless dharma.

He arrives in Varánasi and goes to the deer park where the five mendicants who had deserted him earlier see him approach. Although they had agreed not to pay him any honor, the Buddha's presence, resplendent like the sun, makes them spontaneously greet him with respect. They ask how the Buddha can achieve the deathless state when he had abandoned the path of ascetic toil. Buddha replies that he has found the middle path between bodily torture that is unprofitable and indulgence in pleasures that leads to ruin.

The Buddha then teaches the law of causality, the eightfold path to liberation, the doctrine of no-soul, and the four noble truths. After this first sermon, which was the first turning of the wheel of dharma, one of the five mendicants, Kaundínya, obtains insight and grasps the Buddha's doctrine. He becomes the first of the Buddha's disciples. Miraculous events occur at this moment, just as at the birth and the Awakening of the Buddha.

Canto 16: Conversions and Expansion of the Group of Disciples

The four other mendicants then become converted, and the Buddha shines in the midst of his first five disciples like the moon surrounded by five stars.

Then a nobleman named Yashas sees women sleeping in disgusting postures; he leaves his house and comes to the Buddha. Answering the Buddha's call, he understands the dharma and becomes an Arhat while he is still wearing the householder's garb. The Buddha says that the mendicant emblem (*liṅga*) is not the cause of liberation. Soon that garb miraculously converts into the robe of a mendicant. The Buddha utters the initiatory words "Come, mendicant," and Yashas becomes a Buddhist monk.

At that time there was a total of sixty disciples, all Arhats. The Buddha tells them that they must have compassion and help others to pass beyond suffering. He tells them to go around the world individually to preach the dharma. He tells them that he himself will go to Gaya to convert the Brahmanical forest hermit Áuruvila Káshyapa and his five hundred disciples.

Arriving at Káshyapa's residence, the Buddha asks for a residence in the hermitage. He is given the fire stall with a fierce snake. The mighty snake hisses fiercely at the Buddha, and the fire of his wrath sets the fire stall alight. The fire, however, does not touch the Buddha's body. Seeing the Buddha in the middle of that conflagration, the snake pays homage to him. The Buddha then takes the snake in his begging bowl, shows it to Káshyapa, and performs many miraculous deeds. Áuruvila Káshyapa and his five hundred disciples become converts. Then Áuruvila's two brothers, Gaya and Nadi, arrive there and are also converted.

On the Gaya·shirsha hill the Buddha delivers a sermon to the Káshyapa brothers and their disciples on fire. The world is consumed by the fire of love and hate; the world is scorched by the fire of sins. Fire is a theme that runs through the Buddha's preaching in this chapter.

Remembering his promise to Shrenya, the king of Mágadha, the Buddha then sets out to Raja·griha. Hearing of his arrival, the king goes on foot to meet him. The Buddha asks Káshyapa to do the preaching here, and Káshyapa's sermon focuses on the giving up of fires, both the ritual fires of the Brahmanical religion and the metaphorical fires of passion. Káshyapa also performs many miracles that astonish the people. When such a great ascetic pays homage to the Buddha, all the people are amazed and begin to have faith in the Buddha. His own sermon dwells on the lack of permanence in anything, the absence of a soul. He preaches the doctrine of causality encapsulated in the formulation of Dependent Origination. Shrenya is converted and becomes a lay disciple.

Canto 17: Initiation of the Major Disciples

King Shrenya then donates the grove Venu·vana to the Buddha. He lives there in the company of celestial beings headed by Brahma.

Then Ashva·jit, a new disciple of the Buddha, enters Raja·griha and encounters Upatíshya, a Kápila ascetic following the Sankhya doctrine. Upatíshya is impressed by the demeanor and calmness of Ashva·jit and asks whether he knows the final truth and who his teacher is. Ashva·jit answers that his teacher is the omniscient descendent of the Ikshváku line. He does not know the doctrine in its entirety because he is still a novice, but he tells that the Buddha has explained the causes of the elements (dharma), their suppression, and the means to achieving their suppression. Upatíshya is then converted to this new doctrine. When he returns he encounters Maudgalyáyana, who is astonished at Upatíshya's transformation. After the explanation of the new doctrine, Maudgalyáyana is also converted, and the two along with their disciples go to see the Buddha in person.

The Buddha sees them coming and announces that they will be his two chief disciples. The two are described as carrying tripods and wearing matted hair. By the power of the Buddha they are miraculously transformed into monks wearing ochre robes.

Then a householder named Káshyapa leaves his wife and family and becomes an ascetic in search of liberation. He comes to the Buddha and is instructed in the new doctrine. He is also converted and becomes Maha·káshyapa. The Buddha shines in the middle of these three great disciples.

Canto 18: Instruction of Anátha·píndada

From Kósala in the north comes a householder named Su·datta. He approaches the Buddha at night, and the Buddha teaches him the doctrine of impermanence and the lack of a permanent core called a soul. The world is empty, and it was not created by someone, such as a Creator God. He expounds the theory of causality and the impossibility of the world having a personal creator. The Buddha also shows the fallacy of the doctrine that posits Nature as the source of creation; a single nature cannot produce the multiplicity of the universe. The world could not have proceeded from some unmanifest source or from Man (*puruṣa*). Nor could it have arisen without a cause, by accident or chance.

Su·datta is convinced by the Buddha's arguments and is converted. He offers the Buddha a dwelling he owns in Shravásti. The Buddha praises giving (*dāna*) and presents a long discourse on the merits of giving.

Su·datta goes to Kósala accompanied by Upatíshya and finds the beautiful grove of Jeta, who, however, does not want to part with it. Su·datta covers the land with wealth and offers that as the purchase price; at this sign of generosity, Jeta is converted and gives the entire grove to the Buddhist community. Su·datta, now named Anátha·píndada, quickly builds a monastery in that grove, now named Jeta·vana.

Canto 19: The Buddha Meets his Father

After vanquishing all the teachers of other doctrines, the Buddha leaves Raja·griha for the city of his father, accompanied by his thousand disciples. The chaplain and minister inform the king about the arrival of his son. The king goes out to meet him, along with the citizens of the capital.

The king is unsure whether to call him "Mendicant" or "Son," and laments that his son has to eat almsfood when he should be ruling the world. The Buddha, knowing his father's mind, performs numerous miracles by flying into the sky and touching the chariot of the sun. He plunges into the earth as if it were water and walks on water as if it were dry land.

The Buddha tells Shuddhódana that he will give what no son has ever given a father. He will explain to him the path to deathlessness. The king is convinced and praises his son for abandoning the kingdom in search of the truth.

Seeing this conversion of the king, many citizens and princes leave their homes to become monks, including Anánda, Nanda, Krímila, Anirúddha, Nanda, Upanánda, and Kuntha·dhana, as well as Deva·datta, who was to become a false teacher and to challenge the Buddha. Udáyin, the chaplain's son, also becomes a monk, as also Upáli, the son of Atri.

After their conversion, the Buddha enters the city of Kápila·vastu. Women begin to eulogize him. They wonder what he will do when he sees his son, Ráhula, whether he will still have a father's affection toward him.

Canto 20: Acceptance of the Jeta·vana Monastery

The Buddha leaves Kápila·vastu and travels to Shravásti, the capital of King Praséna·jit. There he enters the newly constructed monastery at Jeta·vana, and Su·datta presents it to the Buddha. Praséna·jit comes to Jeta·vana to see the Buddha and eulogizes him. The Buddha is pleased and preaches to him the duty to govern the kingdom according to dharma. He then preaches the Buddhist doctrine of impermanence and instructs the king to follow the correct path.

Then leaders of other sects, seeing that the Buddha had converted the king, challenge him to perform magical deeds. He becomes as bright as the sun and vanquishes his opponents. He then converts his mother, who is in heaven, and spends the rainy season in Jeta·vana.

Canto 21: Further Conversions and the Challenge by Deva·datta

Returning from heaven after converting his mother and gods desirous of liberation, he travels around the world preaching and converting numerous people. Among these are King Ajáta·shatru, the mother of Nanda, the brahmin Kuta·datta, and the Sankhya teachers Pañcha·shikha and Ásuri. He also converts various kinds of *yakṣas* and evil beings in various parts of the earth. In Varánasi he converts Katyáyana, the nephew of the sage Ásita. The fame of the Buddha thus spreads wide across the earth.

Deva·datta, however, becomes jealous of the Buddha's fame and instigates a schism within the Buddhist community. Then he rolls down a large rock from the Gridhra·kuta mountain at the Buddha, but the rock splits in two and does not hurt him. Then he lets loose a huge mad elephant who causes widespread carnage in Raja·griha. But when the elephant approaches the Buddha, he kneels down. Ajáta·shatru, the king of Raja·griha, is amazed at this feat, and all the citizens praise the Buddha. Deva·datta is plunged into hell.

Canto 22: Visit by the Courtesan Amra·pali

The Buddha continues with his missionary activities by visiting various towns and villages, including Pátali·putra, where the Mágadha king's minister, Varshakára, had constructed a fort to keep the Líchchavis in check. The Buddha predicts the future glory of this city.

Finally, he arrives in the city of Vaisháli and sets up residence in the grove of the courtesan Amra·pali. Seeing her approach, the Buddha warns his disciples about the dangers women pose to men. He gives a long discourse on the ways in which women tempt men and lead them astray. Women using their wiles entrap men. He instructs his disciples to see women as impermanent and not to be attracted to them. It is better to prick one's eyes with a red-hot iron pin than to look at a woman.

Amra·pali pays homage to the Buddha, who speaks highly of her devotion to the dharma. He says that it is difficult especially for a young woman to give up attachment to sensual pleasures and to pursue dharma. Dependence on others and the pangs of child-birth are the lot of women. Feeling disgust for sensual pleasure, then, Amra·pali abhors the activities of her profession and becomes a convert.

Canto 23: Visit by Líchchavis and Sermon on Discipline

After Amra·pali goes home, the leaders of the Líchchavis visit the Buddha. They come dressed in royal splendor. The Buddha tells them that their devotion to dharma is more splendid than all their fine clothes and jewelry. The land of the Vrijjis is fortunate to have leaders who are devoted to dharma. He praises discipline as the highest virtue. He warns against the dangers of passion, which is stronger than a fire, and of anger.

The Líchchavi leaders ask the Buddha to visit them, but he tells them that he must first visit Amra·pali. She gives him almsfood, and he spends the rainy season at her grove. He then returns to Vaishàli, where Mara again accosts him. He tells the Buddha that when he requested the Buddha to enter Nirvana previously, the Buddha had told him that he had to help people to end suffering before he did so. Mara tells him that now many have been converted, so he should enter Nirvana, namely, that he should die. The Buddha tells him to be patient; he will enter Nirvana in three months.

When the Buddha goes into a trance to fix his remaining days, the earth shakes, firebrands fall from the sky, mountains lose their peaks, and there is thunder and lightning everywhere as if the world was coming to an end.

Canto 24: Compassion for the Líchchavis

When Anánda sees the earthquake, his hair stands on end, and he asks the Buddha the reason for it. The Buddha replies that the reason is that he had fixed his life span; he will die in three months. Anánda is deeply troubled and weeps: the eye of the world is about to close, the lamp that lighted the road is about to be extinguished.

The Buddha comforts him: everything is impermanent, I have taught you the path, the only thing you need is the dharma body I have preached, not my physical body. From now on dharma will be your lamp.

Hearing about the impending death of the Buddha, the Líchchavis come to see him in a hurry. The Buddha preaches the impermanence of all beings, including the gods. All the previous Buddhas have entered Nirvana like lamps whose fuel has been exhausted. He too, likewise, must do the same. Then follows the lament of the Líchchavis.

Canto 25: The Final Journey

The Buddha leaves Vaisháli making that city lose its luster and throwing it into mourning. Out of grief people do not cook or eat; they simply weep. Then follows the lament of Sena·pati Simha at the impending death of the Buddha and an eulogy of him as the rescuer of the world. The Buddha turns around for one last look at Vaisháli and says: "O Vaisháli, I will not see you again!"

The Buddha then reaches a town called Bhoga·nágara. There he tells his followers that after he is gone they must fix their attention on the dharma. Whatever is not found in the Sutras or in the Vínaya is against his principles and should be rejected. He warns them against false views that pretend to be those of the Buddha. All views should be tested against the Sutras and the Vínaya as one tests gold. After these last instructions, the Buddha goes to the town of Papa, where the Mallas honor him.

The Buddha takes his last meal at the house of Chunda. Then he goes to Kushi·nágara and, accompanied by Chunda, crosses the river Irávati and goes to the city park. He then tells Anánda, who was full of grief, to prepare a place for him to lie down between two *śāla* trees; that night he will enter Nirvana. He asks Anánda to tell the Mallas about his impending death. The Buddha gives his final sermon to the Mallas telling them that it is not sufficient merely to look at him; they must practice his dharma. The Mallas then return to Kushi·nágara.

Canto 26: The Maha·parinirvána

Then, an ascetic named Su·bhadra, who was carrying a tripod, the symbol of a Brahmanical ascetic, asks Anánda for permission to see the Buddha. Thinking that he has come to enter into a debate with the Buddha, Anánda tells him that it is not the proper time. But the Buddha sees into the heart of Su·bhadra and tells Anánda to let him in.

The Buddha preaches the Eightfold Path to that brahmin, who understands it and rejects the philosophy of Sankhya that he had followed. He goes into the reasons why the Sankhya tenets cannot bring liberation to anyone. He realizes that the world is caused by desire and that one is liberated by destroying desire. He then becomes awakened and does not want to see the Buddha die. He himself then by his own power enters the final stage, and the Buddha asks his disciples to cremate him; he will be the last disciple of the Buddha.

The Buddha then gives his final instructions to his disciples by telling them that after he is gone they should consider the Pratimóksha, the code of monastic rules, to be their guide. There follows a long discourse on how the monks should conduct themselves. He asks them whether they have any doubts. Anirúddha proclaims that the wind may lose its movement, the sun may become cold, and the moon may become hot, but the four truths discovered by the Buddha will never be proven to be false. They have no doubts. The Buddha then gives his final words to his disciples, telling them that the time for his entering Nirvana has come. He asks them not to grieve.

The Buddha then enters the trances one by one and finally enters Nirvana. At that time the earth shook; a fire without smoke and not fanned by the wind arose in the four quarters; fearsome thunderbolts fell on the earth; the wind blew violently; the moon's light waned; an eerie darkness fell even though the moon was shining in a cloudless sky; rivers ran with boiling water; *śāla* trees nearby bent down and showered beautiful flowers out of season on the Buddha's body; and various other supernatural phenomena occurred. Mara and his cohorts laughed in joy.

Canto 27: Eulogy of Nirvana

Then heavenly being and seers utter eulogies of the Buddha and discourses on the impermanence of all life. Anirúddha, who had overcome passion, then speaks about the Buddha's final Nirvana. The Sage has gone to peace after conquering all his foes. He speaks of all the great acts of the Buddha. He laments for the world that has lost its leader; it is left like the sun without its light.

Then those disciples who had not yet conquered their passions utter loud laments and weep, but those who had become Arhats reflect that it is the nature of the world to pass away.

Then in due course the Mallas hear the news and come there quickly uttering laments of grief. They place the Buddha's body on a bier of ivory inlaid with gold. They take the bier through the city and across the river Hirányavati to a Chaitya called Kúkuta. There they make a pyre with costly aloe and sandalwood. Although set alight, the wood does not burn, because Káshyapa was on his way with the desire to see the body of the Buddha. When he had paid his obeisance, the pyre lights by itself. Although the fire is able to burn the skin, hair, and flesh, it is unable to burn his bones. Placing the bones in jars, the Mallas joyfully take those relics to the city.

Canto 28: The Division of the Relics

The Mallas worship the relics for some days, and then ambassadors from seven kings come there seeking to obtain some of the relics. The Mallas out of pride and devotion do not want to part with the relics and decide to fight the other kings. The armies of the seven kings then lay siege to the town, and the Mallas mobilize the people for battle.

The wise brahmin Drona makes a speech to the kings asking them to give up the fight and to abide by the dharma of the Buddha. They agree and send Drona as their ambassador to the Mallas. He enters the city and tells the Mallas that the kings are not after wealth or territory. They are as much devoted to the Buddha as they and merely want a share of his relics. The highest gift is the gift of dharma; this is what the kings are requesting. The Mallas feel ashamed and tell Drona that they will share the relics.

The Mallas then divide the relics into eight parts, keep one part for themselves, and give the other seven to those kings. The kings take the relics and all erect *stūpa*s over them; at that time there were eight *stūpa*s. The brahmin Drona also takes a jar of relics to his own people, the Písala, and erects a *stūpa* there.

Then five hundred Arhat disciples of the Buddha assemble at Raja·griha to collect the teachings of the Buddha. They agree that it is Anánda who had heard all the sermons and ask him to recite them. Anánda recites them, prefacing each with the words "Thus have I heard" and specifying the time, place, and occasion of each sermon and the person addressed.

In due course Ashóka is born. The Maurya king is faithful to the dharma; from being known as Chandashóka (Ashóka the Fearsome) he came to be known as Ashóka the king of dharma. He takes the relics from seven of the *stūpa*s and constructs eighty thousand majestic *stūpa*s across the land. He does not get the relics from the eighth at Rama·pura, which is guarded by serpents. Without relinquishing household life, Ashóka thus attains the first fruit of the faith. Likewise, anyone who worships the relics of the Buddha with faith will obtain a similar fruit.

This poem, which is in keeping with the Scriptures, was produced for the good and happiness of all people and not to display skill in poetry or learning.

NOTES

Bold *references are to the English text;* ***bold italic*** *references are to the Sanskrit text. An asterisk (*) in the body of the text marks the word or passage being annotated.*

1.10 **Aurva** was the son of Chyávana through his wife Árushi, who was the daughter of Manu. Aurva was born by splitting open the thigh of Árushi: see the *Mahābhārata* (MBh, Critical Edition (CE) 1.60.45. The birth of **Prithu** from the hand of his father Vena is narrated in MBh CE XII.60.105–41. **Mandhátri**, according to the Brahmanical narrative, was born from the side of his father, Yuvanáshva; but according to the Buddhist legend in the *Divyāvadāna* he was born from the head. **Kakshívat** is known as the son of king Kalínga, but no information is available about his birth through the armpit. Perhaps this legend is related to his name, *kakṣa* meaning the armpit.

1.12 For the identification of the Buddha with the sun, see the Introduction, p. xx. The statement in verse 11 that "he gleamed as if he had fallen from heaven" may also refer to this identification. See also the simile in verse 13. The comparison to the "**young sun**," that is, the morning sun, evokes the reddish and golden color of his body. His comparison to the **moon**, that is a constant feature of the poem, makes him participate in the best qualities of the two great lights of heaven (see note to 1.16).

1.14 The **seven seers** are Maríchi, Ángiras, Atri, Pulástya, Vasíshtha, Púlaha, and Kratu, who are the mind-born sons of Brahma. They are identified with the seven stars of the Ursa Major or the Big Dipper. Here he is compared to these seven great seers of Brahmanical mythology, while his first steps are compared to the seven shining points of light in the firmament.

1.16 I take ***candra/marīci*** as a *dvandva* compound, *marīci* referring to the **rays of the sun**. Thus, the simile parallels the hot and cold streams of water that fell on the baby's head. The simile also could refer to the fact that Buddha has connection to both the solar and the lunar royal lineages. JOHNSTON takes the compound as a *tatpuruṣa* "rays of the moon" and translates: "clear as the rays of the moon."

1.20 JOHNSTON argues against taking ***tathāgata*** as the common epithet of the Buddha, because Ashva·ghosha, according to him, does not apply the term to him before his Awakening. However, Ashva·ghosha never uses this expression to mean simply "in this fashion." Further, in verse 19 he says that the serpents had performed the same service to past Buddhas, implicitly calling the present one also a Buddha; even the previous ones were not Buddhas when the serpents performed this service.

Gods of the pure realm (*śuddh'|âdhivāsa*) are a particular class of deities within Buddhist mythology. They constitute the highest group of gods and are charged with announcing the approaching birth of a Buddha.

1.21 The reference may be either to Meru, the great mountain in the middle of the earth around which the sun revolves (see 1.36, 5.43) or to Mandára, the mountain that served as the churning stick (see 6.13; MBh CE I.16–7).

1.26 The sound of the drums here probably refers to thunder. The miraculous nature of this sound is signaled by the statement that it came from a cloudless sky.

1.38 Eyes that are not blinking are viewed as a sign of a god. Thus, for example, in the famous epic story, Damayánti recognizes the gods, who had assumed the form of Nala, by the fact that their eyes did not blink: MBh CE III.54.21–4.

1.41 The tradition that **Brihas·pati** and **Shukra** (also known as Úshanas) were the founders of the science of politics (*artha|śāstra*) is recorded in the MBh CE XII.59. Brihas·pati is viewed in the epics as the priest of the gods, while Shukra is the priest of the demons. The former was the son of Ángiras, and the latter the son of Bhrigu.

1.42 **Sarásvata** was the son of Dadhícha and the river Sarásvati. He was brought up by his mother and learnt the entire Veda from her. The seers who knew the Veda were dispersed during a drought of twelve years. After that they went around the world trying to find the Veda, and one of them encountered Sarásvata reciting the Veda. All the seers then came to Sarásvata and requested him to teach them the Veda (MBh CSL IX.51 = CE IX.50). **Vyasa**, the reputed author of the epic *Mahābhārata*, is the one who divided the Veda into its current sections. **Vasíshtha** was Vyasa's great-grandfather.

1.43 Ashva·ghosha knew **Valmíki**'s authorship of the epic *Rāmāyaṇa*, considered the first verse composition (*padya*); he is viewed as the *ādi/kavi*, the first poet (see JOHNSTON 1984: xlvii–l; HILTEBEITEL 2006: 247–54). His relationship to **Chyávana** is unclear, although Ashva·ghosha appears to make such a connection.

1.43 **Atréya**, according to Cháraka, the author of the earliest extant medical text, the *Carakasaṃhitā* (*Sūtra/sthāna* 1.1–2), was the first to edit the science of medicine from which is derived Cháraka's own version. Atréya was a descendant of **Atri**, one of the seven seers (cf. note to 1.14).

1.44 **Kúshika** was an ancient king, who was the father of Gadhin. The latter's son was the celebrated sage Vishva·mitra, who, although born a kshatriya, was able through his austerities to attain the status of a twice-born, that is, a brahmin. Even though the term *dvija* can refer to the three upper classes of society (*varṇa*), its meaning is often narrowed to just brahmins, and this is the meaning with which the term is regularly used by Ashva·ghosha.

1.44 **Ságara** was a king born in the lineage of **Ikshváku**. When his sacrificial horse was stolen by demons, his 60,000 sons dug the earth and found the horse grazing near the sage Kápila. When accused of stealing the horse, Kápila burnt them all to ashes. Ságara's great grandson, Bhagi·ratha, brought the heavenly river Ganga down to earth and filled the hole dug by his forefathers, thus creating the ocean, which is called Ságara. Although it is unclear what setting boundaries on the ocean means, the reference must be to this episode.

1.45 King **Jánaka** of Vidéha is already celebrated as a wise man in the Upaniṣads. He appears as a teacher of Yoga and Sankhya philosophy in the *Mahābhārata*. The point of the story is that normally brahmins are the teachers; Jánaka inverts this relationship by becoming a teacher of brahmins. Jánaka is connected with several early Sankhya teachers such as Pañcha·shikha and Paráshara. The most famous instance of Jánaka instructing a brahmin is his discourse to Shuka, the son of Vyasa: MBh CE XII.313.

1.49 The identity of **Ásita** is unclear. The most famous sage by that name in Brahmanical mythology is Ásita Dévala. He was a disciple of Vaishampáyana, the reciter of the *Mahābhārata*, and is credited with reciting the epic to the ancestors (MBh CE I.1.64). This identification is supported by the story of the Buddha's birth narrated in the introduction to the Pali *Jātaka*s (I.54), where the seer is identified as Kala-Dévala. Although MALALASEKERA (1937–38: I.208–9) insists on distinguishing Ásita from Ásita Dévala who appears in the *Assalāyana Sutta* of the *Majjhima Nikāya*, there is clearly an overlap between the characters of the two. See DE JONG 1954: 314–5.

1.50 The repeated use of ***brahman*** here is noteworthy. The meaning of the term in this context, however, is not altogether clear, although it probably refers to the Veda.

1.52 **Anti·deva**, also called Ranti·deva, the son of Sánkriti, is renowned for his generosity. The episode of his encounter with Vasíshtha is found in MBh CE XII.226.17, where Anti·deva went to heaven by offering lukewarm water to Vasíshtha. Also in the *Mahābhārata*, in a passage relegated to the Appendices in the Critical Edition (XIII App. 14B, 12–13), Anti·deva went to heaven by giving the welcome water (*arghya*) to Vasíshtha.

1.57 These words could not have been addressed to Ásita but to King Shuddhódana, although he did not actually hear them. Only Ásita did by the power of his Yoga. Otherwise, the *iti* clause should be construed as simply indirect speech: "I heard a divine voice saying that a son is born to you for Awakening." But given the reference to Ásita hearing these words in the very next verse, it appears likely that these were the exact words he heard.

1.60 The bodily characteristics noted here are part of the list of thirty-two marks of a Great Man who will become either a universal monarch or a Buddha. These are already listed in the *Mahāpadāna Suttanta* of the *Dīgha Nikāya*; see THOMAS 1949: 220–1. The last mark listed by Ashva·ghosha is unclear, because of the ambiguity of the term ***vasti***. In the Pali, the expression is *kosohita/vattha/guhyo*, where *vattha/guhyo* simply refers to "what is enclosed by a cloth," i.e., the genitals. It is unclear whether the reference in either case is to the penis or the testicles. The reading in the *Lalitavistara* (MITRA 1877: 121) is *koś'/ôpagata/vasti/guhyaḥ*. The correspondence to the Pali is noteworthy, and I think *vasti* in Ashva·ghosha stands for *vasti/guhya*, probably a wrong back-formation from Pali into Sanskrit (the correct one should be *vastra/guhya*). JOHNSTON takes *vasti* as testicles, and I think he may be right, even though the term *vasti/guhya* has a more general meaning of genitals. The comparison with an elephant is also found in the Pali. An elephant's testicles are within the abdomen and, therefore, do not hang down. If the expression refers to the penis, then the meaning would be that the penis is enclosed in a sheath of skin; an elephant can extend the penis out of this sheath when urinating. I have used "**genitals**" to maintain the ambiguity of the original.

1.61 The son of Agni, the fire god, is probably Skanda, also known as Subrahmánya. Agni carried the seed that Shiva had deposited on earth, which the earth was unable to bear. Agni then deposited it in Ganga, and she in turn deposited the fetus in the Údaya mountain where the sun rises. When the child was born, the six divine mothers called Kríttika nursed him. The simile here may refer either to these Kríttikas (then the translation would be "on the lap of the goddesses") or to Ganga, or even to Párvati, the wife of Shiva. For an analysis of Skanda's birth, see O'FLAHERTY 1981: 93–110.

1.64 **Time** here refers to the destructive aspect of time, and thus it is an epithet of Death personified. The reference here is to the fact that a son is born to offer food and water to his ancestors. If the child dies prematurely, then it is as if Death has drunk up that ancestral water. See the similar use of "time" in verse 1.68.

1.81 There appears to be an abrupt transition here to a discourse by an unidentified person who has not been introduced in Ashva·ghosha's narrative. He is simply called "**that holy** (or good) **man**" (*sa sādhuḥ*). JOHNSTON does not note this problem. COWELL identifies the person as Nara·datta on the basis of the *Lalitavistara* (MITRA 1877: 123). But in that narrative, Nara·datta is the nephew of Ásita and returns with Ásita to his hermitage after visiting the Buddha. Further, Nara·datta has no speaking role in the *Lalitavistara*. If we are to follow Ashva·ghosha, this individual is only identified as the maternal uncle of Shuddhódana.

1.83 After the birth of a child, the members of the immediate family are considered impure for ten days. During this period they cannot perform ritual activities.

1.84 See the parallel at *Bṛhadāraṇyakopaniṣad* 3.1.1, where King Jánaka gives one thousand cows, to each of whose horns are tied ten pieces of gold.

1.89 The **wealth-giving god** is Kubéra.

2.1 The comparison here is between the growing prosperity of the king in terms of money, elephants, horses, and allies, and the four major tributaries of the river Indus. They are probably Jhelum, Chenab, Ravi, and Sutlej.

2.6 Ancient Indian political science (*artha/śāstra*) envisaged the political geography of a kingdom as consisting of several concentric circles. This is called the *maṇḍala* (circle) theory, where the states contiguous to a particular kingdom are its natural enemies, the states beyond the immediate circles are that kingdom's natural allies, while some within this expanding circle would be deemed neutrals. His son's power left Shuddhódana without any enemies; all other kings became his allies or, at worst, remained neutral.

2.8 The Sanskrit here is not altogether clear. I take ***tā eva*** (a problematic expression) as referring to the **medicinal herbs** commonly found in the kingdom. Those same plants now became more potent in curing sicknesses.

2.10 The expression **those who have taken the vow** (*vratin*) probably refers to those who are in religious orders of life, such as Vedic students and mendicant ascetics, who are required to beg their food.

2.14 We have here a clear reference to the triple set (*tri/varga*), the goals a human being should pursue: pleasure (*kāma*), wealth (*artha*), and religious/moral acts (*dharma*). Here, **dharma** refers specifically to ritual sacrifices that often involved the immolation of an animal. In Shuddhódana's realm, however, people are depicted as pursuing dharma without causing injury to living beings.

2.36 This **constellation** is probably Pushya presided over by Brihas·pati, who is regarded as the son of Ángiras (hence called Ángirasa). The astronomical text *Bṛhatsaṃhitā* of Varáha·míhira (ch. 48) prescribes that the king should take a bath during the full moon falling within Pushya, considered the most powerful of the constellations, so as to assure the prosperity of his family and subjects.

2.41 This difficult riddle has been variously explained. The "**one**" probably refers to the person of the king; "**seven**" being guarded refer to the seven constituents of a kingdom. They are: king, minister, countryside, fort, treasury, army, and ally (*Arthaśāstra*, 6.1.1). The "**seven**" to be abandoned are the seven vices of a king. The *Arthaśāstra* (8.3.4, 23, 38) lists three springing from anger: verbal abuse, physical assault, and plunder of property; and four springing from passion: hunting, gambling, women, and drink. The "**five**" is somewhat unclear, but probably refers to the policies (*upāya*) of the state in its dealing with other kingdoms. Although the *Arthaśāstra* (7.1.2) gives six, we see five listed in MBh

CE III.149.42: conciliation, giving gifts, fomenting dissension, war, and staying quiet. For the **triple set** he attained, see note to 2.14. The triple set he understood may refer to three kinds of kings: enemy, ally, and neutral. The first **double set** is probably good policy and bad policy, and the second **double set** is probably anger and lust.

2.46 Here we have a play on the name of **Yasho·dhara**, literally, "bearer of fame," with the statement about her **breasts** (*payo/dhara*, "bearer of milk") and the fact that she was actually bearing her own fame and not merely the name. Likewise, **Ráhula**'s face is said to be like the moon, which is the enemy of the demon **Rahu**, whose periodic swallowing of the moon was viewed as causing lunar eclipses.

2.49 The comment about not **casting off his white clothes** refers to the common practice of ascetics to wear dirty or ochre-colored clothes. "White" thus became symbolic of the householder's state. Shuddhódana thus practiced asceticism without giving up home and becoming an ascetic. Sacrifices frequently involved the killing of animals. Here, Shuddhódana is depicted as performing rituals that did not involve animal sacrifice.

2.51 The verses of the **Self-existent** (*Svayaṃ/bhū*) cannot be identified; but the Buddha himself is often referred to as Self-existent by Ashva·ghosha. The **difficult deeds** probably refer either to rites and/or to austerities; the creator god is viewed as having performed difficult austerities (*tapas*) in order to bring out the creatures from his own body.

2.56 Here the term "**bodhisattva**" (literally, "being destined for Awakening," it is the term used for the Buddha before he actually became Awakened) is juxtaposed with the term ***an/upama/sattva***, "one whose *sattva* is unrivaled or incomparable." The term *sattva* in the second example may have a wide range of meanings, including intelligence, goodness, and courage. My use of "**spirit**" is intended to capture this range. See the similar usage at 9.30.

2.56 The **cause** here is probably the mental faculties that would yield Awakening in this life, and this cause had **deep roots** because the future Buddha had gone through numerous lifetimes preparing for this event.

3.7 **Sniffed his son's head**: it is done here in a manner similar to what an animal does to its young. See OLIVELLE 1998: 589.

3.12 For the presence of **humpbacks**, **dwarfs**, and **Kairátakas** in the houses of kings and wealthy persons, see the *Arthaśāstra* 1.21.1.

3.12 The Sanskrit does not make it clear whether the comparison is between the way they bowed and the way flags are carried behind gods in processions, or between the future Buddha and the flags. JOHNSTON opts for the latter and translates "all bowed down as to the flag in the procession of the god." It is more likely that the future Buddha riding down the road is compared to the god being carried in procession, and the people bowing behind him to the flags being waved behind.

3.24 The **flower-bannered god** is Kama, the god of love. In Buddhism he is identified with Mara, the god of death: see below 13.1–2.

3.26 **Gods of the pure realm**: see note to 1.20.

3.26 The term ***prayātuṃ*** is probably used with the meaning of *pravrajati*, "to go forth," which is a technical term to indicate the initial departure of an ascetic from home into a life of homeless wandering. It often refers also to the initiatory rite (*pravrajyā*) an ascetic generally undergoes prior to his assuming the life of an ascetic.

3.61–2 The terms ***pramādyati*** in verse 3.61 and ***pramatta*** in verse 3.62 have a range of meanings, including being heedless or negligent, being intoxicated, being given to inordinate joy. JOHNSTON and COWELL opt for the first meaning. Although that sense is present, I think the reference is to people continuing to be merry while death is threatening, much like a drunken man (second meaning). Note that the future Buddha was on his way to a pleasure garden.

3.62 The term ***sa/cetana*** is used, I think, with a double entendre: a man who is conscious and self-aware, and a man who is intelligent and wise. See the similar use of the term at 4.59. At 4.60

we have the opposite *a/cetana*, a man who is unconscious, and a man who is unintelligent; there I use "senseless" to capture the ambiguity. See the comparison to a tree at 4.61, which does not grieve when another tree is cut down. Here too we can see that the tree lacks self-awareness and sensation. My "**sensible**" attempts to capture this ambiguity.

4.5 The term ***saumyatva*** ("gentleness") is derived from *soma*, a name for the moon. Further, ***dhairya*** ("firmness, fortitude") can also mean steadiness; and this could be an oblique reference to the moon, which, unlike the stars, does not flicker or twinkle but shines with a steady light. These qualities, then, make the women think that he may be the moon himself.

4.8 The term ***praṇaya*** means not just love (so JOHNSTON and COWELL) but in the present context more specifically the **displays of love**, flirtations, and the like that the courtesans were supposed to be engaged in so as to divert the mind of the future Buddha. See 4.101 where the term clearly means displays of love.

4.10 The Kurus were a dynasty of kings of early India to which most of the major kings of ancient India belonged, including those celebrated in the epic *Mahābhārata*. The land of the Kurus, together with that of the Pañchálas, was located in north-central India around the river systems of Yámuna and Ganga. The "**Kurus of the north**" (***uttarān kurūn***) were those living to the north-west of this region, but this land soon came to be imagined as located in the Himalayas. In this idyllic land, people live for thousands of years and miraculous trees providing sweet fruit grow.

4.13 I read ***niyuktānām*** in *pāda* b rather than *viyuktānām* of the edition. The single Nepali manuscript of the Sanskrit text is written in a version of the Bengali script, and in most north Indian scripts the letters "v" and "n" are similar and can be confused. Further, it is difficult to see how the locative ***sva/gocare*** could be syntactically connected with *viyuktānām*, which would normally require an ablative or instrumental. Taken this way, the first half-verse neatly contrasts with the second.

4.15 I have restored the reading of the Sanskrit manuscript (*iti*). It makes perfect sense here, and the emendation of JOHNSTON (*itaḥ*) is unnecessary.

4.16 **Kashi·súndari** may be a reference to the shudra maid of Ámbika, the princess of Kashi. Her maid may also have been from Kashi and may have been called Kashi·súndari ("lovely woman from Kashi"). One trait that emerges in the epic discussion of Vyasa, to whom is ascribed in one way or another most of the major Brahmanical scriptural texts, is that his celibacy is often compromised. The specific episode of Kashi·súndari kicking Vyasa, however, is not recorded elsewhere. On this episode, see HILTEBEITEL 2006: 246.

4.17 JOHNSTON thinks that this verse is spurious. The names and the episode are not known from other sources.

4.18 The story of Gáutama Dirgha·tamas (probably a variant of **Dirgha·tapas**) is found in MBh CE I.98. He was born blind because he was cursed by Brihas·pati while he was still in the womb. He was sent floating down the Ganges in a raft by his sons who did not want to support him in his old age. He was rescued by a king named Balin, who got him to father sons through his wives. The queen was repelled by him and sent her servant woman to have sex with the sage. It is unclear whether the reference here is to this episode or to another story.

4.19 The story of **Rishya·shringa**, a son of a forest hermit who had never seen a woman is narrated in the *Rāmāyaṇa* I.9. He was ensnared by courtesans, brought to the palace of king Roma·pada, and made to marry Shanta, the king's daughter.

4.20 **Vishva·mitra** is one of the most famous seers to whom are ascribed some of the most colorful stories of Indian mythology. **Ghritáchi** is probably the same as Ménaka, who enticed Vishva·mitra while he was engaged in ascetic toil. Their association resulted in the daughter Shakúntala immortalized in Kali·dasa's play. The *Rāmāyaṇa* (IV.34.7) contains a verse which could be the model used by Ashva·ghosha: *Ghṛtācyāṃ kila saṃsakto daśa* *varṣāṇi, Lakṣmaṇa, aho 'manyata dharm'|ātmā Viśvāmitro mahā|muniḥ.* "Enamored of Ghritáchi, they say, the great sage Vishva·mitra, who was devoted to dharma, thought ten years to be a single day, Lákshmana."

4.28 The identity of **Vivásvat** is unclear. The term normally refers to the sun, but he is not usually associated with *apsaras*es or with the **Vibhrája** (or Vaibhrája) **park.** JOHNSTON thinks that here the term may refer to Indra. At 8.78 he is identified as the father of Manu.

4.32 Note the double entendre here. She is asking the prince to make a decorative line (***bhakti***) on her body that is still wet with unguents. But the term *bhakti* can also mean devotion or love; thus she is commanding the prince to be devoted to her.

4.36 The identity of **Padma·shri** is unclear, although the name is applied in Buddhist literature to bodhisattvas, including Avalokitéshvara. It is more likely that the epithet is applied to the goddess of beauty and sovereignty, Shri.

4.39 The Sanskrit here is ambiguous and has been subject to different interpretations. JOHNSTON reads *samāpnotu* and translates "Finish it," with the meaning "Cap that, if you can" or "Improve on my joke." I take the word division as ***sa mā āpnotu***. I think this interpretation fits the context better, especially because in the very next verse we see him running. I think the context is the girls and the prince playing tag and trying to catch each other. But the very ambiguity of the expression may have been deliberate, inviting multiple readings. One can read it to say: "Seize (these earrings)!" or "Seize (me)!"

4.44 Mango blossoms are yellowish in color. The poet here imagines the **mango tree** in bloom as a **golden cage**. See also 4.46.

4.45 **Ashóka tree** (*Jonesia Asoka Roxb.* or *Saraca Indica*) is a tree that occupies a central position in the Indian poetic imagination. The custom of a beautiful young girl touching an *aśoka* tree with her foot to bring it into bloom is mentioned in Sanskrit literature (see Raja·shékhara's *Karpūramañjarī*, 2.43). Meaning literally "without sorrow," it was under an *aśoka* tree that Sita, abducted to Lanka by Rávana, lamented her separation from Rama (*Rāmāyaṇa* V.12). The **fire** probably refers either to the orange-red blossoms of the *aśoka* and/or to its young leaves that are copper colored (see 4.48).

4.46 Mango blossoms are golden in color (see note to 4.44). **Tílaka** (*Clerodendrum phlomoides*) is a medium-sized tree with white flowers. The poet imagines the two gold- and white-flowered trees embracing each other.

4.47 **Kúrubaka** is a variety of *Barleria* with bright red flowers (red Amaranth). Its bright red color is compared to the red nails of the women.

4.48 Here also (see note to 4.45) the copper color of the young leaves of the *aśoka* tree is compared to the red coloring on the hands of the women.

4.49 **Sindu·váraka** (*Vitex negundo*) is a small shrub. The comparison is unclear. If we take the lake as the woman, then the *sinduvārakas* on the bank would be the white clothes. The tree is said to have whitish stems, and this may be the point of comparison.

4.52 The expression ***na tu cintayato '/cintyaṃ*** is ambiguous. JOHNSTON translates: "who reflects on what he should not reflect on." The term *a/cintya*, however, refers probably to what is unthinkable or beyond thought, rather than to something that one should not think about. It suggests that Siddhártha is engaged in a fruitless pursuit.

4.54 The Sanskrit is impersonal: ***martavyam***. It can mean generally "one must die" or more specifically, "I must die." In any case, the reference is to the inevitability of death.

4.59–60 See my note to 3.61–2 on "sensible" and "senseless."

4.65 JOHNSTON's edition reads *parāñ/mukhaḥ*, even though the Sanskrit manuscript reads *parāñ/mukhaṃ*. I have adopted the latter reading, along with COWELL. It also makes better sense to ascribe this adjective to the prince rather than to Udáyin, who is here censuring the prince for turning his back on the **goals of man** (***puruṣ'/ârtha***).

4.71 The Sanskrit is quite unclear, and JOHNSTON expresses doubt about his own translation. He suggests taking the first line as: "Just try accepting them with a feeling that does not go beyond courtesy." But then this verse does not say anything different from the previous one.

4.72 The reference is to the famous episode where Indra became infatuated with **Ahálya**, the wife of the sage Gáutama. Indra takes on the appearance of Gáutama, when the latter is away from home, and has sex with Ahálya.

4.73 The creation of **Lopa·mudra** by **Agástya** and his later marriage to her are narrated in MBh CE III.94–108. The story of Agástya courting **Róhini** cannot be traced, but at MBh CE III.94.24 Lopa·mudra is compared to the star Róhini.

4.74 Brihas·pati's lust for Mámata, the wife of his older brother Utáthya, is narrated in MBh CE I.88.7–18. In this telling of the story, however, Brihas·pati is unable to father a child because Mámata was already with Utáthya's child, whom Brihas·pati curses to be blind; the child thus becomes Dirgha·tamas. However, in other tellings it appears that the son of Mámata is identified with Bharad·vaja (see MANI 1975: 116).

4.75 Chandra (**Moon**) was a pupil of Brihas·pati. Tara, one of Brihas·pati's wives, fell in love with the young Chandra. From their union was born **Budha**, who is identified with the planet Mercury. See MANI 1975: 164, 170.

4.76 **Kali** is also known as Sátyavati. Her birth from a fish is narrated in MBh CE I.57. **Paráshara**'s sexual escapade with Kali is also recorded in MBh CE I.54.2, I.57.69. The son born of this union was the famous Vyasa.

4.77 **Aksha·mala** is also known as Arúndhati. However, some accounts make Arúndhati the wife of Vasíshtha in his first birth, and Aksha·mala (Arúndhati's second birth) his wife in his second birth. There is no information, however, about Aksha·mala being the daughter of an outcaste woman. See MANI 1975: 834–35.

4.78 **Yayáti**'s story of recovering youth in his old age is recounted in MBh CE I.70–80. He indulged in all sorts of pleasures with the help of his new youthfulness. For his dalliance with **Vishváchi**, see MANI 1975: 869.

4.79 **Pandu** shot a deer and a doe as they were copulating. The deer turned out to be a sage named Kíndama, who cursed Pandu to die the next time he had sex. In the narrative as told in MBh CE I.116, Pandu, overcome by lust, had sex with his second wife Madri in spite of the curse and as a result died.

4.80 **Karála·jánaka** is said to be from Vidéha. See *Arthaśāstra* 1.6.5. CHARPENTIER (p. 230) notes that the name Jánaka may have been applied to any king of Vidéha, like Brahma·datta of Benares in the *Jātaka* tales. Karála is mentioned in MBh CE XII.291, where little information is given about him. The *Majjhima Nikāya* (II.82) and *Jātaka* (541) identify Karála·jánaka as the son of Nimi, the king of Míthila. Kalára is said to have brought his royal line to an end.

4.101 **Displays of love**: for the term ***praṇaya***, see note to 4.8.

5.3 For the problems associated with the simile, see the note on this verse by JOHNSTON. The **drumábja** is also known as *karṇikāra* (*Pterospermum acerifolium*), whose fragrant yellow flowers are used for dressing the hair. They were put at the top of a flag pole carried into battle. Sleeping girls at 5.51 are compared to *karṇikāra* branches torn down by an elephant. This may be an allusion to their wearing *karṇikāra* flowers on their hair.

5.10 The meaning of the term ***an/āsrava*** in this context is unclear. JOHNSTON translates: "which is supramundane in quality." The term, I think, refers to the absence of *āśrava*s, the evil inflows which are caused by desire and action and which are tendencies that produce rebirth. See "Handsome Nanda" 16.3, where

Ashva·ghosha also connects the absence of *āśrava*s with stages of meditation.

5.12–3 Johnston translates ***vijugupsate*** as "pay no heed." I think this is mistaken. The reference, I think, is to people who treat a dead man or an old man with contempt.

5.21 Johnston translates ***dharma/saṃjñā*** as "awareness of dharma." I think, however, here *saṃjñā* has the meaning of a sign or emblem; the mendicant garb is the **emblem of dharma**, that is, a sign that the man wearing it is devoted to renunciation. This expression somehow must be a reference to the god who appeared wearing the mendicant garb; this emblem showed the way to release, as a result of which the Buddha decided to leave home.

5.32 On the meaning of ***vikrama*** in Ashva·ghosha, see Olivelle 2007.

5.36 The term ***a/krama*** has the meaning of "in violation of the right order or sequence" (see 5.32, 9.66, 10.23). It can have this meaning here also, but more likely it is used in more general sense of "wayward" or "improper." See the pun here also, with the Buddha's reply (5.37) that "if this is impossible (*krama*)," using the term with a different nuance, and the term *niṣkramiṣuḥ*, "wishing to go out," again from the same verbal root √*kram*.

5.45 The **Lord of Wealth** is Kubéra, and his son is Nala·kúbara (see 1.89).

5.49 The simile appears to be as follows: the **river** is the body/chest, the **foam** is the white dress, the breasts are the **lotuses**, and the **row of bees** is the flute.

5.51 For this simile, see the note to 5.3.

5.52 The simile here is clearly taken from sculpture, probably the gateways around a *stūpa* such as those of Sanchi. There women bent to a side and touching a *śāla* tree are depicted at the very edge of the gateway, as if they were almost about to fall down.

5.53 The simile appears to be as follows: the **lotus** is the face, the **stalk** is the neck, the bird is the earrings. ***Kāraṇḍava*** is probably the common coot, although the term is also applied to any water bird. See DAVE 2005: 298–301.

5.57 JOHNSTON's edition reads *babhuḥ*, which is incorrect. As his note to 5.54 and the edition of COWELL show, the reading should be the negative ***na babhuḥ***.

6.1 The identity of **Bhárgava** (descendant of Bhrigu) here and at 9.2–9.3 is unclear.

6.3 The term ***anuvartitā*** is obscure. JOHNSTON translates it as "politeness." I take it in its literal sense, "follow;" I think the reference might be to the obedience of a pupil to a teacher, whom he follows from behind literally and metaphorically. The Buddha is now a novice and acts in keeping with his subservient status.

6.34 Note the connection in Sanskrit between Yasho·dhara, literally "bearer of fame," and the "**bearer of dharma and fame**" and "highest fame." See also note to 2.46.

6.36 **Sumántra** was the chief minister of Dasha·ratha, the father of Rama (= Rághava, or descendent of Raghu). It was Sumántra who was sent to the forest to bring back Rama; he too returned empty-handed. The journey of the minister to the Buddha is clearly crafted in imitation of the Rama story.

6.37 The meaning of the expression ***ucita|darśitvāt*** is somewhat unclear. JOHNSTON translates: "since I am in the habit of seeing what is proper;" and COWELL: "by way of telling them good news." Given the context of Chanda telling the Buddha what he will be obliged to do after returning to the palace, the expression must refer to the reason why he must talk to the women of the seraglio. Normally they would be out of bounds to men; but, as the groom, he is in the habit of interacting with them. I take *ucita* as "accustomed."

6.49 The first half-verse is difficult. Is the separation from the leaves or from the color of the leaves? The Sanskrit, if read literally, appears to favor the latter. Accordingly, JOHNSTON translates: "Trees are parted from the colouring of their leaves, though it is connate with them." So also COWELL. I prefer to see the simile in the falling of leaves as they discolor and turn brown, although I have been forced to take ***sahajena*** as implying *parṇena*, and the compound ***parṇa/rāgena*** as giving the reason and the timing for the separation of the leaves from the tree.

6.62 The contrast between the clothes of an ascetic, which are ochre, and the white clothes of householders is a constant theme in ascetic literature. For an ascetic, donning white clothes is tantamount to giving up the ascetic life and returning home. The Buddha is constantly equated to the sun and the moon by Ashva·ghosha. See also note to 2.49.

6.65 **The king of stars** is the moon. **Wrapped in twilight clouds**, the moon would look orange in color, thus resembling the Buddha wrapped in his ochre robe.

6.68 Johnston's edition reads *avasa*, and he does not note this in his list of corrections. But I take it to be a typo; both Cowell and Schotsman read *avaśaḥ*.

7.1 **Siddha** refers to a particular class of deities. Given the meaning of the term ("perfected one"), it also refers to the supernatural attainments of these beings. Here, Ashva·ghosha clearly makes a connection between such a deity and the very name of the Buddha, Sarvártha·siddha.

7.3 The purpose of the **yoke poles** is unclear. But other more specific terms of the ascetic vocabulary, such as *khārī/kāja*, *khārī/bhāra*, and *khārī/vidha*, refer to a pole to whose end was attached a bundle containing the ascetic's belongings.

7.5 It is a general belief expressed in poetry that peacocks burst into joyous song at the coming of the rains. Ascetics following the **deer-vow**, that is, imitating the life style of deer by grazing like them, are recorded later by Ashva·ghosha himself at 7.15.

7.7 **Vasus** are a group of eight gods variously identified in different sources. The **Ashvins** are twin gods renowned for their beauty. They are the physicians of the gods.

7.8 **King of gods** is Indra.

7.15 It is a common theme in the epic literature that an ascetic who sits immobile in meditation for long periods of time could become an **anthill**; termites would build their mound around him. The *Mahābhārata* (CE III.122) describes how the sage Chyávana turned into an anthill in that manner. Seeing his eyes beneath the earth, Sukánya did not know what to make of it and pricked the eyes with a thorn.

7.28 If merit comes from the purity of one's food, then the deer should acquire a lot of merit, because they eat only grass, leaves, and berries, which are all pure food. And if simple poverty or lack of wealth is meritorious, then even outcastes and other people normally excluded from religion should acquire merit because they are poor from birth or due to some misfortune.

7.30 Bathing at a **sacred ford** (***tīrtha***) is considered purifying. And **water** used for various kinds of sipping and ablution is also considered similarly purifying. One may also see the use of *tīrtha* as a reference to the parts of the hand also called *tīrtha* used to sip water at various rituals.

7.34 The third line of the Sanskrit text is corrupt and difficult to restore. The translation is tentative. See JOHNSTON's note regarding the alternative readings.

7.41 This appears to anticipate Siddhártha's journey later to the Vindhya mountains in the south to visit the sage Aráda Kaláma.

7.46 Following JOHNSTON's suggestion, I emend the reading *saṃprati* (now, at the present time) to ***taṃ prati*** (with regard to it) in my translation.

7.49 The expression ***pūrva/yuga*** probably refers to the first and golden age in which men were perfect. JOHNSTON takes it as referring more generally to previous times and translates "the primeval ages."

7.54 **Vindhya·koshtha** literally means a cave or similar enclosure in the Vindhya mountain range. It is unclear whether the term has a more specific meaning, referring to a particular place. JOHNSTON poses the question whether the Sankhya system of philosophy was associated with the Vindhya regions; there is also a Sankhya teacher with the name Vindhya·vasin, "resident of Vindhya."

7.55 The compound ***tattva/mārga*** may simply mean "path of truth." But given the Sankhya context, I agree with JOHNSTON that *tattva* here refers to the twenty-five cosmological principles of that system enumerated somewhat unclearly at 12.18–20. It is, of course, unclear what kind of Sankhya was known to Ashva·ghosha; most likely, it was an early form and not the later classical system of the *Sāṃkhyakārikā*.

8.8 **Dásharatha** is the son of Dasha·ratha, namely, Rama. After Rama went into exile in the forest, his chariot returned to the capital empty: *Rāmāyaṇa* II.51. As I have pointed out in the Introduction, it appears that Ashva·ghosha's narrative of the departure of the Buddha, the return of Chanda, and the lamentations in the city and the palace, is modeled after that of Rama in the *Rāmāyaṇa*, although cast within a Buddhist theological and moral background.

8.11 The expression ***phal'/ôttham*** is not altogether clear. If the meaning is that the mind rises from *phala*, as I have taken it, the *phala* must refer to the fruits of former actions that determine the state of one's mind in this life.

8.13 The myth of **Indra** killing **Vritra** is an old one, already recorded in the *Ṛgveda*. Later elaborations of the myth considered Vritra to be a brahmin; his killing resulted in Indra becoming guilty of one of the most serious of sins, the killing of a brahmin. The *Mahābhārata* (CSL V.10.45–46 = CE V.10.43–44) says that Indra ran to the end of the world to hide and dwelt there concealed in the waters.

8.20 **Autumn clouds**, coming after the rainy season, are white. The comparison appears to be to the white palace, the rushing women being compared to the unexpected lightning in a white cloud.

8.36 The comparison probably has many facets. Siddhártha remains steadfast and real like the earth or the Himalayas, but yet unconcerned and withdrawn. He exists, but is of no use. Alternatively, the compound ***himavan/mahī/same*** can also refer to the uplands of the Himalayas where Chanda left him.

8.48 For these episodes see 6.57–6.63 above.

8.77 For this episode, where **Suvárna·nishthívin** is killed by a lightning bolt disguised as a tiger released by the demons Bala and Vritra, see MBh CE XII.31.

8.79 The **son of Aja** is Dasha·ratha, the father of Rama. He dies soon after Rama went into exile. See the note to 8.8.

8.80 The expression *jal'|âñjaliḥ* (handful of water) is a reference to the son who will offer libations to the father when he is dead. See note to 1.64.

8.81 For the lament of Dasha·ratha when Rama went into exile, see *Rāmāyaṇa* II.34.

9.2 For the identity of **Bhárgava**, see the note to 6.1.

9.9 **Vama·deva** was the minister of Dasha·ratha, the father of Rama. The identity of **Aurvashéya** (the son or descendant of Úrvashi) is unclear. JOHNSTON has argued that he is Vasíshtha, the chaplain (*purohita*) of Dasha·ratha; there is early Vedic evidence for Vasíshtha being the son of Úrvashi and Váruna (see *Ṛgveda* 7.33.11), even though this was not part of the Vasíshtha story in the epics.

9.10 **Ángirasa** here is probably Brihas·pati, the teacher of the gods; he is probably viewed here as the chaplain of the king of gods, Indra, paralleling the chaplain of Shuddhódana of the story. If the parallel holds, then Shukra should be the counselor of Indra. Shukra is often depicted as the preceptor of the *asuras*.

9.11 Here the Buddha is compared to the moon. The twin asterism (*nakṣatra*) Punar-Vasu is the seventh in the Indian list. They are the α and β Geminorum.

9.12 **Jayánta** is the son of Indra. I have not been able to identify a story such as the one hinted at here. The simile could simply be based on the assumption that Brihas·pati, Indra's chaplain, would have given fatherly advice to Indra's son.

9.16 The parallel is that the wind grates, i.e., disperses, clouds, sun dries up water, fire burns hay, and a thunderbolt shatters a mountain.

9.18 The **emblem** (*linga*) of an ascetic consists of such things as shaven head, ochre dress, begging bowl, and walking stick. That these are not what brings about liberation is repeatedly stated even in Brahmanical texts (MBh CE XII.308.47–8), with the oft-repeated adage: *na liṅgaṃ dharma/kāraṇam*, "the emblem does not produce dharma."

9.21 There are two difficulties with the Sanskrit text of this verse. First is ***ubhau pi***, which is impossible sandhi. COWELL's manuscripts had *ubhe 'pi*, which may be the result of copyists trying to correct the original. Could the *pi* be the result of a Prakritic influence? Note that *api* is regularly rendered *pi* in Pali. The second difficulty affects the meaning. The Nepali manuscript, the only extant one in Sanskrit, reads *vitt'/ādhipatyaṃ*, but, as JOHNSTON notes, such a meaning ("dominion over wealth") is impossible in the context. The appeal is to the possibility that the Buddha can both rule the kingdom and follow dharma. JOHNSTON takes *vitta* to mean knowledge simply on the basis of its connection to √*vid* "to know." I have opted to go with COWELL's reading found in the copies of the Nepali manuscript he had access to, namely, ***citt'/ādhipatyaṃ***. In northern Indian scripts, the orthography of *ci* and *vi* is very similar. Another possibility is *vṛtt'/ādhipatyaṃ*. The *Mahābhārata* passage cited by JOHNSTON (*dharmam anye vittam anye dhanam īhanti c' âpare*) as given in the Pune Critical Edition (XII, App. 1.4, line 34) actually reads *vṛttam anye*. With that reading the translation would be "dominion over proper conduct." The reading, however, remains doubtful.

9.25 **Bhishma** was the son of Shántanu. Shántanu fell in love with Satya·vati, a fisherman's daughter, who extracted the promise that Satya·vati's son would succeed to the throne. To help his father, Bhishma voluntarily gave up his right to the kingdom. **Rama** also voluntarily went into exile in the forest so his father could redeem his pledge and make his younger son the heir to the throne. **Rama, the son of Bhrigu**, commonly known as Párashu·rama, killed the entire race of kshatriyas to avenge the death of his father.

9.26 Agástya's departure to the southern regions of India is a well-known myth. He is regarded as still dwelling in the south, and thus the south, the region of death, is identified as **Agástya's region**. Not going to Agástya's region means that she had not died yet.

9.28 For the myth of Rahu and its connection to Ráhula, the Buddha's son, see note to 2.46.

9.30 For the play on the words **bodhisattva** and ***paripūrṇa/sattvaḥ***, see note to 2.56.

9.35 The word "**here**" (***iha***) may well refer to the side of the road where the Buddha and the two envoys were talking. **Travelers** would usually have gathered to rest under a tree, just like the Buddha, before each went his own way.

9.36 The trickery here may consist in the relatives thinking that their link to him is permanent.

9.63 **Íshvara** means simply "Lord," but it can have a more specific meaning with reference to Shiva. It is unclear whether in the present context the term refers to Shiva or more generally to the creator god.

9.65 The use of ***mokṣa*** here may be similar to its usage in Manu (see OLIVELLE 2004: note to 1.114), where it means simply renunciation. Thus Manu says at 6.35–7 that a man may set his sights on *mokṣa*, i.e., renunciation, only after he has paid his three debts.

9.66 For the use of the term ***vikrama*** with the meaning of "violating an established sequence or order," see OLIVELLE 2007.

9.69 **Ambarísha** was the son of Mandhátri. Even though we have stories about many of his exploits, there is none that accords with the one hinted at by Ashva·ghosha. The reference in the second story of this verse is probably not to Rama but to Párashu·rama, who rid the world of Árjuna Kartavírya (MANI 1975: 570).

JOHNSTON, I think, is mistaken in translating "surrounded by his subjects;" the verb *√vṛ* here is to choose or request rather than to cover or surround.

9.70 JOHNSTON identifies this **king of Shalvas** with Dyumatséna, who lost his kingdom and went to the forest. But he regained his kingdom through the marriage of his son Sátyavan to Sávitri, the daughter of King Ashva·pati. The persistence of Sávitri saved her husband from death and won back the kingdom for her father-in-law (MBh CSL III.293–299 = CE III.277–283). For **Anti·deva**'s connection to Vasíshtha, see the note to 1.52. The story of his accepting sovereignty from Vasíshtha, however, is not recorded elsewhere.

10.2 The reference is to the city of Raja·griha that has five hills surrounding it, as well as hot springs. The reference of **Svayam·bhu** (the Self-existent One) is unclear (see 2.51). It may refer to the self-existent creator Brahma (see Manu 1.1–7). The Buddha himself is called by that name, but given the simile the reference must be to some other divine person.

10.3 Shiva is the god who has the bull on the banner; he is known by the epithet Sthanu, which can mean a **pillar** or anything or anyone that is immobile. According to the myth as narrated in MBh CE X.17, Brahma asks Shiva to create living beings. But Shiva plunged into water and performed ascetic toil for a long time. His remaining still in this manner appears to have been the reason for his getting the epithet Sthanu. For a detailed discussion, see SHULMAN 1986 and KRAMRISCH 1981: 117–22.

10.17 The **Pándava** mountain is the north-easterly of the five hills around Raja·griha, and the name is a clear reference to the *Mahābhārata* episode where Krishna, Árjuna, and Bhima approach the city across these hills to kill its king, Jara·sandha. For a more complete study of this, see HILTEBEITEL 2006: 257–9. The "**bouncing mane**" may be a comparison to the head-dress of the king that would have a long white cloth streaming behind (see 6.57).

10.19 The expression ***dharmasya nirmāṇam*** is not altogether clear. JOHNSTON translates it as "some being magically projected by Dharma." I follow EDGERTON (1953: 302) in taking *nirmāṇa* more metaphorically as a "projection" and therefore a picture or image of dharma. For Svayam·bhu, see note to 10.2.

10.20 According to Manu 2.127, the polite way to greet a kshatriya is to **ask about his health** (*an/āmaya*). Ashva·ghosha is following this custom in his composition.

10.22 The **friendship** (***prīti***) alluded to here probably refers to a hereditary alliance that the two royal houses had forged.

10.23 On the meaning of *krama* and its opposite *vikrama*, see note to 9.66.

10.39 The last half of the verse is problematic with the repetition of ***nāka/pṛṣṭham***. If both mean the same thing, then it is tautological. The Chinese translation appears to read the first one as *nāga/pṛṣṭham* (the back of the serpent), and if this was correct then we could take *adhiṣṭhāya hi nāga/pṛṣṭham* as "mounting the back of the serpent," i.e., killing the serpent. Then the translation would be: "For having killed the serpent, even Marútvat attained the crest of heaven by means of sacrifices."

11.2 For the difficulties in the reading of this verse, see JOHNSTON's note to it. **Haryánka** (or Haryánga) is a Brihad·ratha king, said to have been the founder of the dynasty of Raja·griha.

11.14 For the sin incurred by Indra when he killed Vritra, see note to 8.13. It is unclear which story of **Náhusha** the verse alludes to. Náhusha, however, was elected to replace Indra when he hid himself after killing Vritra; but he was not satisfied with this and craved for Indra's wife. As a result he was cursed to become a snake on earth, regaining his original form only after seeing the Pándavas.

11.15 For **Aida**, see the note to 13.12. His downfall came when he stole the property of some brahmins.

11.16 On the divine kingship going from Indra to Náhusha, see note to 11.14. **Bali** was the leader of the *asuras*, the enemies of the gods. He was anointed as Indra, the king of gods, by Shukra (see note to 1.41). It was after his defeat by Vishnu that Indra was able to resume the role of king (Mani 1975: 103). Note that in this verse Ashva·ghosha cleverly uses the two meanings of ***viṣaya***, object of sense and realm/kingdom.

11.18 The killing of **Ugráyudha** by Bhishma is mentioned in MBh CE XII.27.10. The story is laid out in greater detail in the *Harivaṃśa* 15.30ff.

11.31–32 The destruction of the **Kurus** was the result of the *Mahābhārata* war in which the Pándavas were victorious. The **Vrishni-Ándhakas** are mentioned frequently in the epic as an allied group. Not much is known about the **Mékhala** (or Mékala) or the **Dándakas**. As Johnston observes, it may well be that these groups of peoples are associated with the four vices arising from lust: dice, drink, hunting, and women. The Kurus are associated with dice, the Vrishni-Ándhakas probably with drink, and the Mékhala-Dándakas with hunting. The two demon brothers, **Sunda and Upasúnda**, are then associated with lust for women. The story is that both fell in love with the same woman, Tilóttama; in the ensuing fight both were killed. On the early kings coming to ruin because of their lack of discipline, see also Manu 7.40–2.

11.70 For details of this enigmatic verse and the many meanings of the verb ***ava***, see Johnston's note to it.

11.71 **The enemy of cold** is both fire and the sun. **Fire** is called "twice-born" in the Vedas, probably because of his birth in heaven as the sun and on earth as fire. Water comes from **clouds** that are formed by **smoke** produced by fire; and when water encounters its cause, fire, it makes the fire leave its visible form and return to its latent form. Likewise, the king should kill the **darkness** that is the enemy of the sun, which, like fire, is also the enemy of the cold. Then, like the fire, the mind goes back into a latent state.

12.17–20 We are dealing here with a very ancient form of Sankhya philosophy. **Primal nature** (***Prakṛti***) is the material principle of all material entities, and **Transformation** (***Vikāra***) is the evolutionary process whereby material entities are evolved from Primal nature. In early Sankhya *prakṛti* is viewed as consisting of eight (see verse 18) and *vikāra* as consisting of sixteen (see verse 19), thus constituting the twenty-four material principles of the cosmos. "**Being**" here probably means the totality of material reality as opposed to the Spiritual being called "**Knower of the field**," field being the "knowable" reality, which is material.

12.21 **Kápila** is considered the founder of the Sankhya system. Here he and his pupils are identified with the spiritual principle of the cosmos, whereas **Praja·pati**, the old creator god, is viewed as the personification of the material universe. I take the Sanskrit ***iha*** to mean "in this system or doctrine" rather than "in this world" (JOHNSTON).

12.30 The term ***namaḥ***, indicating veneration, occurs in many invocations of gods (e.g., *Gaṇeśāya namaḥ*). The ritual exclamation ***vaṣaṭ*** accompanies many fire offerings in Vedic rituals.

12.33 JOHNSTON identifies the "**wise one**" as the great Sankhya teacher Várshaganya. See also JOHNSTON (1930: 861–2).

12.58 JOHNSTON takes **Great** (***bṛhat***) to be *brahman* or the Absolute. The term *bṛhat*, however, could have other meanings especially within the Sankhya cosmology of Aráda, particularly with reference to Primal nature or *prakṛti*. Ashva·ghosha is also playing with this term in its multiple meanings when he uses it three times in this verse.

12.67 **Jaigishávya** is cited as an early Sankhya teacher in MBh CE XII.222. For **Jánaka**, see note to 1.45. **Elder Paráshara** is probably the same as the famous Sankhya teacher Pañcha·shikha.

12.70 In the Sankhya system the eight *prakṛtis* (see note to 12.17–20) act as a **seed**, giving birth to other entities within the evolutionary process. When such qualities are present, someone cannot be said to be fully liberated. The term ***dharma*** here has the meaning of **quality** or characteristic.

12.77 As BRONKHORST (2005) has shown, **number** here refers not to Sankhya, as had previously been thought, but to a category in the Vaishéshika system of philosophy. "Number" (*saṃkhyā*) appears in a list of fourteen qualities in a soul. According to Vaishéshika, the first nine disappear in a liberated soul, whereas some of the remaining five headed by "number" remain. The Buddha says that when such qualities are present, a person cannot be viewed as liberated. BRONKHORST has shown that the entire argument of the following verses is also directed at doctrines of Vaishéshika rather than Sankhya.

12.85 These states of consciousness reached during meditative trance are expressed in Buddhist terminology.

12.101 The reference is to the Buddha's previous meditative trance described at 5.8–15.

13.5 The identity of this king of **Vidéha** is uncertain, but he could be Karála-Jánaka alluded to in 4.80 (see the note to it).

13.11 An **enemy of fish** is mentioned twice by Ashva·ghosha in "Handsome Nanda" (8.44, 10.53). There it is said that he fell in love with a woman named Kumúdvati. He is known elsewhere as an enemy of Kama, the god of love. At 10.53 of "Handsome Nanda" we hear that this person was reduced to ashes by passion.

13.12 **Aida**, the son of Ida, is the same as Purúravas. His father was Budha, the son of Moon. Purúravas was cursed by Kama, the god of love, to go mad when separated from his wife Úrvashi. King **Shántanu**'s infatuation with Ganga and his shaking uncontrollably when separated from her is recorded in "Handsome Nanda" 7.41. For the story of Shántanu, see MBh CE 1.91–3.

13.16 The story of Kama preparing to strike Shiva (= **Shambhu**) with his arrow is well known in Indian mythology. In the commonly told version, Shiva notices Kama and reduces him to ashes before he can discharge his arrow. Apparently, Ashva·ghosha knew a different version of the story. In any case, Shiva did fall in love with Párvati, which was the intent of Kama.

13.38 It is unclear whether this is a reference to a mythological episode or simply a description of what happens to mountain outcrops when struck by lightning. If it is the former, it may refer to a time when mountains had wings. Indra struck them in order to clip their wings and to make them immobile. See MANI 1975: 325.

14.5 Along with JOHNSTON, I think the reading ***ca kriyāḥ*** is erroneous. The original probably was *cakriyaḥ*.

14.15 **Forest with leaves of swords** (*asi/pattra/vanam̩*) is the name of one of the hells in Brahmanical mythology: see MANI 1975: 58. It is unclear whether Ashva·ghosha is here alluding to this particular hell or simply describing a particular place these people go to.

LIST OF METERS

The following meters are used in this text:

anuṣṭubh 4.1–96, 6.1–55, 12.1–115, 14.1–31

aparavaktra 7.58

aupacchandasika 5.1–78

mālinī 2.56, 13.72

praharṣiṇī 9.81, 9.82, 10.41

puṣpitāgrā 1.80–89, 5.79–87, 8.81–87

rucirā 3.64, 3.65, 12.121

śikhariṇī 4.103

upajāti 1.8–24, 1.40–79, 2.1–55, 3.1–62, 6.56–65, 7.1–57, 9.1–71, 10.1–39, 11.1–57, 13.1–69

vaṃśastha 3.63, 4.97–102, 6.66–68, 8.1–80, 9.72–80, 10.40, 11.58–73, 12.116–120, 13.70, 13.71

unidentified due to lacunae 1.1–7, 1.25–39

GLOSSARY OF NAMES

ADÍTYA son or descendent of Áditi, especially applied to the sun.

AGÁSTYA a sage already mentioned in the *Ṛgveda* in connection with Lopa·mudra. He is said to have gone to the south, and thus is connected with the southern region (9.26): see note to 4.73.

AGNI the fire god.

AHÁLYA the wife of the seer Gáutama: see note to 4.72.

AIDA the son of Budha and Ida who conquered the whole world. He is also known as Purúravas, whose wife was Úrvashi: see note to 13.12.

AJA the father of Dasha·ratha, who was the father of Rama.

AKANÍSHTHA name of the fifth and highest class of Shuddhavása deities in Buddhist mythology.

AKSHA·MALA the wife of Vasíshtha: see note to 4.77.

ÁLAKA the capital city of Kubéra located in the Himalayas.

AMBARÍSHA the son of Mandhátri: see note to 9.69.

ANARÁNYA little is known about this king from Brahmanical sources. He is mentioned in the list of kings in MBh CE 1.171–9. Clearly, Ashva·ghosha had access to a narrative in which he ruled over a very prosperous and peaceful kingdom.

ÁNGIRAS an ancient seer born from the mind of the creator god Brahma. One of the seven seers: see note to 1.14.

ÁNGIRASA son or descendant of Ángiras, often identified with Brihas·pati: see 2.36, 9.10.

ANTI·DEVA also called Ranti·deva, he is the son of Sánkriti and is well known for his generosity: see note to 1.52.

ÁPSARAS a class of female divine beings associated with water. They are extremely beautiful and are experts in dance. They are often coupled with *gandharvas*.

ARÁDA the name of a philosopher-ascetic to whom the future Buddha went for instruction. He left Aráda, dissatisfied with his teaching.

ASHÁDHA A king named Ashádha is mentioned in MBh CE 1.61.58, but nothing else is known about him. The passage at 9.20 indicates that he aspired to liberation while remaining a householder.

ÁSITA a Brahmanical seer, often called Ásita Dévala: see note to 1.49.

ASHÓKA the name of the tree *Jonesia Asoka Roxb.* or *Saraca Indica*: see note to 4.45.

ASHVIN a twin divinity identified with medical knowledge.

ATRÉYA regarded as the first person to create a text on medicine: see note to 1.43.

ATRI an ancient seer, the father of Atréya associated with medical texts.

AURVA the son of Chyávana. He was born by splitting the thigh of his mother: see note to 1.10.

AURVASHÉYA perhaps the same as Vasíshtha. For the identity of this figure see note to 9.9.

BALI at 11.16 he is identified as the king of the gods from whom sovereignty passed to Indra, and at 9.20 he is said to be a king who aspired to liberation while still a householder. In other accounts he is identified as a king of the *asura* demons.

BHARAD·VAJA the son of Brihas·pati: see note to 4.74.

BHÁRGAVA the identity of this sage is unclear: see 6.1, 9.2.

BHAVA another name for Shiva.

BHISHMA the eldest son of Shántanu and a main figure in the *Mahābhārata*; see note to 9.25.

BHRIGU an ancient seer who was the progenitor of the Bhárgavas: see note to 1.41.

BRIHAT·PHALA a class of Buddhist deities dwelling within the realm of form (*rūp'|âvacara*).

BRIHAS·PATI the son of Ángiras and the teacher of the gods, he is viewed as the author of a text on political science: see note to 1.41.

BUDHA identified with Mercury, he is the son of the Moon by the wife of Brihas·pati: see note to 4.75.

CHÁITRARATHA a lovely forest known for its beauty in which many episodes in the *Mahābhārata* took place: see MANI (1975: 166).

CHAKRA·VAKA the ruddy sheldrake or the "Brahmini Duck," the name being derived from its call that resembles the sound of a wheel. The attachment of a pair and their faithfulness is celebrated in Sanskrit poetry: see DAVE (2005: 450–51).

CHÁNDA(KA) the groom who accompanied Prince Siddhártha, the future Buddha, during his great departure with the horse Kánthaka.

CHYÁVANA an ancient seer, the son of Bhrigu, famous for recovering his youth when he was very old: see note to 1.43.

DARBHA a type of grass used for ritual purposes, most commonly the same as *kuśa*; specifically the grass *Saccharum cylindricum*. Sometimes, *darbha* can mean simply a tuft or bundle.

DASHA·RATHA the father of Rama.

DÁSHARATHA the patronymic of Rama, the son of Dasha·ratha.

DHRUVA his identity is unclear. JOHNSTON identifies him with the god Brahma. The *Viṣṇupurāṇa* (1.12) has an account of one Dhruva who through austerities became a great king and attained the highest heaven.

DRUMA he is identified as the king of the Shalvas who returned to his city and resumed his kingship. He is probably the same as Dyumat·sena, the father of Sátyavan and the father-in-law of Sávitri.

DRUMÁBJA: also known as *karṇikāra*, it is the flower of the plant *Pterospermum acerifolium*: see note to 5.3.

GADHIN the father of the celebrated sage Vishva·mitra: see note to 1.44.

GANDHÁRVA a class of male divine beings associated with the female *apsarases*. *Gandharvas* are experts in music.

GÁRUDA the name of the mythical bird and the vehicle of Vishnu. He is considered the divine king of birds.

GÁUTAMA a famous sage whose wife, Ahálya, was raped by Indra: see note to 4.72.

GÁUTAMA DIRGHA·TAPAS a sage who was born blind due to a curse: see note to 4.18.

GÁUTAMI the name of Prince Siddhártha's foster mother, who was the sister of his biological mother, Maya.

GAYA a royal seer by this name is recorded in MBh CE III.93, where he is said to be son of Amúrta·rayas.

GIRI·VRAJA another name for Raja·griha.

GHRITÁCHI the name of an *apsaras*, probably the same as Ménaka: see note to 4.20.

HARYÁNKA Haryánka (or Haryánga) is a Brihad·ratha king, said to have been the founder of the dynasty of Raja·griha.

IKSHVÁKU the son of Manu and the one who established the solar dynasty of kings.

INDRA the king of the gods, also called Shakra especially in Buddhist literature.

ÍSHVARA literally "lord," the name given to the creator god or specifically to Shiva.

JAIGISHÁVYA see note to 12.67.

JÁNAKA the famous king of Vidéha. He appears in the *Upaniṣad*s as a wise king and the *Mahābhārata* makes him a teacher of yoga and of the path to liberation: see note to 1.45.

JANGHA See note to 4.17.

JAYÁNTA the son of the god Indra.

KA another name for the creator god Praja·pati or Brahma.

KAILÁSA located in the Himalayas, it is the mountain residence of Shiva.

KAIRÁTAKA this term probably refer to a group of tribal or lower-class people known as Kirátas. Buddhist texts show that humpbacks, dwarfs, and Kirátas regularly lived in establishments of courtesans.

KAKSHÍVAT a king who was born from the armpit: see note to 1.10.

KALAVÍNKA a generic name for a variety of sparrow-like birds, perhaps including finchs: see DAVE 2005: 487.

KALI another name for Sátyavati, the mother of Vyasa: see note to 4.76.

KAMA the god of love.

KÁNTHAKA the horse that carried Prince Siddhártha, the future Buddha, to the forest.

KÁPILA (1) name of the capital of the Shakya kingdom, Kápila·vastu; (2) name of a famous sage and philosopher viewed as the founder of the Sankhya system of philosophy.

KÁPILA·VASTU the capital city of the Shakya clan where Shuddhódana was king.

KAPIÑJALÁDA a son of Vasíshtha through Aksha·mala: see note to 4.77.

KARÁLA·JÁNAKA a king from Vidéha: see note to 4.80.

KARÁNDAVA A kind of waterfowl, probably the common coot: see note to 5.53.

KARNIKÁRA the flower of the plant *Pterospermum acerifolium*: see note to 5.3.

KASHI·SÚNDARI the identity of this woman is unclear: see note to 4.16.

KUBÉRA the guardian deity of the north and the lord of wealth.

KURU a dynasty of kings of early India to which most of the major kings of ancient India belonged, including those celebrated in the epic *Mahābhārata*.

KÚRUBAKA the red Amaranth tree: see note to 4.47.

KÚSHIKA an ancient king who was the grandfather of the famous Vishva·mitra: see note to 1.44.

LODHRA a small tree (*Symplocos racemosa*) about eighteen feet high with a red bark and white flowers turning pale yellow as they fade.

LOPA·MUDRA the wife of Agástya: see note to 4.73.

LÚMBINI the birth-place of Siddhártha, the future Buddha.

MADRI one of the two wives of Pandu: see note to 4.79.

MÁGADHA the major kigdom in north-eastern India (today's Bihar) during the time of the Buddha with its capital at Raja·griha, and later at Pátali·putra.

MÁGHAVAN another name for Indra.

MAHA·SUDÁRSHA mentioned as a forefather of Siddhártha at 8.62.

MÁMATA the wife of Utáthya, the elder brother of Brihas·pati: see note to 4.74.

MÁNDARA a mythical mountain used as the churning stick during the original churning of the ocean: see MBh CE I.16–17.

MANDÁRA the coral tree, *Erythrina Indica*, also viewed as one of the five trees of paradise.

MANDHÁTRI a righteous king who ruled the whole world (see 10.31; MANI 1975: 476). His craving for sensual pleasures is noted in 11.13. For his extraordinary birth, see note to 1.10.

MANTHÁLA GÁUTAMA appears as a seer at 4.17. Nothing else is known about him: see note to 4.17.

MANU the first man, the first king, and the first law giver. Ashva·ghosha may have been familiar either with the actual *dharma/śās-tra* or legal treatise ascribed to Manu or knew the legend of Manu being the first propounder of law.

MARA the god of death, identified here with Kama, the god of love (see 1.27).

MÁRUTA his identity is unclear. At 4.74 he is said to be the father of Mámata.

MARUTS gods associated with the wind and storm, regarded as companions of Indra.

MARÚTVAT the son of Dharma by Marútvati, the daughter of Daksha.

MAYA the mother of Siddhártha, the future Buddha. Maya is also the consort of Vishnu.

MÉKHALA-DÁNDAKAS for the identity of this obscure group of people, see note to 11.31–2. The Mékalas are referred to in MBh CE VI.10.39 as one of the regions.

MERU the great mountain in the middle of the earth around which the sun revolves.

NÁGARI the name of a hermitage recorded at 12.89. No further information is available.

NÁHUSHA the father of Yayáti. Náhusha's genealogy is: Brahma, Atri, Chandra, Budha, Purúravas, Ayus, Náhusha.

NAIRÁÑJANA called *Nerañjarā* in Pali, this is the river near which the Buddha stayed after his Awakening. It is identified with the modern Nilájana (Lílajan), which joins the Móhana to form the Phalgu.

NALA·KÚBARA the son of Kubéra.

NÁNDANA a park in heaven, especially associated with the abode of Indra.

PADMA the great elephant of the south that supports the earth on its head: see *Rāmāyaṇa* 1.39.16–17.

PADMA another name for Shri, the goddess of fortune and consort of Vishnu.

PADMA·SHANDA the name of a park in the Shakya capital.

PÁNDAVA the five brothers headed by Yudhi·shthira who are the main protagonists in the epic *Mahābhārata*.

PANDU the father of the five Pándava brothers in the *Mahābhārata*: see note to 4.79.

PARÁSHARA (1) the father of Vyasa; (2) probably another name for the Sankhya teacher Pañcha·shikha.

PRAJA·PATI the creator god.

PRITHU a righteous king born from the right hand of his evil father Vena: see note to 1.10.

PUNAR a particular constellation: see note to 9.11.

PURAN·DARA an epithet of Indra.

PUSHYA name of a lunar asterism.

RÁGHAVA patronymic of Rama, the descendant of Raghu.

RAHU the celestial demon responsible for the eclipses of the sun and the moon.

RÁHULA the son of Prince Siddhártha, the future Buddha, by his wife, Yasho·dhara.

RAJA·GRIHA the early capital of the kingdom of Mágadha.

RAMA the hero of the epic *Rāmāyaṇa*, he came to be viewed as an incarnation of the god Vishnu.

RAMA BHÁRGAVA also known as Párashu·rama, he killed the entire race of kshatriyas to avenge the death of his father: see note to 9.25.

RÓHINI one of the stars and the wife of Moon: see note to 4.73.

RISHYA·SHRINGA a young ascetic who was totally ignorant of the female sex: see note to 4.19.

SÁGARA an ancient king, whose sons were responsible for digging up the earth, which became the ocean (*sāgara*): see note to 1.44.

SANAT·KUMÁRA one of the four mind-born sons of Brahma, sometimes identified with Skanda, who also bears the name Kumára.

SARÁSVATA the son of Dadhícha and the river Sarásvati. He recited the lost Veda: see note to 1.42.

SARVÁRTHA·SIDDHA the personal name of the future Buddha, also called Siddhártha.

SÉNAJIT the identity of these kings is uncertain, but several are mentioned in the *Mahābhārata*.

SHACHI the wife of Indra.

SHAKRA another name for Indra, the king of the gods.

SHAKYA the clan in which the Buddha was born.

SHALA the tree *Vatica Robusta*, renowned for its beautiful flowers.

SHALVA the name of a region in northern India: see MBh CE VI.10.37.

SHAMBHU another name for Shiva.

SHAN·MUKHA literally, "six-faced," the name of Shiva's son Skanda or Karttikéya.

SHANTA the daughter of King Roma·pada who married the sage Rishya·shringa.

SHÁNTANU the father of Bhishma through Ganga.

SHAURI the patronymic of Krishna; Shura was Krishna's grandfather.

SHIBI the name of a famous ancient king in both Buddhist and Brahmanical mythology. His generosity was tested by gods. Indra took the form of a hawk that chased Agni (Fire) in the form of a dove. The dove sought refuge with Shibi, who refused to give him up. The hawk asked for an equal amount of Shibi's flesh. As Shibi cut up and placed his flesh on the scale, the dove became more and more heavy. Finally Shibi put his whole body on the scale. The deities reveal themselves and recognize the generosity of Shibi. The story also forms the basis of a *Jātaka* tale where Shibi is identified with the Buddha in a previous life as a bodhisattva, where the gift is not of flesh but of an eye.

SHRENYA the king of Mágadha, also known as Bimbi·sara.

SHRI the goddess of fortune; it is also the sovereign power of the king personified as a divinity and viewed as the wife of the king.

SHUBHA·KRITSNA a class of Buddhist deities (Pali: *subha/kiṇṇa*) dwelling within the realm of form (*rūp'/âvacara*).

SHUKRA also known as Úshanas, he is the teacher of the *asura*s and the author of a text on political science: see notes to 1.41 and 9.10.

SHURA Krishna's grandfather.

SHÚRPAKA the name of a person identified as an enemy of fish: see note to 13.11.

SIDDHA a class of gods, also means a "perfected one:" see note to 7.1.

SIDDHÁRTHA the personal name of the future Buddha, also called Sarvártha·siddha.

SINDU·VÁRAKA the shrub *Vitex negundo*: see note to 4.49.

SITA·PUSHPA could be either *Tabernaemontana Coronaria* (or *Divaricata*), known as East Indian Rosebay (a shrub growing to about six feet in height with white fragrant clusters of flowers), or Jasmine.

SUMÁNTRA the chief minister of Dasha·ratha, the father of Rama: see note to 6.36.

SUNDA one of a pair of demon brothers, the other being Upasúnda: see note to 11.31–2.

SUVÁRNA·NISHTHÍVIN the son of King Sriñjaya: see note to 8.77.

TÍLAKA the tree *Clerodendrum phlomoides* with white flowers: see note to 4.46.

UDÁYIN the son of King Shuddhódana's chaplain (*purohita*).

ÚDRAKA also known as Údraka Rama·putra, he is the second Brahmanical philosopher to instruct the future Buddha.

UGRÁYUDHA a king killed by Bhishma in MBh CE XII.27.10.

UPASÚNDA one of a pair of demon brothers, the other being Sunda: see note to 11.31–2.

ÚRVASHI an *apsaras* who was the wife of Purúravas: see note to 13.12.

UTÁTHYA the older brother of Brihas·pati: see note to 4.74.

VAIBHRÁJA it is not possible to identify this king or god recorded in 9.20.

VÁISHRAVANA: the patronymic of Kubéra.

VAISHVÁNTARA the name of a hermitage at 11.73.

VAJRA·BAHU probably an epithet of Indra, who is said to have inherited the sovereignty among gods from Bali: 11.16.

VÁLABHID an epithet of Indra.

VALMÍKI the reputed author of the *Rāmāyaṇa*: see note to 1.43.

VAMA·DEVA a minister of Dasha·ratha, the father of Rama.

VASÍSHTHA a great seer already recorded in the *Ṛgveda*. He was the great-grandfather of Vyasa: see note to 1.42.

VASU a group of eight gods. The term also refers to a particular constellation (9.11).

VIBHRÁJA also called Vaibhrája and Vaibhrájaka, it is a pleasure grove in the heavens, associated by Ashva·ghosha with Indra and his heaven.

VIDÉHA a kingdom in the northeastern part of India ruled by the famous king Jánaka.

VINDHYA the mountain range across northern India that divides the northern region from the Deccan.

VINDHYA·KOSHTHA a place in the Vindhya mountain range: see note to 7.54.

VISHVÁCHI listed as one of the six great *apsaras*es in MBh CE 1.68.67.

VISHVA·MITRA one of the most famous sages of ancient India who fathered Shakúntala: see note to 4.20.

VIVÁSVAT his identity is unclear: see note to 4.28.

VRISHNI-ÁNDHAKA mentioned frequently in the epic as an allied group of people: see note to 11.31–2.

VRITRA a demonic being that is the chief enemy of Indra whom Indra killed with his bolt, the Vajra. In later myth, Vritra is viewed as a brahmin; thus the killing of Vritra made Indra guilty of the sin of killing a brahmin.

VYASA the seer to whom is ascribed the division of the Veda, as well as the authorship of the *Mahābhārata*: see note to 1.42.

YAKSHA generally a term for demons, but in Buddhist terminology refers to a class of divine beings.

YÁMUNA the second major river of north-central India, along with the Ganges.

YASHO·DHARA the wife of Prince Siddhártha, the future Buddha.

YAYÁTI an ancient king, the son of Náhusha, who reigned for a thousand years. When he reached old age, Yayáti asked his sons to give him their youth. Only one, Puru, agreed to do so. As a result, Yayáti gave his kingdom to Puru before he left for the forest. See the narrative in MBh CE 1.70–80.

INDEX

Sanskrit words are given in the English alphabetical order, according to the accented CSL pronuncation aid. They are followed by the conventional diacritics in brackets.

THE CLAY SANSKRIT LIBRARY

The volumes in the series are listed here in order of publication.
Titles marked with an asterisk* are also available in the
Digital Clay Sanskrit Library (eCSL).
For further information visit www.claysanskritlibrary.org

1. The Emperor of the Sorcerers (*Bṛhatkathāślokasaṃgraha*) (vol. 1 of 2) by *Budhasvāmin*. SIR JAMES MALLINSON
2. Heavenly Exploits (*Divyāvadāna*). JOEL TATELMAN
3. Maha·bhárata III: The Forest (*Vanaparvan*) (vol. 4 of 4)* WILLIAM J. JOHNSON
4. Much Ado about Religion (*Āgamaḍambara*) by *Bhaṭṭa Jayanta*. CSABA DEZSŐ
5. The Birth of Kumára (*Kumārasaṃbhava*) by *Kālidāsa*. DAVID SMITH
6. Ramáyana I: Boyhood (*Bālakāṇḍa*) by *Vālmīki*. ROBERT P. GOLDMAN
7. The Epitome of Queen Lilávati (*Līlāvatīsāra*) (vol. 1 of 2) by *Jinaratna*. R.C.C. FYNES
8. Ramáyana II: Ayódhya (*Ayodhyākāṇḍa*) by *Vālmīki*. SHELDON I. POLLOCK
9. Love Lyrics (*Amaruśataka, Śatakatraya & Caurapañcāśikā*) by *Amaru, Bhartṛhari & Bilhaṇa*. GREG BAILEY & RICHARD GOMBRICH
10. What Ten Young Men Did (*Daśakumāracarita*) by *Daṇḍin*. ISABELLE ONIANS
11. Three Satires (*Kaliviḍambana, Kalāvilāsa & Bhallaṭaśataka*) by *Nīlakaṇṭha, Kṣemendra & Bhallaṭa*. SOMADEVA VASUDEVA
12. Ramáyana IV: Kishkíndha (*Kiṣkindhākāṇḍa*) by *Vālmīki*. ROSALIND LEFEBER
13. The Emperor of the Sorcerers (*Bṛhatkathāślokasaṃgraha*) (vol. 2 of 2) by *Budhasvāmin*. SIR JAMES MALLINSON
14. Maha·bhárata IX: Shalya (*Śalyaparvan*) (vol. 1 of 2)* JUSTIN MEILAND

15. Rákshasa's Ring (*Mudrārākṣasa*)* by *Viśākhadatta*. MICHAEL COULSON
16. Messenger Poems (*Meghadūta, Pavanadūta & Haṃsadūta*) by *Kālidāsa, Dhoyī & Rūpa Gosvāmin*. SIR JAMES MALLINSON
17. Ramáyana III: The Forest (*Araṇyakāṇḍa*) by *Vālmīki*. SHELDON I. POLLOCK
18. The Epitome of Queen Lilávati (*Līlāvatīsāra*) (vol. 2 of 2) by *Jinaratna*. R.C.C. FYNES
19. Five Discourses on Worldly Wisdom (*Pañcatantra*)* by *Viṣṇuśarman*. PATRICK OLIVELLE
20. Ramáyana V: Súndara (*Sundarakāṇḍa*) by *Vālmīki*. ROBERT P. GOLDMAN & SALLY J. SUTHERLAND GOLDMAN
21. Maha·bhárata II: The Great Hall (*Sabhāparvan*) PAUL WILMOT
22. The Recognition of Shakúntala (*Abhijñānaśākuntala*) (Kashmir Recension) by *Kālidāsa*. SOMADEVA VASUDEVA
23. Maha·bhárata VII: Drona (*Droṇaparvan*) (vol. 1 of 4)* VAUGHAN PILIKIAN
24. Rama Beyond Price (*Anargharāghava*) by *Murāri*. JUDIT TÖRZSÖK
25. Maha·bhárata IV: Viráta (*Virāṭaparvan*) KATHLEEN GARBUTT
26. Maha·bhárata VIII: Karna (*Karṇaparvan*) (vol. 1 of 2) ADAM BOWLES
27. "The Lady of the Jewel Necklace" & "The Lady who Shows her Love" (*Ratnāvalī & Priyadarśikā*) by *Harṣa*.* WENDY DONIGER
28. The Ocean of the Rivers of Story (*Kathāsaritsāgara*) (vol. 1 of 7) by *Somadeva*. SIR JAMES MALLINSON
29. Handsome Nanda (*Saundarananda*)* by *Aśvaghoṣa*. LINDA COVILL
30. Maha·bhárata IX: Shalya (*Śalyaparvan*) (vol. 2 of 2)* JUSTIN MEILAND
31. Rama's Last Act (*Uttararāmacarita*) by *Bhavabhūti*. SHELDON POLLOCK. Foreword by GIRISH KARNAD

32. "Friendly Advice" (*Hitopadeśa*) by *Nārāyaṇa* &
"King Víkrama's Adventures" (*Vikramacarita*). JUDIT TÖRZSÖK
33. Life of the Buddha (*Buddhacarita*)
by *Aśvaghoṣa*. PATRICK OLIVELLE
34. Maha·bhárata V: Preparations for War (*Udyogaparvan*) (vol. 1 of 2)
KATHLEEN GARBUTT. Foreword by GURCHARAN DAS
35. Maha·bhárata VIII: Karna (*Karṇaparvan*) (vol. 2 of 2)
ADAM BOWLES
36. Maha·bhárata V: Preparations for War (*Udyogaparvan*) (vol. 2 of 2)
KATHLEEN GARBUTT
37. Maha·bhárata VI: Bhishma (*Bhīṣmaparvan*) (vol. 1 of 2)*
Including the "Bhagavad Gita" in Context
ALEX CHERNIAK. Foreword by RANAJIT GUHA
38. The Ocean of the Rivers of Story (*Kathāsaritsāgara*) (vol. 2 of 7)
by *Somadeva*. SIR JAMES MALLINSON
39. "How the Nagas were Pleased" (*Nāgānanda*) by *Harṣa* &
"The Shattered Thighs" (*Ūrubhaṅga*) by *Bhāsa*.*
ANDREW SKILTON
40. Gita·govínda: Love Songs of Radha and Krishna (*Gītagovinda*)*
by *Jayadeva*. LEE SIEGEL. Foreword by SUDIPTA KAVIRAJ
41. "Bouquet of Rasa" & "River of Rasa" (*Rasamañjarī & Rasataraṅgiṇī*) by *Bhānudatta*. SHELDON POLLOCK
42. Garland of the Buddha's Past Lives (*Jātakamālā*) (vol. 1 of 2)*
by *Āryaśūra*. JUSTIN MEILAND
43. Maha·bhárata XII: Peace (*Śāntiparvan*) (vol. 3 of 5)*
"The Book of Liberation" (*Mokṣadharma*). ALEXANDER WYNNE
44. The Little Clay Cart (*Mṛcchakaṭikā*) by *Śūdraka*.
DIWAKAR ACHARYA. Foreword by PARTHA CHATTERJEE
45. Bhatti's Poem: The Death of Rávana (*Bhaṭṭikāvya*)*
by *Bhaṭṭi*. OLIVER FALLON

46. "Self-Surrender," "Peace," "Compassion," and "The Mission of the Goose": Poems and Prayers from South India (*Ātmārpaṇastuti, Śāntivilāsa, Dayāśataka & Haṃsasaṃdeśa*) by *Appayya Dīkṣita, Nīlakaṇṭha Dīkṣita & Vedānta Deśika*. YIGAL BRONNER & DAVID SHULMAN
Foreword by GIEVE PATEL
47. Maha·bhárata VI: Bhishma (*Bhīṣmaparvan*) (vol. 2 of 2)* ALEX CHERNIAK
48. How Úrvashi Was Won (*Vikramorvaśīya*) by *Kālidāsa* VELCHERU NARAYANA RAO & DAVID SHULMAN
49. The Quartet of Causeries (*Caturbhāṇī*) by *Śūdraka, Śyāmilaka, Vararuci & Īśvaradatta*. CSABA DEZSŐ & SOMADEVA VASUDEVA
50. Garland of the Buddha's Past Lives (*Jātakamālā*) (vol. 2 of 2)* by *Āryaśūra*. JUSTIN MEILAND
51. Princess Kadámbari (*Kādambarī*) (vol. 1 of 3) by *Bāṇa*. DAVID SMITH
52. The Rise of Wisdom Moon (*Prabodhacandrodaya*)* by *Kṛṣṇamiśra*. MATTHEW T. KAPSTEIN
Foreword by J.N. MOHANTY
53. Maha·bhárata VII: Drona (*Droṇaparvan*) (vol. 2 of 4)* VAUGHAN PILIKIAN
54. Maha·bhárata X & XI: Dead of Night & The Women (*Sauptikaparvan & Strīparvan*).* KATE CROSBY
55. Seven Hundred Elegant Verses (*Āryāsaptaśatī*)* by *Govardhana*. FRIEDHELM HARDY
56. Málavika and Agni·mitra (*Mālavikāgnimitram*) by *Kālidāsa*. DÁNIEL BALOGH & ESZTER SOMOGYI